GOD'S WARRIORS

GOD'S

WARRIORS

The
Christian
Right
in
Twentieth-
Century
America

CLYDE WILCOX

The Johns Hopkins University Press
Baltimore and London

The Johns Hopkins University Press
701 West 40th Street
Baltimore, Maryland 21211-2190
The Johns Hopkins Press Ltd., London

The paper used in this book meets the minimum requirements of American National Standard for Information Sciences—Permanence of Paper for Printed Library Materials, ANSI Z39.48–1984.

Library of Congress Cataloging-in-Publication Data

Wilcox, William Clyde.
    God's warrriors : the Christian right in twentieth-century America
  / Clyde Wilcox.
        p.   cm.
    Includes bibliographical references and index.
    ISBN 0-8018-4263-8 (alk. paper)
    1. Fundamentalism. 2. Christianity and politics—History—20th century.
  3. United States—Politics and government—20th century.
  I. Title.
  BT82.2W54   1992
  322'.1'09730904—dc20   91-15849

Contents

Tables

Acknowledgments

Although I wrote the first draft of this book in the summer and fall of 1989, I have worked on related projects for several years. The comments of discussants of many conference papers and referees of journal articles, and many conversations with my friends and colleagues in the religion and politics research community all have shaped the final product.

A number of people made valuable comments about earlier drafts of this book. Elizabeth Cook read several versions of each chapter, and her comments were invaluable. Ted Jelen served as a sounding board for ideas and also provided many helpful comments. Both made comments on the substance, the methodology, and the writing, and both provided needed support when the project seemed to be progressing slowly. These two contributed more than they know to the project.

Michael Webber provided useful suggestions on the writing of several chapters, and Ken Wald made substantive suggestions on chapter 2. Kristi Andersen, Aage Clausen, Herb Weisberg, and especially Herb Asher all helped guide the dissertation that was the intellectual predecessor of this book, although the current volume bears little resemblance to the dissertation. Anonymous reviewers of a book prospectus and of this volume all deserve thanks.

Georgetown University provided computer time, and release time through summer grants and a semester off in 1989. The Georgetown University Department of Government provided some funds that helped finance the survey of contributors to presidential candidates. Additional funds came from a research award from the Society for the

Scientific Study of Religion, from Union College, and from the University of Rochester. The survey of the Ohio Moral Majority was funded by a Graduate Research Award from Ohio State University. The Polimetrics Laboratory at Ohio State conducted that survey at a reduced rate, stretching the grant as far as it could go. The Reverend Tom Trammell of the Ohio Moral Majority provided a cover letter urging his members to participate, without which the survey would not have succeeded. Sharon Georgianna provided access to her data on the Indiana Moral Majority. Henry Tom and Jane Warth of The Johns Hopkins University Press provided encouragement and support. Roland Gunn assisted with the index.

A number of journals have published earlier reports of some of this research. I would like to thank *American Politics Quarterly, Social Science History, Journal of Social History, Review of Religious Research, Journal for the Scientific Study of Religion,* and *Social Science Journal* for allowing the incorporation of some of this analysis in the book.

Introduction

The 1980 elections thrust a New Christian Right into the national limelight. Although the Gallup Poll had predicted a dead heat in the presidential election, Ronald Reagan won with surprising ease. Republican challengers upset nine Democratic incumbent senators, giving Republicans control of the upper chamber for the first time in nearly three decades, and Republicans gained seats in the House as well. These surprising results left media analysts scrambling for an explanation. They found in the Reverend Jerry Falwell, head of the recently formed Moral Majority, an articulate and controversial proponent of the argument that conservative Christians (especially fundamentalists and other evangelicals) had elected Reagan and defeated many of the liberal Senate incumbents.

The Moral Majority and its sister organizations (e.g., Religious Roundtable and Christian Voice) spanned the interstitial zone between religion and politics. Falwell and his colleagues claimed to speak for conservative Christians and Jews—"Catholics, Jews, Protestants, Mormons, and Fundamentalists," seeking to restore moral equilibrium to the United States. Falwell claimed that the Moral Majority had hundreds of thousands of members, including tens of thousands of pastors.[1]

1. Estimates of Moral Majority membership varied widely, in part because of the ambiguity surrounding the concept *member*. The national organization was essentially a direct-mail operation, so anyone who ever gave money could be claimed as a member, although this would include numerous citizens who did not support the Moral Majority's agenda. It appears that the official claims of the Moral Majority rested on the number of

The media had actually discovered the New Christian Right earlier during the 1980 campaign and drastically overestimated its support (Reichley 1985), but it was the aftermath of the election that provided the New Christian Right with its most thorough media coverage. Falwell's frequent appearances on televised analyses of the 1980 election provided the Moral Majority with a degree of notoriety which exceeded other current or previous organizations of the Christian Right. Moen (1990a) reported that the Moral Majority received more than eight times as much publicity as all other organizations of the New Christian Right combined.

Falwell claimed to have registered some four million to eight million evangelical and fundamentalist Christians to vote, and that these Christians had provided Reagan's margin of victory. Pollster Louis Harris gave Falwell's claims some credence when he reported that two-thirds of Reagan's vote margin was provided by fundamentalist and evangelical Christians.

Although the Religious Roundtable never got off the ground and Christian Voice generally preferred to shun the media spotlight,[2] Falwell quickly became a national figure. His pronouncements on abortion and gay rights, on Taiwan and South Africa, and on welfare and the gold standard were widely reported. The Moral Majority quickly became an organization of controversy, even among conservative evangelicals.

Falwell and other New Christian Right spokesmen played an even more visible role in the 1984 election. They were prominent figures in the Republican National Convention, and they campaigned actively for Reagan in 1984. New Christian Right efforts have been credited with registering large numbers of white voters in North Carolina in 1984 (Reichley 1985), although the Helms-Hunt Senate race also played a role: Republicans attempted to counter Democratic voter-registration drives in the black community with their own efforts among rural whites.

---

people estimated to have read the *Moral Majority Report,* including those who may have read it secondhand.

2. The Religious Roundtable foundered when the head of the Southern Baptist Convention at a Roundtable-sponsored event proclaimed that God does not hear the prayer of Jews. Christian Voice has generally avoided the spotlight, although its ratings of members of Congress, the "Morality Scorecard," attracted widespread attention when it assigned perfect one hundred scores to one member convicted during Abscam and another censured for an affair with a teen-aged page, and scores of zero to ordained ministers and priests. Nonetheless, Christian Voice is widely regarded to be a more politically sophisticated organization than the Moral Majority had been, primarily because of the role of Gary Jarmin as director.

Soon after Reagan's 1984 victory, the organizations of the New Christian Right began to decline. The revenues of the Moral Majority had come primarily from direct mail, and such appeals depend on the portrayal of immanent crisis to persuade supporters to part with their money. Reagan's campaign of "Morning in America" made it difficult to portray the country as facing crisis, and funds began to dry up. Falwell retired as head of the Moral Majority and folded the organization into a larger Liberty Federation. In June 1989, the Moral Majority ceased operation.

Even before the demise of the Moral Majority, however, its role as leader of the New Christian Right had been eclipsed by the Reverend Marion (Pat) Robertson, a Baptist televangelist who renounced his ministry to seek the Republican nomination for president in 1988. Although Robertson received only a handful of votes at the Republican convention, he raised millions of dollars and defeated the other Republican candidates, including George Bush, in a number of party caucuses. He did credibly in southern primaries as well, although he was soundly trounced in states where he outspent Bush by large margins (Wilcox 1991).

In many ways, Robertson's campaign sounded the same themes as the Moral Majority. His positions on social issues were almost identical with those taken by Falwell, and his conservatism on economic issues, foreign policy, and even racial issues was also in line with that of the Moral Majority. Yet Falwell endorsed not Robertson but Bush during the Republican primaries, and he committed the Moral Majority to supporting Bush's candidacy. This split between the two leading spokesmen for the New Christian Right reflected more than just their rivalry as competing televangelists. Longstanding religious tensions were also at work between fundamentalists on the one hand and charismatics and pentecostals on the other. In chapters 8 and 9, the consequences of these tensions for the Robertson candidacy will be evident.

The rise of the New Christian Right aroused considerable interest among scholars. A flood of articles by political scientists and sociologists examined the New Christian Right from a variety of viewpoints. Social scientists studied the New Christian Right for a variety of motives, but the general tone of many studies suggests a concern among scholars that a successful movement from the religious Right would threaten democratic civility, and perhaps reverse recent trends toward growing social and political tolerance. Many feared that mobilizing previously apolitical evangelicals into religiously based political action would lead to a group of self-assured, uncompromising political activists whose self-righteousness might lead to dangerous political conflict and, if they proved successful, a compromising of civil liberties. History has quieted those fears and now allows us an opportunity to examine the Christian Right in a more dispassionate manner.

Such an assessment must put the New Christian Right of the 1980s into historical context. The Moral Majority and its fellow travelers were called the New Christian Right to distinguish these organizations from earlier Christian Right groups. During the twentieth century, two other waves of New Christian Right activity have occurred—one that opposed the teaching of evolution early in the twentieth century, and a second that trumpeted the dangers of domestic and foreign communism in the 1950s. These earlier groups differed from the Moral Majority and the Robertson campaign in important ways, but were similar in many others.

A number of works have described the origins of the organizations of the New Christian Right (Zwier 1982; Guth 1983a; Johnson and Bullock 1986), and others have described the activity of these organizations, in lobbying (Moen 1989) and in electoral campaigns (Johnson and Bullock 1986; Latus 1983, 1984; Wilcox 1988b). These and other related works have greatly expanded our understanding of the organizational imperatives of the New Christian Right, but they tell us little about what motivates individuals to support or join New Christian Right organizations.

This book examines the sources of individual support for the Christian Right, as well as the political consequences of that support. The analysis will be closely tied to an examination of data from surveys of the general public, of political elites, of evangelical Christians, and of activists in organizations of the Christian Right. Because there is no survey data on support for the Christian Right in the 1920s, the discussion will focus primarily on Christian Right groups in the 1950s through 1980s. The book seeks to answer several questions:

1. Who were the supporters of the Christian Right in these two eras, and how did they differ from other Americans? How do the supporters of the Christian Right differ from those who supported other right-wing groups? What theories best explain support for the Christian Right? How did supporters of one organization or leader differ from those who supported different organizations? How do religious differences contribute to and limit support for the Christian Right?

2. Who were the members of the Christian Right, and how did they differ from what we know of other political activists? How did they differ from those who merely supported the Christian Right, but were not active in it? What theories best account for activism in the Christian

Right? How did activists in one organization differ from those in other Christian Right organizations?

3. What have been the consequences of the Christian Right? Did Christian Right organizations mobilize large numbers of conservative Christians into political action? Did they participate in a realignment among evangelicals?

4. How unified were the supporters of and activists in the Christian Right groups in these two eras behind the platforms of their leaders? Was there support for the platforms among nonsupporters as well?

5. What was the potential for Christian Right organizations? Was there a constituency that remained untapped? How might Christian Right leaders have more fully mobilized support? What are the prospects for a renewed New Christian Right in the 1990s or beyond? Was there once and does there remain a potential black constituency for the Christian Right?

The first section of the book provides a context for the study. Chapter 1 reviews the history of the Christian Right in this century. Chapter 2 presents a set of competing theories which has been used to explain support for the Christian Right, and reviews the results of empirical studies that have attempted to test these theories. Some of these theories see support for the Christian Right as resulting from social or psychological strain, while others portray the sources of support as coming from political and religious values. Chapter 3 provides an introduction to the target constituency of the Christian Right— white evangelical Christians. There are important theological and political fault lines in the evangelical community, which are explored in this chapter. One of the most important cleavages is between fundamentalist evangelicals, who generally believe in a literal interpretation of the Bible; pentecostal and charismatic evangelicals, who believe in the gifts of the Spirit; and other evangelicals, who fall into neither the fundamentalist or pentecostal camp. Finally, I briefly examine black evangelicals as a potential constituency for the Christian Right.

The second section explores support for and activism in the fundamentalist Right of the 1950s through the 1980s. Chapter 4 explores support for the Christian Anti-Communism Crusade in 1964, and chapter 5 examines support for the Moral Majority from 1980 to 1987. Both chapters begin by testing the various theories of support for the Christian Right. Next, I contrast the supporters of the fundamentalist Right with those who supported other organizations commonly considered as part of the political Right—the John Birch Society in 1964, and the prolife movement in the 1980s. There are important differences between the supporters of the Christian Anti-Communism

Crusade and the John Birch Society, and between the Moral Majority and the prolife movement. There are differences between the John Birch Society and the prolife movement supporters as well. Although the data confirm that supporters of the John Birch Society were indeed from the political Right, support for the prolife movement came from liberals as well as conservatives. Both chapters explore black support for the fundamentalist Right, and they conclude with an analysis of the political importance of these Christian Right organizations.

Much of the scholarship on the Right has failed to distinguish between those who merely support these organizations and those who are members or other sorts of activists. Although members of the Christian Right vary in their level of activism within the organizations, they are all political activists in the sense that joining a political organization is a rare activity. Chapter 6 focuses on activists in the Christian Anti-Communism Crusade in 1962 and in the Moral Majority in 1982. Throughout this book, I refer to members of the Christian Right and those who have attended their rallies as activists. The interest-group literature uses the term *activist* somewhat differently, and it often seeks to determine what makes members of groups become more active. Yet compared with passive supporters, those who join the Moral Majority or attend its meetings and rallies are political activists. I therefore use the term *activist* in a manner consonant with the literature on political behavior, though not necessarily with some interest-group research. Although my discussion of Christian Right activists draws heavily on data from two small, single-state surveys of activists, I cite findings from other surveys which confirm the general results.

The third section explores support for the pentecostal/charismatic Right in the 1980s—primarily the presidential campaign of Pat Robertson. Chapter 7 examines support for Robertson among the general public during the primary season, especially in southern primaries. Chapter 8 examines support for Robertson among political elites—those who contributed $200 or more to a presidential candidate in 1988 and those who served as delegates to the Republican National Convention. I compare these results to those of Guth and Green (1988), who examined support for Robertson among those activists who contributed early in 1987 to the Political Action Committees (PACs) associated with presidential candidates. In contrast, the survey that provides much of the data for chapter 8 includes those whose total contributions to a single presidential candidate totaled $200. This includes members of Robertson's 1988 Club, who pledged to contribute $19.88 each month to the campaign.

The final section explores the potential of the Christian Right. Chapter 9 examines the lingering support for New Christian Right groups and for Robertson in November 1988, after the demise of the Moral Majority and after Robertson's announced withdrawal from presidential politics. Chapter 10 examines the potential Christian Right. This chapter discusses support for the New Christian Right platform in 1988, and it explores various constituency groups that future Christian Right movements might tap. Finally, I examine changes in evangelical politics during the past two decades which might influence the likelihood of another future emergence of the Christian Right.

The final chapter summarizes the main conclusions of the book and assesses the role of the Christian Right in American society.

Although I explore a number of questions in this book, I make four main arguments. First, there are important continuities and discontinuities between Christian Right movements in this century. There were important continuities in themes and approaches in the various manifestations of the Christian Right, but supporters of the Christian Anti-Communism Crusade were much more moderate than supporters of the Moral Majority, and some of Robertson's supporters were also moderate on many issues. Religious differences existed also between supporters of the Moral Majority and Robertson. Sectarian differences between competing subgroups of white evangelicals kept the Robertson forces from gaining the support of Moral Majoritarians in the 1980s.

Second, support for and activism in the Christian Right can best be understood as the result of a particular set of religious and political beliefs. Many previous writers have suggested that support comes from personality disorders, from preoccupation with status concerns, or from other social or psychological strains. I find no evidence for these theories and argue that support for the Christian Right is not different in kind from support for any other political group.

Third, although there is some evidence that the New Christian Right of the 1980s may have influenced the partisanship and voting of its supporters, these effects were generally small. Contrary to some claims, the Christian Right did not mobilize a core of previously apolitical and Democratic evangelicals into Republican politics. At least in the 1980s, however, it seems that the Christian Right did influence the partisanship of some of its followers, as well as increase slightly their political activism.

Finally, there has been a potential black constituency for the Christian Right throughout this century, which has remained largely untapped. Most previous scholarship has ignored the possibility of black support, but in this book blacks are found to be slightly *more* supportive than whites of the Christian Right. Although it would be difficult to mobilize this black constituency into Republican politics, it could provide political support for an issue agenda that focused on social issues while ignoring or taking populist positions on economic matters. There is a supportive constituency in the black community for morally conservative political action.

GOD'S WARRIORS

CHAPTER 1

The Christian Right in Twentieth-Century America: Continuity and Change

Although the rise of the New Christian Right has produced an enormous volume of scholarly research, there has been little published writing to date which seeks to put support for the New Christian Right in any historic context. The New Christian Right is only the most recent organizational manifestation of right-wing politics among conservative Protestants. To fully understand the New Christian Right, it is important to understand the political history of evangelical, fundamentalist, pentecostal, and charismatic activity in this century, especially its right-wing manifestations of evangelical politics. Although various segments of the evangelical community have also supported liberal causes, including a sizable effort by evangelical elites in support of George McGovern in 1972, these efforts are not relevant to a historical understanding of the New Christian Right.

In addition, a complete understanding of the New Christian Right today requires a grasp of the doctrinal and religious differences that divide evangelical, fundamentalist, pentecostal, and charismatic Christians. These differences are an important limitation on the ability of the Christian Right to form a unified coalition. The Moral Majority has little appeal for pentecostal and charismatic Christians, whereas Pat Robertson seems to have attracted the support of pentecostals and charismatics, but had little fundamentalist backing. Thus it is also important to be aware of the doctrinal divisions within conservative Christianity which led to this split in the New Christian Right.

THE FUNDAMENTALIST REVOLT

Religious Conflict at the Turn of the Century

Fundamentalism developed out of evangelicalism early in the twentieth century. Fundamentalism's theological roots were firmly planted in millenarianism (Sandeen 1970). The doctrinal heritage of fundamentalism included three main tenets: premillennialism, dispensationalism, and biblical inerrancy. Protestants at the turn of the century were widely involved in a debate involving the timing of the Second Coming of Christ. For the postmillennialists, Christ would come after the millennium, a thousand-year period of perfect peace and tranquility. In contrast, the premillennialists believed that Christ would return prior to the millennium and defeat the Antichrist in a major battle. The Second Coming, also known as the Rapture, was widely believed to be imminent, and it was commonly believed that it would be triggered by a worsening of the world situation, as well as the growing successes of the Antichrist in the world.

These doctrinal disputes had important political consequences. If Christ's return is to be preceded by a period of perfect peace, then politics may be a viable means of improving the world. If, however, Christ's return is triggered by the success of the Antichrist, and this return is imminent, then political solutions to the world's problems are not possible. Turmoil and discord are to be expected and may signal the end of the world. There is little incentive for Christians to try to save a doomed world: instead, Christians should withdraw from politics and keep themselves pure and holy. Turner and Guth (1989) report that contemporary premillennialists retain this pessimism about the utility of temporal reform.

The second doctrinal element of millenarianism which is important in fundamentalist thought is dispensationalism (Jorstad 1970). This doctrine argued that God has dealt with humankind through different means over the centuries. History unfolds under different dispensations, or covenants, between God and humanity. The most accepted variant on this theme was that there were seven dispensations and that the world is now in the sixth. Because the seventh and final dispensation was the kingdom, this doctrine served to reinforce the notion that the Second Coming was imminent.

Finally, the fundamentalists drew upon the millenarian belief in the inerrancy of the Scriptures. Most accepted an even stronger view—that the Bible was literally true. This doctrine, which originated in the nineteenth century, has become an important component of the creed of contemporary fundamentalism (Ammerman 1987).

The latter part of the nineteenth century and the early years of the twentieth were times of great strain within Protestantism. Revivalists of the pietistic tradition and denominational conservatives of the Calvinist tradition who accepted the doctrinal positions discussed above were concerned with the growing liberalism of the clergy (Marsden 1980). Theological modernists, who sought to make religious teachings consistent with contemporary understanding of science and culture, were making impressive gains within the denominations. With the publication of *The Fundamentals* in 1910, the conservatives went on the offensive. These volumes of collected writings were largely ignored by liberals and academics (Hunter 1987), but provided a rallying point for conservative Protestants. Throughout the decade, the split between these conservatives and the liberals widened. In 1919, the formation of the World's Christian Fundamentals Association (WCFA) marked the beginning of a bitter religious battle. Fundamentalism had emerged as a distinct movement within evangelicalism. The fundamentalist leadership, including William Riley, James Gray, Clarence Dixon, and John Straton, immediately initiated a series of more than one hundred conferences to preach the fundamentals throughout the United States and Canada. The Baptist and Presbyterian churches were deeply divided, and organizational splits occurred. Fundamentalists had always believed that it was important to remain separate from a sinful world, but this separatism now began to entail a separation from nonfundamentalist Protestants.

Although the fundamentalist-modernist dispute was the most important religious battle of the period, another development would have some later importance. The turn of the century marked not only the origins of fundamentalism but also the birth of the pentecostal movement in the United States (Quebedeaux 1983). Unlike the contemporary charismatic movement, this early manifestation was largely confined to newly formed denominations, such as the Church of God, the Church of God in Christ, and the Pentecostal Holiness Church, all of which emerged from the revivalist tradition (Smidt 1989). The roots of these churches were in the Methodist tradition of the second blessing (Poloma 1982), but a second stream developed from the Reformed tradition and led to the formation of the Assemblies of God churches (Marsden 1980). The movement was characterized by the formation of a number of new denominations (e.g., the Nazarene Church was formed from a split with the Methodists) and of independent congregations.

Although there are important doctrinal differences among them, the pentecostal, holiness, and charismatic churches share a belief in the importance of the gifts of the Holy Spirit. The most frequent manifestations of these gifts are in glossolalia, or speaking in tongues, and in faith healing. The pentecostals shared with the fundamentalists an opposition to modernism and a belief in the inerrancy of the Scriptures, and many considered themselves to be fundamentalists (Marsden 1980), but the fundamentalist response to pentecostalism was strongly negative. Reuben Archer Torrey, dean of the Los Angeles Bible Institute and a prominent fundamentalist leader of the period, stated that the movement was "the last vomit of Satan" (Quebedeaux 1983). While this vehemence was not shared by most fundamentalist leaders, the fundamentalists were generally antagonistic toward pentecostals (Marsden 1980). The doctrinal debate between the two camps centered on dispensationalism. Whereas the pentecostals felt that the early 1900s were the "Age of the Spirit," the fundamentalists believed that the gifts of the Spirit were part of an earlier dispensation, ending with the age of the apostles.

The pentecostals did not play a visible role in the political actions of the 1920s or the 1950s, but are an important part of the contemporary New Christian Right. They proved the most supportive denominational constituency for the presidential candidacy of Pat Robertson in 1988.

Political Battles over Evolution in the 1920s

Although the fundamentalists joined their liberal colleagues in support of Prohibition, the two camps were deeply divided by the teaching of evolution in public schools, an issue that marked the formation of the first set of Christian Right groups in this century. Fundamentalist leaders saw the teaching of evolution as striking at the heart of their doctrine of biblical literalism, as well as representing the worst excesses of the modernist movement. A variety of political organizations were formed by fundamentalist elites around the evolution issue. Precisely why fundamentalist energy became so concentrated on the evolution issue is not entirely clear. Szasz (1982) argued that William Jennings Bryan became convinced that the German militarism that led to World War I was based more on the writings of Charles Darwin than on Nietzsche and that the theory of evolution was one of the causes of World War I. Szasz argued that it was Bryan's enthusiasm for the subject that mobilized support among fundamentalists, although Bryan himself did not hold to strictly fundamentalist doctrine.

Furniss (1968) provides a detailed account of the various fundamentalist organizations that actively opposed the teaching of evolution. The WCFA led the fight, but other groups were quite active. The Bible League of North America (formed in 1902, before the WCFA) attempted to argue the case against evolution at an intellectual level. The well-funded Bible Crusaders of America, which drew its support primarily from Baptists, lobbied effectively in Florida and Mississippi, but was less effective in Louisiana and North Carolina. The Defenders of the Christian Faith sponsored a series of rallies in the Midwest which were sponsored by a part of the organization known as the "Flying Fundamentalists." Each of these organizations was founded by a fundamentalist entrepreneur, who remained influential in the organization through the years. In addition, a number of state-level organizations were formed, such as the Anti-Evolution League of Minnesota.

The efforts of the Christian Right to affect state legislatures were fairly sophisticated. Elite members of the organizations attempted to persuade individual legislators of the validity of their position, while other spokespersons mobilized public opinion, often by addressing church congregations and public rallies. The Flying Fundamentalists organized a series of rallies in a variety of states: in 1926 they appeared in over two hundred Minnesota cities. This combination of inside and outside lobbying strategies brought effective pressure to bear on state senators and representatives. Furniss cites as evidence of the strength of this pressure the efforts by one Louisiana representative to curtail the efforts of the Bible Crusaders of America through an old state antilobbying law. Prominent spokespersons (especially Bryan) spoke before state legislatures, urging action.

Far more common, however, were rallies and mass speeches. Many fundamentalist leaders (e.g., John Straton) participated in public debates on evolution, others (e.g., Frank Norris) held mock trials of religious institutions that taught evolution in their colleges. In an attempt to ban the teaching of evolution at the University of Minnesota, Riley gave a series of lectures on campus in 1926 (Russell 1976).

The anti-evolution groups had mixed success. They stirred passions in some northern cities that today would seem unlikely candidates for Christian Right influence,[1] but their successes came primarily in southern and border states. In all, thirty-seven anti-evolution bills were introduced in twenty state legislatures (Hunter 1987), but most failed to pass. Some were withdrawn before votes, and still others died in committee. (In Delaware the bill died in the Committee on Fish, Game, and Oysters, presumably because the language of the bill proscribed theories that man had evolved from lower organisms. For a complete description of the fate of various bills, see Furniss 1968.) Bills to limit the teaching of evolution passed in Oklahoma, Florida, Tennessee, and

---

1. Early support for fundamentalist churches was strong in northern urban areas and among the well educated. It was not until the 1930s that the pattern of support in the South and Midwest among those of lower socioeconomic status developed.

Mississippi. In other states (e.g., Louisiana), school boards prohibited the teaching of evolution. Yet even these successes were limited: for example, the Florida bill contained no penalty for violation.

In the early 1920s, the movement seems to have had fairly broad backing among conservative Protestants, but by 1926 support was largely limited to extreme fundamentalists (Marsden 1980), and funding became precarious (Cole 1931). As support for the anti-evolution campaign waned, the leaders began to shift their emphasis to anticommunism, a theme that had been present in the movement since 1919. Some fundamentalist leaders from this period continued to sound the anti-Communist theme until the early 1950s, when that message began to gain more popularity (Russell 1976).

Anticommunism was a natural cause for the fundamentalists for several reasons. First, the premillennialist teachings concerning the Second Coming of Christ were often interpreted as predicting a final battle between the forces of God and the Antichrist, in which the latter forces would come from the geographic area now occupied by the Soviet Union. Second, the atheism that Communist leaders professed was consonant with the belief that communism was the doctrine of the Antichrist in the world. Finally, the tendency of fundamentalist leaders to see world history as an arena for battle between good and evil (Hofstadter 1967) was conducive to interpreting the contemporary world as a battleground between a nation of God and one opposed to God, from which the forces of the Antichrist were to come. However, the anti-Communist rhetoric failed to generate the same level of popular sentiment among the fundamentalist rank and file as had the anti-evolution crusade.

Although many fundamentalist leaders responded enthusiastically to the anti-evolution crusade, others were troubled by the mixture of religion and politics, which seemed to contradict the premillennialist creed (Sandeen 1970). Some prominent fundamentalist leaders withdrew their membership from organizations that became involved in anti-evolution activity, and still others complained that the religious fervor that marked the foundations of fundamentalism was being absorbed into political activity (Szasz 1982).

It should be noted that although fundamentalists became politicized in the 1920s, "this politicization was haphazard" (Marsden 1980). Their consensus did not extend much beyond opposition to the teaching of evolution and to communism. Fundamentalist doctrine steered its adherents away from politics and admonished them to remain separate from the sinful, secular world. Indeed, Marsden has argued that fundamentalists developed no coherent political theory during this period and so were more easily swayed by conspiracy theories and extremist politics that were offered by some fundamentalist leaders during the Great Depression.

It should also be noted that many of the spokespersons for the Christian Right in the 1920s were not consistently conservative. The most visible example was Bryan, who prosecuted the Scopes case. Bryan's economic populism focused primarily on opposition to the role of large national banks and corporate interests. Unfortunately, the anti-evolution movement rose and fell before the advent of survey research. Although historians have documented the beliefs of the leaders of the Christian Right in the 1920s, we know little about the beliefs of supporters and members. However, it seems likely that many rank-and-file fundamentalists who opposed the teaching of evolution were supportive of liberal economic policies.

POLITICAL RETREAT AND RELIGIOUS TURMOIL: THE 1930S AND 1940S

During the 1930s and 1940s, many of the fundamentalist political organizations of the 1920s continued to exist, albeit without widespread support. Many of the leaders of these organizations began adopting the language of racism, anti-Semitism, and anti-Catholicism. This language was often embedded in some description of a larger conspiracy. Some of the early leaders of the fundamentalist movement, such as Gerald Winrod, openly advocated Fascist ideas (for an excellent history of the Christian Right in the 1930s and 1940s, see Ribuffo 1983). Winrod had been active in the anti-evolution crusades, but his openly bigoted pronouncements made him the obvious prototype for the character Buzz Windrip in Sinclair Lewis's *Elmer Gantry* (Furniss 1968).

The Great Depression fit well with the premillennialist prediction of a collapse of the social and political order that would precede the Second Coming, and many prominent preachers foresaw an immediate end to the world. Opposition to the New Deal provided a focus to the efforts of these fundamentalist leaders, but proved an unpopular position among the economically disadvantaged fundamentalist rank and file. Indeed, rival religious leaders, such as Gerald L. K. Smith, preached a populist fascism that advocated radical redistribution of wealth (Ferkiss 1962). However, among all of these leaders, strident anticommunism remained a major theme. Although fundamentalist and other religious figures attracted a good deal of attention during these two decades, they do not seem to have attracted widespread support among rank-and-file fundamentalists, evangelicals, or pentecostals. Moreover, much of the attention that these leaders attracted was quite negative: some were involved in legal battles (including the indictment of Gerald Winrod for sedition), several drifted into a vehement anti-Semitism, and others were discredited in other ways (Ribuffo 1983).

It may seem that these fundamentalist leaders should have been able to attract widespread support during this period. The Great Depression fit well with premillennialist theology, for it appeared that the secular world was deteriorating, which might hasten the Second Coming. Moreover, the suffering it caused was consistent with the teaching that spiritual salvation, not the pursuit of worldly goods, was of paramount importance, for worldly treasures were ephemeral. Hunter (1987) argued that the religious tendencies of fundamentalists during this period became "privatized"; that is, religion became a private matter of spiritual concern. Revivals were the preferred form of expression of the fundamentalist impulse, not political action. Indeed, perhaps the perceived immanence of the Second Coming made political action seem all the more futile.

Although fundamentalists were relatively quiet on the political front during this era, they continued to make progress on the religious front. Bible colleges were built, and fundamentalist churches grew. In 1941, fundamentalist leaders organized the American Council of Christian Churches (ACCC). Designed to be an organization that represented the independent and separatist fundamentalist churches, the organization was headed by the fiery anti-Communist Carl McIntire. He roundly attacked liberal Protestants, Catholics, and pentecostals in preaching a militant separatism.

Alienated by the intolerance of the ACCC, more moderate fundamentalist leaders in 1942 formed the National Association of Evangelicals (NAE), which they intended to be a more inclusive organization than the separatist ACCC (Carpenter 1984). This neo-evangelical movement shared much of the religious doctrine with the fundamentalists, but was considerably more moderate. The new evangelicals rejected the anti-intellectualism of the fundamentalists (Speer 1984) and welcomed cooperation with pentecostals and liberal Protestants. There were doctrinal differences as well, with fundamentalists generally holding that the Bible is literally true, and evangelicals frequently accepting a view of the Scriptures as inerrant, but not literally true. This evangelical-fundamentalist split is still present among conservative Christians, and it has important political ramifications.

THE SECOND FUNDAMENTALIST CRUSADE:
ANTICOMMUNISM IN THE 1950S AND 1960S

The anticommunism that became a major theme in fundamentalist political thought in the late 1920s and that had continued through the 1930s and 1940s found expression in the second wave of organized Christian Right activity in the 1950s. Many prominent fundamentalist leaders preached vigorously against the Communist menace in the latter part of the 1940s, but it was not until the McCarthy campaign began in earnest that Christian Right organizations began to form. Fundamentalist leaders cooperated closely with McCarthy and urged investigation of prominent modernist religious leaders as possible Communists or fellow travelers.

Sociologists have stressed the role of sympathetic organizations in mobilizing resources into social action (McCarthy and Zald 1977), and political scientists have also emphasized the importance of supportive organizations (Walker 1983). The resource mobilization theory fits well the establishment of the Christian Right organizations of the 1950s. By 1953, all of the future leaders of the anti-Communist organizations were associated with the ACCC (Jorstad 1970). Even as McCarthy began to self-destruct, these leaders were forming, with the aid of the ACCC, organizations that would constitute the Christian Right of the 1950s. Billy Hargis formed the Christian Crusade, Fred Schwarz founded the Christian Anti-Communism Crusade (CACC), and Edgar Bundy formed the Church League of America. During this era, some of the organizations from the 1920s also experienced a revival of public interest. For example, the Defenders of the Christian Faith grew rapidly during the 1950s, although it never rivaled the newly formed organizations in numbers (Ribuffo 1983).[2]

Like the organizations of the 1920s, the Christian Right groups of the 1950s sounded one major theme—this time anticommunism. Although some of these organizations took positions on domestic issues, these positions were generally related to communism in some manner. For example, the CACC opposed Medicare because it would open the door to socialism in the United States (Wilcox 1987b). Like the groups of the 1920s, the anti-Communist groups took strong stands on education issues. Sex education in the schools was attacked not because it contributed to the lowering of moral standards per se, but because it was part of a Communist plot to undermine the United States' moral

---

2. The founder of the Defenders of the Christian Faith, Gerald Winrod, was unable to buy radio time in the United States after his sedition trial. This undoubtedly limited support for the organization.

foundations. School prayer was supported to thwart the Communist attempt to separate the United States from God (Clabaugh 1974).

The leaders of these organizations used nationwide radio shows to communicate with their followers, who contributed increasing amounts to the cause (Jorstad 1970). In addition, some leaders, such as Schwarz of the CACC, conducted traveling "schools of anti-communism" (Wolfinger et al. 1969).

The fundamentalist efforts did not attract widespread support, even within the conservative Christian community. Evangelical leaders, while sharing a general anti-Communist orientation, were critical of the tactics of these fundamentalist groups (Hunter 1987). Moreover, the public seems to have been largely unaware of these groups. Even among those who attended fundamentalist churches, the majority were unaware of the Christian Right of this period.

Activists in the Christian Right during this period were, like all political activists, well-educated, affluent individuals. Chapter 5 provides more details on activists in the Crusade. Although they were strongly anti-Communist, they were not doctrinaire conservatives. Predictably, they were overwhelmingly Republican. The anti-Communist message seems to have appealed not only to fundamentalists but also to more secular rightists. These secular rightists were more conservative than the fundamentalists.

Mass support for the Crusade was highest among fairly well-educated fundamentalists. As was the case among activists, a set of secular supporters can be identified, and, when these are excluded from the analysis, Crusade supporters were quite moderate on most issues, although strongly anti-Communist. Unlike activists, they were not disproportionately Republican.

In 1964, the Christian Right organizations shed their separatist tendencies and allied themselves with more secular organizations in open support of the presidential candidacy of Barry Goldwater. Goldwater's repudiation in the election seems to have dealt a major blow to the Christian Right, whose financial base soon began to evaporate. Although some of these organizations survive today, their influence waned quickly after the 1964 election.

THE THIRD COMING OF THE FUNDAMENTALIST RIGHT: THE 1970S AND BEYOND

The period between 1965 and 1976 was marked by a good deal of change in the political behavior of evangelicals and fundamentalists. A sizable minority bloc of evangelicals supported liberal causes and in

1972 endorsed McGovern. Although evangelical and fundamentalist elites had previously accepted a doctrine which indicated that Christians should remain separate from the secular world, evangelical elites began to pay increasing attention to politics, as the content of their publications demonstrates (Wuthnow 1983). In 1976 the Jimmy Carter candidacy mobilized the evangelicals as no candidate had done before. Carter was a professed "born-again" Christian and a Southern Baptist. His campaign brought increased media attention to evangelicals: *Newsweek, Time, U.S. News and World Report,* and national television news all carried features on evangelicalism in 1976 or 1977.

Fundamentalist elites were less favorable to Carter, and responded negatively to his *Playboy* interview, in which he admitted to having committed adultery in his heart. Nevertheless, substantial numbers of fundamentalists joined their evangelical brethren in casting their votes for the first avowedly evangelical candidate in over fifty years.

The Carter candidacy had two important consequences for the future of the Christian Right. First, the mobilization of previously apolitical evangelical voters by the campaign demonstrated to secular political elites the existence of a new potential voting bloc. Leaders of the secular New Right immediately began to devise strategies to further mobilize these evangelicals and woo them to Republican activism. Second, because Carter argued that Christians had an obligation to participate in politics, his candidacy helped to break down the longstanding feeling among evangelicals and fundamentalists that electoral politics were not the proper realm for Christian activity.

The period between 1965 and 1976 was also marked by the development of a number of networks which improved the communications between fundamentalists (Ammerman 1987). Christian bookstores grew rapidly during this period, and they stimulated the sale of books by fundamentalist religious and political leaders. One of the best-selling books of the 1970s was Hal Lindsey's *The Late Planet Earth,* a Far-Right tract with a strongly premillennial message of the imminent Second Coming. Christian magazines also grew in circulation. Christian radio and television stations were established, giving fundamentalist, evangelical, and pentecostal preachers access to wider audiences.

Fundamentalist Christian schools also grew rapidly during this decade. This growth was spurred by a number of factors, including school desegregation efforts, but also by the teaching of evolution, which was part of the increased emphasis on science that followed *Sputnik,* and by the changing content of public-school textbooks in the areas of history, politics, and sex roles.

Wald (1987) has suggested that local political movements in the 1970s facilitated the return of evangelicals and fundamentalists to politics, thus creating a potential constituency for the New Christian Right. He cites a textbook protest in Kanawha County, West Virginia, the Dade County, Florida, gay rights referendum, and the various state and local campaigns against the proposed Equal Rights Amendment (ERA) as attracting support among fundamentalist and evangelical Protestants. They also attracted the attention of secular political leaders, who were important forces in the formation of the New Christian Right.

During the late 1970s, the organizations of the New Christian Right were formed. The two most important organizations, Christian Voice and the Moral Majority, were both founded in 1978. Christian Voice was established as an effort to extend the work of several local antigay and antipornography groups in California. Its membership has come primarily from the independent Bible churches, independent Baptist churches, and other fundamentalist churches, as well as the pentecostal Assemblies of God (Guth 1983b), located in the West and South.

The Moral Majority was formed by Falwell after he had been approached by leaders of the secular New Right and promised support in the form of direct-mail lists, organizational support, and training of state and regional leaders. The Moral Majority made a concerted effort to build state organizations, primarily through the networks of Falwell's denomination, the Bible Baptist Fellowship (Liebman 1983). Falwell claimed organizational success in nearly every state, but actual state chapters were established in fewer than twenty (Guth 1983a), and many of these were quite small. Although Falwell publicly sought to forge a coalition of fundamentalists, evangelicals, pentecostals, and conservative Catholics, Jews, and other Protestants, this effort floundered because of the relative intolerance of the fundamentalist pastors who headed the state and local organizations (Wilcox 1987d). These pastors, schooled in a tradition of anti-Catholic and antipentecostal rhetoric, were unable to overcome this tradition in their political dealings.

In many ways, the organizations of the New Christian Right resembled those of the Christian Right in earlier days. Like these earlier organizations, the New Christian Right was headed by fundamentalist ministers who relied on existing religious and political organizations to build their groups. Whereas the organizations of the 1950s spread their message through radio, the new organizations used television and direct mail to communicate with their followers. As was the case in the 1920s and 1950s, these organizations were fairly well funded. Their message included a vehement anticommunism, as well as a rejection of modernism in the classroom, this time in the form of an attack on the teaching of "secular humanism." However, unlike these earlier organizations, the New Christian Right took positions on a range of issues, from South Africa and the Contras to the balanced budget amendment and the gold standard to gay rights and the ERA.[3]

The New Christian Right attracted a good deal more media attention than had the earlier manifestations of the fundamentalist Right. The new communication channels that the fundamentalists had established, particularly the televised sermons of sympathetic preachers, served to alert potential converts. Moreover, new technology, such as computerized direct mail, enabled the organizations to more accurately target sympathetic individuals and approach them with carefully designed messages. The mass media paid a good deal of attention to the New Christian Right, particularly in the aftermath of the 1980 elections. The net result of all of these factors was that the general public was significantly more aware of the existence and message of the New Christian Right than it had been of its predecessors.

Studies suggest that support for the Christian Right in the 1970s and 1980s was not widespread, however. Among the general public, support hovered between 10 percent and 15 percent of the population (Buell and Sigelman 1985; Wilcox 1987c; Sigelman et al. 1987). Among white evangelicals, support was somewhat higher, but limited to around 25 percent.

Supporters of the fundamentalist Right of the 1980s were similar in many ways to those of the Christian Right in the 1950s. Support was strongest among evangelicals and fundamentalists who attended church regularly (Sigelman et al. 1987; Shupe and Stacey 1983; Johnson and Tamney 1984). However, unlike supporters of the Christian Right in the 1950s, they tended to be Republican and conservative on economic, social, and foreign-policy issues. Activists in the Moral Majority were remarkably similar in demographic profile to those of the CACC some twenty years earlier. Unlike the Crusaders, however, the Moral Majority activists were fairly consistent conservatives. Moreover, unlike the Christian Right of the 1950s, the New Christian Right did not attract a sizable secular group of supporters.

The 1980 election brought a good deal of attention to the leadership of the New Christian Right, and in particular to Jerry Falwell. The results of this scrutiny were not positive: Falwell's positions on a number of issues (such as South Africa) were widely publicized, and he became an unpopular figure. Although the New Christian Right played a visible role in the 1984 Republican convention, by 1987 the fundamentalist Right was in retreat. Falwell had retired as head of the

3. The Moral Majority took positions opposing sanctions against South Africa, favoring military aid to the Contras, favoring a balanced-budget amendment and a return to the gold standard, and opposing gay rights and the Equal Rights Amendment.

Moral Majority, which had experienced an erosion of its financial base and been incorporated into an umbrella organization known as the Liberty Federation. Christian Voice had discontinued its Moral Government Fund, again due to falling revenues. Finally, in 1989, Falwell announced the disbandment of the Moral Majority, claiming that it had achieved its goals.

The collapse of the organizations of the new fundamentalist Right should not be taken as an indication that their political message was unpopular among fundamentalists, evangelicals, and pentecostals. A number of studies (Simpson 1983; Stockton 1984; Kellstedt 1988) have suggested that the platform of the New Christian Right had substantially more support than did the organizations themselves, particularly among evangelicals, and the data in chapters 8 and 9 suggest a lingering support for the Christian Right and its platform.

THE RISE OF THE PENTECOSTAL RIGHT:
PAT ROBERTSON'S PRESIDENTIAL CAMPAIGN

During the 1960s, a second wave of pentecostal and charismatic activity occurred. Unlike the earlier movement, which was confined to a set of newly created splinter denominations, in the 1960s charismatic activity grew within mainstream Protestant churches, such as the Methodists, Presbyterians, and Lutherans, and among Catholics as well. In addition, this latter movement was not confined to poor whites and blacks, but was largely a middle-class and suburban phenomenon (Smidt 1989). The middle-class orientation of this charismatic movement was evident in the formation and rapid spread of charismatic businessmen's associations.

Although there are subtle doctrinal differences between charismatics and pentecostals, none of the surveys used in this book allows us to distinguish between them. The primary difference between charismatic and pentecostal theology lies in the role of speaking in tongues. Although both groups believe in a wider range of gifts of the Spirit, pentecostals generally assign glossolalia a central role among spiritual gifts, while charismatics often view it as merely one of many gifts (Smidt 1989). Charismatics cannot be distinguished from other Christians based on denominational affiliation, although there are explicitly pentecostal denominations.

Charismatic and pentecostal ministers, like their fundamentalist colleagues, took their message to the airwaves in the 1970s and 1980s. Jim and Tammy Bakker, Jimmy Swaggart, and Pat Robertson preached the blessings of baptism of the Holy Spirit on their respective television programs. Swaggart and especially Robertson included in their programs a healthy dose of conservative politics.

The 1980s witnessed the first flowering of a new type of Christian Right activity—this time by pentecostal and charismatic Christians. Robertson, the Baptist minister who hosted the televised "700 Club," in 1987 declared his candidacy for president. During his career on the "700 Club," Robertson clearly established himself as a charismatic. During his early years on the program, he spoke in tongues, and he practiced faith healing throughout his tenure on the program. He also endorsed a premillennialist view of the future and often interpreted contemporary political events as harbingers of the Second Coming.

Although most polls showed that Robertson lacked widespread support, his campaign showed considerable muscle in Michigan and in early straw polls, where the degree of dedication of a candidate's followers could influence the results. His early fundraising was immensely successful: his first submission to the Federal Election Commission (FEC) to qualify for federal matching funds (for $4.5 million) contained the names of over seventy thousand contributors, and it had to be brought to the FEC in a sixteen-foot truck.

Robertson won the endorsement of several prominent charismatic and pentecostal religious leaders, but the fundamentalist and evangelical response was lukewarm. The two major organizations of the fundamentalist right (Moral Majority and Christian Voice) did not spring to his support, and Falwell endorsed George Bush despite earlier feelers from Robertson. Moreover, studies suggested that Robertson's support among evangelical pastors was weak (Langenbach 1987). One early study of the major financial contributors to the Robertson campaign found that nearly one-half were members of charismatic and pentecostal churches, especially the Assemblies of God, and that only 4 percent were members of fundamentalist churches (Guth and Green 1987c).[4]

Robertson's political platform was quite similar to that of the fundamentalist Right. He called for the elimination of the vestiges of secular humanism from the classroom and condemned the teaching of evolution. His foreign policy was strongly anti-Communist. Like the fundamentalist Right of the 1980s, he took conservative positions on economic issues as well. This expanded issue agenda was evident in the issue positions of his early contributors, who were consistently conservative (Guth and Green 1987c).

4. Although few Robertson contributors belonged to fundamentalist churches, fully 53 percent identified themselves as fundamentalists. The Green and Guth (1988) survey allowed for multiple religious identifications, so most of these fundamentalists also identified themselves as charismatics. It seems likely that these respondents used the label fundamentalist to identify their position on biblical inerrancy.

As the campaign unfolded, Robertson had considerable success in states that selected their delegates by caucuses. Because caucuses typically have very low levels of public participation, small groups of committed activists who turn out in large numbers can dominate the process. Although the caucus results in Michigan were disputed, most analysts reported that Robertson won the first-round balloting. Robertson also surprised Bush and the media by finishing second in Iowa, and he went on to win or do well in caucuses in Hawaii, Washington, and Alaska.

His campaign began to develop problems around the time of the New Hampshire primary. Over a period of a few weeks, Robertson charged that the Soviets had missiles hidden in the caves of Cuba, claimed to have known where hostages were held in the Mideast, and accused the Bush campaign of masterminding the troubles of fellow charismatic Jimmy Swaggart. These events reinforced doubts that conservative Republicans had about Robertson's judgment. Added to these gaffes were other troubles: a libel lawsuit that centered on Robertson's claim to have been a combat Marine and an IRS investigation of the financing of his campaign.

Although Robertson had predicted a good showing in the southern primaries, Bush swept the region. By the time Robertson withdrew from the campaign in early May, he had spent nearly $30 million to garner only thirty-five official delegates. However, in assessing the successes and failures of the campaign, two points must be made. First, Robertson did fairly well for a novice politician. He raised more money than any candidate except Bush, won several states, and got around 20 percent of the vote in each of the southern primaries. Moreover, his campaign succeeded in establishing footholds in state party committees throughout the country—presumably with another bid for the presidency in mind. Second, the delegate totals for Robertson are deceptive. Robertson continued to seek delegates in a number of states where state law bound all delegates to vote for Bush. In Virginia, the Carolinas, and Texas, for example, many of the delegates selected favored Robertson, and they could be counted on to support him on any disputes over the platform or, more importantly, future delegate selection rules.

THE CHRISTIAN RIGHT IN THE TWENTIETH CENTURY: CONTINUITY AND CHANGE

During this century, the fundamentalist Right has shown organizational strength in three periods, and the pentecostal Right has recently organized. These manifestations of the Christian Right have a number of similarities, as well as some important differences. The different sets of organizations are quite similar in their formation, and there are a number of similarities in their platforms and in the characteristics of their supporters and activists.

Political scientists who seek to explain the formation of interest groups have generally offered two sets of explanations. The pluralist theory, best articulated by Truman (1951), sees interest group formation as a response to disturbances in the equilibrium between groups, both active and latent. In contrast, the entrepreneur theory, articulated by Salisbury (1969), sees group formation as the result of the efforts of political leaders who see a potential market for the issue positions and benefits of a group, and form a group to offer these goods. The theories need not be viewed as mutually exclusive: disturbances in the equilibrium may create the market that entrepreneurs seek to mobilize.

Both sets of theories offer explanations for the creation of the Christian Right of the 1920s, the 1950s, and the 1980s. The activity in the 1920s was preceded by a marked liberalization among the clergy in the mainstream Protestant denominations. Thus the anti-evolution groups are usually perceived as a response to the creeping modernism that was evident in many Protestant churches. The activity of the 1950s was facilitated not by an upset to the equilibrium against the fundamentalists, but rather by one in their favor. McCarthyism made the anti-Communist message that many of the fundamentalist preachers had espoused for decades suddenly popular, and it made the formation of political organizations profitable. The fundamentalist and pentecostal activity of the 1980s was preceded by a period of rapid social change, including changes in the role of women and the national legalization of abortion. In each era, the potential market created by these changes was exploited by dynamic preachers, who headed the organizations.

One group of sociologists, in contrast, have stressed the role of resources in the creation of social movement organizations (McCarthy and Zald 1977). The resource mobilization theory (and Jack Walker's related patron theory) suggests that such organizations are more likely to form when they have access to resources from sympathetic organizations. There is considerable support for this theory in each wave of Christian Right activity as well. The groups in the 1920s relied on the resources of the newly formed fundamentalist religious organizations to launch themselves. During the 1950s, the ACCC provided an organizational umbrella under which the fledgling Christian Right leaders were trained and sent forth. In the 1980s, the secular New Right leaders supplied the Moral Majority and the Christian Voice with the technology of direct mail to help fund the organizations (Zwier 1982). Moreover, the Moral Majority built its grass-roots efforts around the already existing network of pastors of the Baptist Bible Fellowship (Liebman 1983). Robertson achieved name recognition through the "700 Club," and in late 1987 the Federal Election Commission began investigating the possibility that his Christian network channeled resources to his presidential campaign. The investigation was still in process in 1991.

The similarities between different generations of the Christian Right extend beyond their formation. Two prominent themes echo throughout each crusade. The first, anticommunism, has been present in the message of each Christian Right organization. Indeed, activists of the Moral Majority were as suspicious of the domestic influence of Communists as were activists in the CACC two decades earlier.

The second common theme throughout this century is one of education policy. The century's first crusade was centered on the teaching of evolution in the schools, the organizations of the 1950s were concerned with sex education in the schools, and the fundamentalist and pentecostal movements of the 1980s opposed the teaching of secular humanism (which generally included evolution and sex education) in the classroom. The role of education issues in the activities of the Christian Right cannot be exaggerated. The wave of fundamentalist schools in the 1970s and 1980s was in part a response of fundamentalist activists to the teaching in public schools of doctrines that they believed contradicted their faith. The activities by many state school boards to deny certification to these fundamentalist schools gave impetus to the formation of the New Christian Right organizations in the 1980s (Zwier 1982). In many states, the Christian school organizations were markedly stronger than any other New Christian Right group.

In many ways, however, the organizations of the 1980s were different in kind from those that preceded them. Whereas the organizations of the 1920s confined their messages primarily to evolution, with a secondary emphasis on anticommunism, and the organizations of the 1950s rarely strayed from the anticommunism theme, those of the 1980s took positions on a broad range of public-policy issues. As a consequence, whereas activists and supporters of the anti-Communist groups were not consistently conservative, activists and supporters of the New Christian Right of the 1980s were.

Moreover, the widespread television coverage of the New Christian Right and the new technology of direct mail made the groups of the 1980s a more visible part of public life. Whereas the majority of Americans had not heard of the Christian Right in the 1950s (and probably few Americans had heard of the groups in the 1920s), the Moral Majority of the 1980s was widely known. As a consequence, it had a somewhat larger support base than had the earlier organizations, but it also aroused more heated and organized opposition.

There are also similarities between the organizations of the 1920s and the 1980s, which do not apply to those of the 1950s. Like the anti-evolution groups of the 1920s, the New Christian Right has attempted to influence government by lobbying the legislature, as well as through electoral politics. Although the anti-Communist groups in the 1950s were involved in electoral politics, they made no appreciable effort to influence legislation. Moreover, the groups in the 1920s often worked at the grass-roots level, building local organizations in order to attempt to influence state legislatures. Similarly, the New Christian Right attempted to build grass-roots organizations in the early 1980s, although these attempts were largely unsuccessful. Like the anti-evolution groups, and unlike the anti-Communist organizations, the New Christian Right seems to appeal almost entirely to highly religious evangelicals and fundamentalists.

Finally, the new charismatic Right, though it shares a common agenda with the fundamentalist organizations, differs in one potentially important way. By embracing the support of evangelicals, conservative Catholics, and other Christians, the charismatic Right may have the potential to build a coalition of conservative Christians, which the intolerance of the fundamentalists has prevented. Smidt (1989) has noted that the contemporary charismatic movement is the most ecumenical religious movement in recent history, a sentiment echoed by others (e.g., Rifken and Howard 1979). Robertson himself has endorsed an ecumenical perspective. Harrell (1988) quotes Robertson: "In terms of the succession of the church, I'm a Roman Catholic. As far as the majesty of worship, I'm an Episcopalian; as far as the belief in the sovereignty of God, I'm Presbyterian; in terms of holiness, I'm a Methodist; in terms of the priesthood of believers and baptism, I'm a Baptist; in terms of the baptism of the Holy Spirit, I'm a Pentecostal. So I'm a little bit of all of them" (pp. 102–3).

Although the pentecostal churches may not fully share this ecumenical spirit,[5] a charismatic Right could welcome pentecostals, fundamentalists, other evangelicals, and conservative Catholics. Moreover, although the fundamentalist leaders continue to condemn the pentecostals, Ammerman (1987) suggests that fundamentalist members may view charismatic and pentecostal Christians as potential allies. If the rank-and-file fundamentalists begin to see the many similarities

5. Whereas the charismatic movement is inclusive, pentecostalism has historically been more sectarian. See Harrell (1981) for a description of sectarian conflict in the early days of the pentecostal movement. Moreover, Wilcox and Jelen (1990) report that pentecostals are the most intolerant of politically unpopular groups of the Right and the Left, although their study did not focus on religious tolerance.

between the charismatics and themselves, then the possibility of a truly important Christian Right may emerge. This possibility might be further enhanced by Robertson's popularity among blacks, perhaps due in part to his choice of a black as cohost of the "700 Club," and in part to the frequently charismatic nature of black religious services.

If the charismatic Right could gain the support of most white charismatics and pentecostals, some white evangelicals, some white fundamentalists, and a portion of the black evangelical and charismatic movements, it would constitute a sizable political force. However, there are several barriers to the formation of this larger movement. First, there are important religious differences between the various original pentecostal churches and the charismatic movement in mainstream Protestant and Catholic congregations (Poloma 1982). Whereas the original pentecostal churches splintered from the mainstream denominations and retain elements of this religious particularism, the new charismatic movement is one of renewal of faith within established denominations (Quebedeaux 1983). Doctrinal differences have long been a source of disunity among conservative Protestants, and doctrinal differences between separate pentecostal denominations and Catholic and mainstream Protestant charismatics might prevent the formation of a unified Christian Right. Yet Poloma notes that "the spirit of unity among charismatics bridges both denominational and interdenominational differences."

Moreover, like evangelicals, charismatics and pentecostals are not consistently conservative (Poloma 1982; Smidt 1989). Indeed, Smidt found that self-identified charismatics were more politically moderate than evangelicals, although other studies (Wilcox and Jelen 1990) find that pentecostals are the most conservative. However, Poloma has argued that one wing of the charismatic movement is quite similar in its political outlook to the fundamentalist Right, calling Robertson the "Moral Majority in charismatic dress." It is from this wing of the charismatic movement that support for the New Christian Right comes.

The fundamentalist Christian Right of the 1920s faded from view after the Scopes verdict, and the fundamentalist Right of the 1950s likewise faded after the defeat of Goldwater in 1964. Recent scandals involving prominent televangelists have weakened the fundraising power of the contemporary movement and may likewise undermine the current charismatic and fundamentalist Right. The task for students of the Christian Right is to develop a clearer understanding of the circumstances that cause the formation and success of Christian Right movements, as well as the dynamics that ultimately end their crusades.

CHAPTER 2

Explaining Support for the
Christian Right

As the various waves of right-wing activity in American politics have
ebbed and flowed, social scientists have attempted to explain support
for right-wing organizations. A number of studies attempted to explain support for the anti-Communist crusade of Senator Joseph Mc-
Carthy, and even more attention was paid to the secular and religious
right-wing organizations of the early 1960s. The rise of the New Right
(and particularly the New Christian Right) has sparked yet another
wave of research. Although some of this later research has been
grounded in the theories and research of students of the earlier right-
wing movements, there are noticeable differences in emphasis between
the most recent set of studies and those that came before.

   Although social science is often alleged to be value-neutral, it is
difficult to study an ideological movement with perfect detachment.
Most researchers who have studied the Christian Right oppose many of
its political goals, and this was emphatically true of those who studied
support for McCarthy and right-wing organizations of the 1950s and
1960s. Unable to imagine that support for right-wing groups might
exist among rational, well-adjusted citizens, many of these scholars
posited a wide variety of types of social and psychological strain as the
source of support. Hofstadter (1955) referred to the "rural-evangelical
virus" that spread prohibition. Often supporters of the Right were
depicted as victims of these groups—and individuals with certain types
of social and psychological strain were seen as particularly "vulnerable"
to their appeals. Support for the Right was generally viewed by these
writers as irrational. This view is seen in many of the essays in Bell's

edited book *The Radical Right* (1963). McAdam (1982) notes: "While perhaps effective as a means of discrediting one's political opponents, such formulations are less convincing as scientific accounts of insurgencies" (p. 13).

In part, the emphasis on nonrational sources of support for right-wing figures and organizations in this era may have been due to the Byzantine conspiracy theories promulgated by some groups, especially those of the secular Right. It is relatively easy to understand support for a mainstream conservative organization as rooted in rational political impulses, but when organizations such as the John Birch Society preach of a centuries-old conspiracy by an offshoot of the Masons which has controlled the history of the world, rationality seems somewhat less relevant. Indeed, some researchers attempted to distinguish between organizations that represented a "responsible" political right and more "irresponsible" right-wing groups. One study (Green, Turner, and Germino 1963) labeled as irresponsible those organizations that hired as speakers individuals with no knowledge of the substance of politics—speakers such as John Wayne and Ronald Reagan.

In contrast, more recent work has generally favored the more parsimonious explanation that the combination of conservative religious and political values leads to support for the Christian Right. Such work generally posits that support for the Christian Right is "rational" in two senses. First, it does not spring from psychopathology. In addition, support for the Right is seen as the politically rational choice given a set of basic values and attitudes, much as support for any other political groups. Rationality in this sense implies a congruence between the values and attitudes of citizens and the groups and candidates they support. The values and attitudes that lead to support for the Christian Right, of course, are in turn the result of the not-always-rational socialization process.

It should be noted that not all writers who attribute support for the Right to social or psychological strain view supporters as irrational. Moreover, the distinction between rational and nonrational explanations for support for the Christian Right is not always a neat one, for some explanations have elements of both. Some conceptions of organized political activity suggest that all members of groups that provide nonexclusive public goods are in some sense nonrational (Olson 1965). In addition, not all writers in the 1950s and 1960s focused on social, psychological, or other strain, and not all scholars in the 1980s have emphasized the role of beliefs and values. It is nonetheless generally true that scholars who wrote about support for the Right in the 1950s and 1960s often saw that support as the result of social or psychological strain, and somehow different from support for other mainstream political groups. Those who have studied support for the Right in the 1980s have conceived of this support as not differing in kind from support for other political and social groups.[1]

EXPLANATIONS FOR SUPPORT FOR THE CHRISTIAN RIGHT

This chapter examines a series of explanations for support for the political Right in American politics. These explanations address a different question from those theories discussed at the end of chapter 1, which focused on the formation of the organizations of the Christian Right. The explanations discussed in this chapter attempt to account for individual differences in support for existing right-wing organizations. These explanations do not generally distinguish between support for the secular and religious Right, so I review studies of support for all types of organizations of the Right. Much of the work that attempts to explain support for the Right neglects to examine the mechanism that drives particular explanations. This chapter therefore pays particular attention to the processes that are assumed by each type of explanation.

PERSONALITY EXPLANATIONS

Among all explanations for support for the Right in American politics, the one most firmly rooted in nonrational sources focuses on the personality characteristics that lead to support for the Right. Many of these explanations rely on the Freudian notion of projection, in which individuals transfer their aggression, resentments, and inadequacies onto out-groups. The authors of *The Authoritarian Personality* (Adorno et al. 1950) reported a personality type that was associated with displacement of aggression to out-groups and with support for right-wing figures. Evidence for these types of personality explanations may be sought by looking for evidence of hostility toward out-groups. In this case, racial and religious prejudice among Christian Right supporters might constitute evidence for personality explanations. Other personality defects have been associated with support for the Right, including

---

1. Wallis has made the distinction between strain theories of support on the one hand and values and socialization theories on the other. Jelen (1991a) refers to pathological and representational theories. Wood and Hughes (1984) distinguish between status discontent on the one hand and culture and socialization theories on the other. In each case, the distinction is similar to the one I am drawing.

dogmatism, strong-mindedness, distrust of others, and excessive nostalgia. Some have also argued that those who support the Right have a simplified cognitive structure and perceive complex realities in terms of simple dichotomies.

How do personality characteristics lead to support for right-wing organizations? Rohter (1969) describes the function that membership in or support of a right-wing group is thought to provide for individuals with certain personality traits. He suggests that right-wing groups help individuals bolster their self-image by projecting their inadequacies onto out-groups. In addition, by strongly voicing a moral conservatism and fervent patriotism, individuals enhance their self-worth— both by associating themselves with traditional symbols of value and by gaining social acceptance from others who share their sentiments. This social acceptance is even more important if combined with active participation in a right-wing group, because such activity can enhance feelings of self-worth. Finally, the simple explanations offered by rightist groups appeal to those individuals who have a strong aversion to ambiguity and a strong need for firm, simple views of the world.

Theorists have also argued that right-wing (and possibly left-wing) ideology may have a particular appeal to individuals with particular personality attributes or styles of cognitive organization. Individuals with dogmatic or authoritarian personalities may be attracted to the Manichean account of the struggle between good and evil, as well as to complex theories of conspiracy. Individuals who compensate for weak feelings of self-worth may be attracted to the authoritative pronouncements such groups make about the values of active patriotism and moral conservatism. However, Elms (1969) has noted that any internally consistent ideology (of the Left or Right) could serve these functions.

The theoretical connection between personality and support for the Christian Right involves two additional arguments that do not apply for the secular Right. First, it may be that religious conservatism, especially fundamentalism, in some way fosters the very personality types most likely to support the Right. Researchers have suggested that fundamentalists are among those most likely to exhibit authoritarian traits (Brown 1962; Rhodes 1960). Some have argued that those individuals who seek the security of an absolute moral code may find it in fundamentalist churches, which may then mold the socialization process in such a way as to create these personality traits in the young. Rohter (1969) posited that the socialization process among fundamentalist Christians produces and reinforces authoritarian personality traits, although Hofstadter (1967) has suggested that authoritarianism is also the result of the socialization practices of status-striving adults, thus merging personality theories with the status theories described below.

Bruce (1988), however, provides a connection between fundamentalism and monistic styles of thought which does not involve personality traits. He notes that the basic tenets of fundamentalism preach a perpetual battle between God and Satan, which explains the complexity of the world. Fundamentalists may use the same cognitive processes to explain complex social and political events. In this way, Bruce argues that rightist notions that the "decline of America" is due to a conspiracy of Communists or secular humanists are attractive to fundamentalists for reasons other than personality characteristics. Fundamentalists may be attracted to such theories because they fit with their religious beliefs, not because they have simplified cognitive structures or dogmatic personalities.

The evidence for a personality explanation for support for the Right is mixed. Lipset (1963a) reported that authoritarianism was associated with support for McCarthy among all educational groups, and Rohter (1969) reported that his group of rightists were markedly more dogmatic, intolerant of left-wing groups, less willing to compromise, and more close-minded than his control group. In his final causal model, Rohter found that personality traits had a strong direct and indirect impact on scores on his radical Right ideology index, although conservative political beliefs had a much stronger link. Elms (1969) conducted in-depth psychological interviews with a small set of members in right-wing groups, and he concluded that some of them had joined these organizations in order to cope with extreme psychological symptoms. Johnson and Tamney (1984) reported that authoritarianism had a strong indirect link with support for the Christian Right, by increasing support for its agenda and by increasing cultural ethnocentrism.

Lipset and Raab (1978) reported consistent evidence that rightists disliked out-groups, which could be interpreted as evidence of projected hostility. The authors find a regular pattern of racism, anti-Catholicism, and anti-Semitism among right-wing organizations in the United States throughout its history, although this hostility is not evident in the members and supporters of all right-wing groups. Jelen (1991a) concludes that negative affect for certain cultural minorities fuels support for the Christian Right, though he does not link this affect to personality sources.

Although these studies have all found relationships between personality traits and support for and membership in right-wing groups, they are far from definitive. Each study suffers from methodological flaws. The authoritarianism index (F scale) has been criticized on methodological grounds (Christie and Jahoda 1969), although later formulations have avoided some of these problems (Altemeyer 1988). Rohter's control group was composed of liberal political activists who were probably more committed to democratic norms than the general public. Elm's study did not include a control group, although he did report interviews with two liberals.

Wald et al. (1989b) has offered a reconceptualization of these personality explanations. Although the authors find no evidence that support for the New Christian Right among Gainesville, Florida, churchgoers is associated with authoritarianism, they do report that Christian Right support is linked to "authority mindedness," which they define as an ideological commitment that values authority and obedience as matters of principle, but is not linked to a personality disorder. They suggest that the fundamentalist's commitment to the inerrancy of the Scriptures as an authority on all matters may lead them to support political movements that promote conformity to biblical values. They note the authority relationships between husband and wife, and they cite Ammerman's (1987) description of the authority of fundamentalist pastors over their flocks as evidence of the fundamentalist ideology of authority. The evidence by Wald et al. supports Bruce's interpretation that religion explains some of the characteristics of fundamentalists which were previously attributed to personality characteristics.

ALIENATION

A second explanation for support for the Right in American politics which is rooted in a nonrational conception of right-wing support is alienation. Although this concept has a rich theoretical heritage, its use in the literature on the Right is more limited. Drawing on the "mass society" literature that saw social change creating large numbers of individuals who are no longer attached to social, community, or political institutions, proponents of this explanation suggested that these rootless individuals would be attracted to extremist symbols and leaders (Kornhauser 1959).

Several processes have been described that would lead these alienated individuals to support extremist causes. Rohter (1969) offered a functional explanation, suggesting that right-wing ideology offers people the means to overcome or compensate for their feelings of social and political powerlessness. Conover and Gray (1981) focused instead on the ease with which alienated individuals might be mobilized by political groups. They argued that "without such organizational involvement in their lives, people are thought to grow restless and alienated . . . such individuals are 'easy prey' for right-wing movements" (p. 4).

The evidence that right-wing activists or supporters are alienated is weak. Rohter found some evidence of alienation in his group of rightists and John Birch Society members in Oregon, and Abcarian and Stanach (1965) found strong themes of alienation in their content analysis of right-wing literature. However, Conover and Gray (1981) reported no relationship between alienation and profamily activism, and Wolfinger et al. (1969) reported that Crusaders who answered their survey were deeply involved in community and political activity and had higher levels of efficacy than a demographically similar group from the national election study. Similarly, Grupp (1969) reported a high degree of civic and political organizational attachment among his sample of John Birch Society members.

There is some evidence in these studies of a somewhat different type of alienation, however. Wolfinger's Crusaders and Grupp's Birchers were generally highly active in partisan politics, but also felt quite distant from government. Crusaders generally believed that the federal government was infiltrated by Communists, whereas the Bircher's were also totally unsatisfied with government. This sort of alienation from government seems common among the Right of the 1950s and 1960s.

SOCIAL STATUS EXPLANATIONS

Among the various explanations for support of right-wing movements, those that focus on social status are by far the most common. Although this set of explanations ultimately is derived from Max Weber's discussion of status groups, its more recent antecedent is Hofstadter's (1967) claim that status politics had replaced class politics in the United States. There are many variants on this general type, which suggests that those who support the Right do so to enhance their social status. These variants differ in the extent to which status concern is seen as the result of sociological strain, or as the rational concern with the preservation of a way of life. However, common to all status explanations is the assumption that individuals are aware of, and concerned about, the prestige that society awards them. In some cases this concern is for the material benefits of high income, but more commonly it is focused on the psychological benefits of socially ratified status.

Individual Social Status

One set of explanations focuses on the importance of individual social status in producing support for the Right. Status crusades are posited to be most common in periods of prosperity, when some groups and individuals experience sharp increases in income. In periods of rapid social mobility, those who have advanced most rapidly (e.g., the newly wealthy) may support the Right because, as McEvoy (1971) says, "the right is the organized and visible segment of society that is most radical in attacking the established power structures within the system while at the same time affirming the . . . legitimacy of hoarding one's own money for oneself" (p. 38). Similarly, those who are passed by on the social ladder may turn to the Right for its nostalgia for past social orderings.

This set of explanations has produced three sets of testable hypotheses. The first comes from the work of Lenski (1954), who suggested that those individuals with discrepant or inconsistent ranks on status dimensions may adopt extreme attitudes. Those with income far in excess of their levels of educational attainment may fear that social change will lower their social status, as better-educated members of a new class pass them on the status ladder. For example, these individuals may be more likely to support the Right because it legitimizes their wealth while asserting the value of traditional status orderings based on wealth. Alternatively, those same individuals may not fear losing social status, but may feel that they are denied the proper status due them by those with inherited wealth, who view them as social Philistines. In this case, these individuals may support the Right because it often involves populist attacks on the upper class, while again asserting the value of wealth.

That the same type of status inconsistency might be expected to lead to support for the Right for two entirely different reasons points to one of the major weaknesses of the status-inconsistency hypothesis. Any type of status inconsistency could lead to support for the Right, because, as Lipset (1963b) noted, "such status incongruities were presumed to have created sharp resentments about general social developments, which predisposed individuals to welcome [rightist] attacks on the elite" (p. 350).

Indeed, any combination of inconsistent social locators has been posited to lead to almost any behavior or attitude. As Bruce (1988) and others have pointed out, status inconsistency has been posited to lead to right-wing extremism, left-wing extremism, liberalism, aggression, susceptibility to illness, spousal abuse, alcoholism, and seeing flying saucers. Yet such findings are not entirely inconsistent with Lenski's initial formulation, which merely stated that status inconsistency led to extreme attitudes and behaviors. Lenski's rationale for expecting more extreme behavior focused on the discomfort that status-inconsistent individuals would feel, for they would perceive their social status as a function of their highest locator, whereas others would perceive their status as a function of their lowest locator.

The evidence that status inconsistency leads to support for right-wing movements, however, is weak. Rush (1967) found evidence that individuals characterized by status inconsistency were more likely than others to be right-wing extremists. However, it is unclear from the work of Rush what is meant by right-wing extremism, and he finds that 21 percent of the population is composed of right-wing extremists, a number that is quite suspect, to put it mildly. Wilson and Zurcher (1976) reported that those individuals with high incomes and discrepant levels of occupational prestige and education were more likely than others to support an antipornography crusade. Lipset (1963a) reported weak but suggestive evidence that status inconsistency led to support for the John Birch Society in California.

Most other studies have reported negative results. For example, Trow (1957) found no evidence that status-discrepant groups responded to McCarthy's appeals. McEvoy (1971) found no evidence of status inconsistency among early backers of Senator Barry Goldwater. Wolfinger et al. (1969) compared their collection of activists in the Christian Anti-Communism Crusade with respondents to the 1964 American National Election Studies and concluded that Crusaders were no more likely to have discrepant-status locators. Grupp (1969) found no evidence of status inconsistency among John Birch Society members, and Stone (1974) reported that Bircher activists were like most other political activists: they had high levels of education, income, and occupational prestige. Wood and Hughes (1984) found little evidence that status inconsistency contributed to support for pornography restrictions between 1973 and 1980.

A second testable hypothesis from the individual status model is that those who experience subjective status anxiety will be more likely than others to support right-wing groups. As Bruce (1988) noted, status-discrepancy theorists assumed a level of status awareness and a conceptualization of social status that seem rare among the general public. However, among those who are concerned with social status, it is possible that evidence for a status explanation can be found.

The strongest support for a status-anxiety explanation comes from Rohter's (1969) study of John Birch Society letter writers in Oregon. Rohter hypothesized that three groups would be most likely to experience status anxiety: those who are declining on the status ladder, those who have newly arrived at the top of that ladder, and those who seek to maintain vanishing lifestyles. He measured status anxiety based on responses to three items: whether the respondent was accepted in the community, whether he or she perceived society to be open or closed, and whether he or she believed that a small set of elites in the community prevented the respondent's advancement. Rohter concluded that his sample exhibited higher levels of status anxiety than his control group. Elsewhere, however, Rohter (1965) concluded that although his measure of status anxiety had the predicted relationship with rightism, "they produced the weakest relationships, while value concerns and personality variables have produced overwhelming differences between rightists and non-rightists" (pp. 20–21). Lipset (1963a) cited an unpublished study by Sokol as providing evidence that "felt status inconsistency" led to support for McCarthy. There have been few other tests of the status-anxiety thesis.

A final testable hypothesis from the personal-status explanation is that those who experience rapid change in social status (either upward or downward) will be more likely to support the Right. Two variants of this hypothesis have been tested: one posits that change in an individual's social status results in support for the Right, while the second suggests that generational change in social status leads to such support. The first variant has never been satisfactorily tested, for few surveys have questions that ask about past income, occupational prestige, or social status. Several studies have attempted to examine the role of generational change in social status on support for the Right. In general, the results have been negative.

Rohter (1969) reported that his rightists were more likely than his control group to have experienced downward intergenerational status mobility. However, Wolfinger et al. (1969) found no evidence that intergenerational social mobility explained activism in the Crusade. Trow (1957) found that present occupation was much more important than social mobility in explaining support for McCarthy.

The explanations that center on individual social status were commonly accepted during the 1960s, and they are found throughout Bell's volume on the Right. However, the paucity of supporting evidence led later generations of social scientists to largely abandon these explanations. Few of the studies of support for the Christian Right have attempted to assess the role of individual social status concerns on support for the New Christian Right.

Status Politics: Group Status

A second major line of explanation centering on social status focuses not on individual social status, but on the status that society affords different social groups. Members of a social group may feel that the prestige of their group or its lifestyle is threatened by social change, and they may support right-wing movements in an attempt to protect that status.

Gusfield (1963) uses this type of explanation to account for support for the temperance movement. Gusfield defined status groups as those that share a common lifestyle or set of values and beliefs. When members of a social group realize that they are no longer accorded the honor and deference to which they have become accustomed, they become distressed. As the realization of such a loss becomes increasingly common among members of a group, members may be mobilized politically to enlist governmental authority in the struggle to preserve or enhance the prestige of the social group. Gusfield argues that the success of Prohibition involved the state in acknowledging the superiority of the values of evangelical, small-town Protestantism, thus preserving such Protestants' threatened social status.

As Bruce (1988) notes, however, Gusfield may give a satisfactory account of the functions of the temperance crusade without really explaining why members were attracted to the movement. Although members may have ultimately believed that the success of their movement validated their values and teetotaling lifestyle, there is little evidence in Gusfield's account that they were initially drawn to the temperance movement to attempt to preserve their declining social prestige.

Smidt (1988b) has argued that the group-status model provides an unsatisfactory account of the mobilization of conservative evangelicals into politics in recent years, because they have not commanded high levels of social status in this century. Moreover, any change in social status experienced by evangelicals immediately prior to their mobilization was surely positive. For example, he notes that both *Time* and *Newsweek* declared 1976 the "year of the evangelicals" and that the latter magazine noted that Carter's candidacy had brought attention to "the emergence of evangelical Christianity into a position of respect and power" (p. 7). In addition, Smidt argued that the 1980 elections pitted three candidates (Carter, Reagan, and Anderson) who claimed a born-again status.[2] Although Smidt is correct in noting that evangelicals had experienced a small increase in social prestige during the 1970s, this may not necessarily mean that a status-politics model is entirely inappropriate for explaining evangelical mobilization. As Bruce (1988) notes, "although most [political and social] movements are directed to the solution of some problem, the remedy of some grievance, or the alleviation of some hardship, the genesis of many social movements follows periods of *improvement* in the circumstances of those mobilized" (p. 46). It is possible that evangelicals became energized by their increase in social prestige and began to believe that it was possible to further enhance (or restore) their status.

---

2. Barry Commoner frequently noted in 1980 that he was the only presidential candidate to have been born only once.

The strongest evidence for the group-status model comes from Wald et al. (1989a). The authors asked congregants in thirty-two Protestant churches in Gainesville, Florida, whether various traditional groups were accorded too little, too much, or the right amount of status by society. Factor analysis revealed a set of groups which elicited similar responses: churchgoers, ministers, hard-working people, law-abiding people, and people like themselves. Those who believed that society currently assigned to these groups (primarily Christians) less prestige than it should were more likely to support the Christian Right than were others.

The Politics of Lifestyle Defense

Another related explanation centers not on the social status of the group or its lifestyle, but on the preservation of its way of life. Whereas other explanations in this set see right-wing supporters as concerned with their social status, this explanation suggests that they are simply concerned with maintaining the integrity of their lifestyle. In this way, the politics-of-lifestyle explanation involves an assumption of rationality which not all social-status explanations accept. Often the attack on lifestyles is seen as coming from the government, which is therefore the appropriate target for political activity. McAdam (1982, 1983) emphasized the role of policies of the state in mobilizing social-movement activists. When government action is seen as threatening the integrity of the lifestyle of a group, it might rationally organize to remedy that government action.

Lipset (1982) has argued that the status of evangelicals' lifestyles and values is under attack by postindustrial ideology and that this attack is the sharpest since the rational humanism of the Enlightenment. However, most writers who stress the politics of lifestyle stress the defense of the integrity of lifestyle, not its social status. Page and Clelland (1978) use this explanation to account for support for a crusade against certain public-school textbooks, and Lorentzen (1980) explained evangelical involvement in the Democratic senatorial selection process as an attempt to preserve their lifestyles. These writers have suggested that evangelicals have become mobilized into political action primarily because they perceive a threat to their lifestyle. This attack is perhaps most keenly felt in the area of education, in which evangelicals (especially fundamentalists) have challenged the textbooks used in public schools and have formed Christian schools at a prodigious rate (Bruce 1988, p. 41; Hunter 1987, p. 6).

The lifestyle-defense explanation has also been used to explain antifeminist activity by evangelical women. Women who perceived that their traditional roles of housewife and mother were threatened by the feminist movement were the most likely to participate in organizations such as Stop ERA and the Eagle Forum (Scott 1982), as they were in the antisuffrage movements earlier in the century (Marshall 1986). Luker (1988) reported that prolife activists also felt that their lifestyle was threatened by feminism and abortion.

Although the politics of lifestyle has become a popular explanation of support for Christian Right causes, there have been few empirical tests of the lifestyle-defense explanation. Miller (1985) argued that lifestyle concerns were not major factors in the genesis of the New Christian Right. Using data from a content analysis of evangelical and fundamentalist publications between 1955 and 1980, he reported that there was not a statistically significant increase in articles that focused on lifestyle concerns, though there was a measurable increase in articles on political matters. Miller argued that we cannot assume that the statements of NCR leaders on the importance of lifestyle concerns accurately mirrors the concerns of members and supporters. Bruce (1987) responded to Miller by noting that the content of periodicals may also fail to reflect the concerns of supporters and activists of the Christian Right, who may read with special interest those articles on lifestyle concerns. Bruce (1988, p. 168) concludes that the New Christian Right of the 1980s was primarily concerned with lifestyle defense.

SYMBOLIC POLITICS EXPLANATIONS

Although symbolic politics explanations have little relationship to status politics theories, they are often linked to explanations that center on the politics of lifestyle. Symbolic politics explanations suggest that the issues upon which social movements focus are symbolic of deeper group conflict, which involves long-held emotional responses. Public reaction to the issue agenda of a social or political movement depends on both the substance and the symbolism (Conover and Gray 1983, p. 35). The symbolism arouses an affective response, which may motivate citizens to support right-wing groups. This explanation is sometimes tied to lifestyle defense: some issues and groups acquire extra-affective strength because they symbolize a larger conflict over lifestyles. In this way, women who oppose abortion are posited to be motivated at least in part by a larger conflict over the integrity of the role of homemakers (Fried 1988).

One type of symbolic politics explanation suggests that those motivated by symbolic concerns will perceive differences between contending sets of social and political groups. Supporters of a right-wing group may see the social-group universe as divided between those sets of groups that support the issue agenda of the Right and those who oppose that agenda. Moreover, certain groups may come to symbolize the substantive-issue conflict and may therefore be laden with negative affect. Therefore, one prediction of the symbolic politics model is that supporters of the Christian Right will have markedly stronger positive affect toward groups that symbolize the traditional values than do other citizens, as well as stronger negative affect toward groups that symbolize the attack on those values.

The symbolic politics literature is relatively weak in delimiting exactly what qualifies as a symbolic attitude. Many writers have focused on racism (Kinder and Sears 1981; Sears et al. 1979), although many other attitudes have been cast in symbolic terms, including partisanship and ideology (Sears et al. 1980), and Kinder and Sears included moral traditionalism into their definition of symbolic racism. Conover (1983) tested a symbolic politics explanation of support for the New Right with measures of ideological self-placement and of gender-role attitudes.

It is difficult to test symbolic politics theory. Sears et al. (1980) regressed partisanship, ideology, and affect toward minorities to measure symbolic politics in presidential voting. But how do we separate the symbolic and instrumental components of partisanship? Another difficulty is in distinguishing between the predictions of certain personality theories, which suggest that hostility will be projected onto outgroups, and symbolic politics theories, which argue that the symbolic components of political conflict may manifest themselves in decreased affect for groups that symbolize the broader scope of the conflict. For example, if a supporter of the Moral Majority is quite cool toward feminists, is he projecting his own internal inadequacies onto an outgroup, or symbolizing the larger conflict over lifestyle definition? Or, for that matter, is he simply responding to political reality, in which feminists oppose the goals that he seeks from politics and consequently engender his dislike? In this latter instance, group affect would be a function of a realistic assessment of group conflict.

The same attitude may have symbolic import for some respondents but not for others. Fried (1988) reported that, for activists, abortion is a condensation symbol for changes in women's roles, in family structures, and in sexual behavior. However, for others abortion has no symbolic component and is instead seen as a complex and nuanced issue.

SUPPORT FROM BELIEF AND VALUE CONGRUITY

A different set of explanations focuses on the role of the belief and value congruity in producing support for right-wing organizations. Support for right-wing groups is seen as not different in kind from support for other political organizations—those who share the goals and values of the Right will support its organizations. These beliefs and values are generally presumed to have been acquired through childhood socialization. Although the socialization process is anything but rational, most scholars who have offered these sorts of explanations have viewed support for the Right as the rational consequence of certain values and beliefs, however they were acquired.

Religion and Support for the Christian Right

Not surprisingly, religious beliefs are most frequently found to predict support for the Christian Right. Several sets of religious attributes have been reported as correlates of support for the religious Right. In general, religious beliefs and practices have been more powerful predictors than religious affiliation. Denominational attachment is at best a weak predictor of passive support for the Crusade and the Moral Majority, although there is a strong denominational component to membership in the Moral Majority (Liebman 1983), and to support for Robertson. However, religious beliefs are powerful predictors.

Religious doctrine has consistently been reported as a strong predictor of support for the contemporary Christian Right. The various studies of Johnson and Tamney (1984, 1985), Johnson, Tamney, and Burton (1989), and Tamney and Johnson (1983) reported that their measure of doctrinal fundamentalism is strongly associated with support for the Moral Majority and Pat Robertson. Sigelman et al. (1987) found that evangelical doctrine was one of the best predictors of support for the Moral Majority in 1984. Various other religious variables are strong predictors of support for the Christian Right.

Political Beliefs

Political beliefs are frequently seen as predictors of support for the Christian Right. One of the most important political attitudes that predicts support for right-wing groups is partisanship. One of the most consistent relationships in the entire literature on social groups is that support for the Right in the United States comes from Republicans. Polsby (1963) reported that partisanship was among the strongest predictors of support for McCarthy, a finding confirmed by Lipset

(1963b). Although this is not surprising in light of the senator's own partisanship, other studies showed that members and supporters of right-wing organizations were considerably more likely to be Republican than the rest of the public. Wolfinger et al. (1969) and Koeppen (1969) both reported that activists in the Crusade were overwhelmingly Republican. Grupp (1969) reported that activists in the John Birch Society were mostly Republicans, and other studies of right-wing activists in the 1950s and 1960s reported similar results (Chesler and Schmuck 1969; Rohter 1969).

In addition, support for the Right is linked to a visceral anticommunism. Indeed, Rohter (1969) uses fervent anticommunism as his operational definition of rightism. Yet the conceptual distinction between anticommunism and support for the Right is an important one, for the correlation between the two speaks clearly to the rationality of right-wing support. Rogin (1967) suggests that anticommunism is the parsimonious explanation for McCarthy support. He rejects status and personality theories, noting that "to many Americans, especially those who were not actively in touch with events in the political world, McCarthy was simply fighting communism. Support for McCarthy meant opposition to communism" (p. 157). Like Polsby, Rogin sees support for McCarthy as a function of anti-Communist Republicanism.

Not surprisingly, support for the Right comes disproportionately from those who hold conservative political views on other issues as well. Although these relationships are not always strong (Wolfinger et al. 1969), most studies have found that supporters of the Christian Right are more conservative than other Americans, particularly on social issues and defense spending. Guth and Green (1987b) found that ideological congruence is the strongest predictor of support for the Moral Majority among contributors to Political Action Committees.

Although many have assumed that support from the Right is highest among those who are consistently conservative on political issues, support for the Christian Right has also been linked to populist ideologies of the Left and Right. One of the leading spokesmen for the Christian Right in the 1920s was Bryan, whose populism was evident in his crusade against banking interests. The right-wing populism of the McCarthy crusade is evident in his attack on the political elite, with their college degrees and social pedigrees. Several political leaders of the Right have blended elements of left- and right-wing populism. George Wallace's racism and militarism were combined with a left-wing economic populism that attacked not only the federal government but also big business. Ronald Reagan's populism was more consistently conservative, although it included a critique of the eastern Republican establishment.

Other Socialization Explanations

Some other explanations for support for the Christian Right are rooted in a socialization model, although they may incorporate additional explanatory elements. Geography has been shown to be a predictor of support for the Right. Those raised in rural areas and the South are more supportive, presumably because of exposure to conservative values and beliefs during the socialization process. Current residents of the South, West, and rural areas are also thought to be more supportive, regardless of where they were born, because of the process of ongoing adult socialization.

Other geographical explanations combine elements of political socialization with those of social strain. Those who have recently moved from the South, or those who have moved from rural to urban areas, are thought to be especially likely to support right-wing groups, in an effort to bolster their traditional values, which may seem alien to their new environments.

POLITICIZED GROUP CONSCIOUSNESS

In the past decade, political scientists have rediscovered the role of group identification and group consciousness in motivating political and social action. A series of studies (Miller et al. 1980; Miller, Simmons, and Hildreth 1986) have reported that those members of disadvantaged groups who share a set of group-related attitudes are more likely to support political organizations that speak for that group, and are more likely to participate in politics. These group-related attitudes include an identification with the group, a belief that the group is disadvantaged, a belief that disadvantage is due to systemic rather than individual sources, and support for collective action to redress that disadvantage (Cook 1987).

These components of group consciousness do not spontaneously emerge, but are rather the result of patient efforts by political entrepreneurs to mobilize the social or political group. The core constituency of the Christian Right has been exposed to a variety of appeals by group leaders to develop a group identity and subsequent group consciousness. Falwell (1981) has written of the common political interests of fundamentalists and of the interests that they share with evangelicals, pentecostals, and conservative Catholics. In this way, religious leaders have attempted to develop a group consciousness among fundamentalist Christians.

Group consciousness implies not only a strong commitment to the group but also a rejection of the societal rationale for the group's disadvantaged status and an agreement on collective action as a solution. Smelser (1963) lists as one important prerequisite of social movements a social strain about which there is an agreed-upon cause and solution. One type of social movement Smelser calls value-oriented, which attempts to restore, protect, modify, or create values in the name of a generalized belief. Smelser suggests that value-oriented movements are common among fundamentalists. However, unless the fundamentalists share a common belief about the cause and solution to the strain (in this case value strain), there can be no social movement. Those who seek to develop group consciousness focus on building consensus on the causes and solutions.

Among those who accept the authority of the Scriptures, one route to building this consensus is to root the argument in biblical truth. Christian Voice, a group from the 1980s, frequently publishes biblical verses, which are used to justify its political positions. If Christian Right leaders can overcome the general reluctance of fundamentalists (and, to a lesser extent, pentecostals and evangelicals) to bridge the gap that separates the religious and political spheres, religion can be used to mold the political beliefs of those with a religious group consciousness. In this way, religious/political elites seek to mold a politicized religious consciousness among their target constituency (Wilcox 1989b).

There has been relatively little research that seeks to test a theory of politicized religious identity as a source of support for the Christian Right. Jelen (1990b) reports that fundamentalist identification is a significant predictor of support for the Moral Majority, for Falwell, and for Robertson. Elsewhere (Wilcox 1990b), I have reported that, among white evangelicals, those with a fundamentalist identity were more supportive of the Moral Majority. In other research (Wilcox 1989b), I have reported that a fundamentalist identity has a greater effect on political attitudes among those exposed to efforts by religious elites to develop a political message for that identity.

RESOURCE MOBILIZATION THEORIES

Among sociologists, the most widely discussed theory of social and political movements focuses on the role of available resources in building social- and political-movement organizations. These resources often come from other organizations—governments provide interest groups with resources, and, more frequently, friendly groups provide assistance (McCarthy and Zald 1977; Moe 1980).

Frequently, political entrepreneurs are able to assemble resources from sympathetic organizations and to create a political organization (Salisbury 1969). They are most likely to undertake this task when an event upsets the political equilibrium, which may both motivate the entrepreneur and create a set of potential organizational supporters.

Although the resource mobilization theory has a great deal of relevance to the formation of the Christian Right (see chapter 1), it is somewhat less relevant to understanding the sources of support for these organizations. From the point of view of a group supporter, the actual mechanics of group formation may be irrelevant. However, resource mobilization theory does help us understand the sources of *membership* in these organizations. When Christian Right organizations make use of preexisting political and social structures, rates of membership will be highest among those with ties to those structures. For example, when the Moral Majority capitalized on a ready-made network of Bible Baptist Fellowship pastors to form its state and county chapters (Liebman 1983; Guth 1983a), its membership was disproportionately Baptist. Moreover, these preexisting structures and networks served to limit the appeal of Christian Right groups. The religious intolerance of Bible Baptist Fellowship pastors served to limit membership in the Ohio Moral Majority.

Himmelstein (1986) suggested that religious networks are important sources of recruitment for right-wing movements. He found that frequency of church attendance is a predictor of support for the right-to-life movement, even after a variety of controls for demographic and religious variables. Himmelstein argues that those who frequently attend church services are more likely to be exposed to appeals from prolife groups. In this same way, those who frequently attend churches in certain denominations doubtlessly are more familiar with Christian Right groups, and more supportive as well.

DISCUSSION

Of course, supporters and members may be attracted to Christian Right groups for a variety of motives. Some of the support may be accounted for with one explanation, while other support may be due to different sources. Many of these explanations may be complementary: there is no conflict among explanations that center on the politics of lifestyle, on symbolic politics, and on group consciousness. Others are directly contradictory: those individuals with group consciousness do not fit the picture of rootless, unattached individuals of alienation explanations. To the extent possible, these various explanations will be tested in some of the chapters that follow.

One criterion for evaluating rival explanations is parsimony. The simplest and most straightforward explanation for support for the Christian Right is that it stems from a set of religious and political beliefs and values. These beliefs may include a politicized religious identity and a belief that the secular change threatens the fundamentalist lifestyle, but they center primarily on the role of religion in witnessing to the nation, as well as on attitudes toward social, defense, and other issues. The evidence in this book suggests that support for the Christian Right can be understood from a rational-choice perspective, without the need for concepts such as status anxiety and inconsistency, authoritarianism, or other sources of strain. In this respect, support for the Christian Right is no different in kind than support for the Sierra Club, the National Organization for Women, or any other political group.

CHAPTER 3

The Evangelical Constituency
of the Christian Right

Although Falwell claimed that the Moral Majority sought a larger coalition of conservative Protestants, Jews, and Catholics, the target constituency of the Christian Right in the twentieth century has been the white evangelical community. Zwier (1982) described that constituency as "the primary audience, or constituency, for these groups was the approximately 50 million evangelicals in the country, and in particular the fundamentalist wing of this community. The aim from the beginning was to mobilize a group of people who had traditionally avoided politics because they saw it as dirty, corrupt business . . . by convincing these people that political involvement was a God-given responsibility" (pp. 9–10).

These white evangelicals were characterized by Menendez (1977) as the "sleeping giant of American electoral politics" (p. 104) because they generally were not active in politics. Some saw the possibility of an united evangelical political movement, whereas others (e.g., Lipset and Raab 1981) argued that political and religious differences would preclude such a movement. This chapter focuses on the target constituency of the Christian Right, evangelical Christians. Because religion and politics have vastly different connections in the white and black evangelical communities, I focus first on white evangelicalism and later on blacks. Although the Christian Right may have a potential constituency among blacks, throughout the twentieth century it has failed to effectively mobilize that constituency. For this reason, most of this chapter focuses on white evangelicals.

DEFINING EVANGELICALS

A good deal of scholarly attention has been devoted to the measurement of evangelicalism, with three general approaches most common
in the literature: those that identify evangelicals by their denominational affiliation, those that identify them by their religious doctrine
and practice, and those that identify them by asking people if they
think of themselves as evangelicals. These three operational definitions
identify somewhat different subsets of evangelicals.

First, evangelicals are sometimes identified by the denominations
of the churches they attend. This measurement strategy assumes that
evangelicalism is a sociological phenomenon, rooted in religious structures. Some denominations are members of the National Association
of Evangelicals (NAE), whereas others are not. Those who attend evangelical denominations are classified as evangelicals.

A denominational classification is useful because survey data on
denominational membership is widely available. Although the denominational coding scheme of the American National Election Studies
(ANES) (at least prior to the 1989 pilot study) leaves something to be
desired, it is possible to identify those who attend evangelical denominations in surveys from 1952 to 1988 and to examine trends in the
politics of evangelicals over time (Kellstedt and Green 1990).[1] Most of
these earlier ANES surveys had few if any items on religious doctrine,
and no items on religious identification, so denominational definitions
are the only ones available to those who wish to do longitudinal analysis.
In addition, denominational definitions of evangelicalism allow researchers to isolate those who attend fundamentalist or pentecostal
churches from those who attend churches of other evangelical denominations (Wilcox and Jelen 1990; Green and Guth 1988).

The limitation of denominational definitions of evangelicalism is
that not all churches affiliated with a particular denomination preach
the same doctrine. While growing up, I attended a fundamentalist
United Methodist church in West Virginia. A denominational definition would not classify Methodists as evangelicals or fundamentalists,
but most of the members of that congregation would profess evangelical and fundamentalist beliefs, and most would classify themselves as
evangelicals or fundamentalists. However, even within congregations,

1. Prior to 1972, the ANES did not probe Baptist respondents to determine if they
were Southern Baptists, American Baptists, or identified with some other Baptist denomination. Those who seek to use the ANES data for longitudinal analysis of the attitudes
and behaviors of evangelicals are forced to classify all Baptists as evangelicals. Although it
is not customary to include American Baptists as evangelicals, most meet the doctrinal
test.

individuals differ in their religious doctrines and identities. Not all members of that United Methodist church held fundamentalist or evangelical views, and not all would have identified themselves as evangelicals or fundamentalists. At least one member would claim to be a charismatic or pentecostal, and others would have reported charismatic experiences.

An alternative approach is to identify evangelicals by their religious doctrine. Kellstedt (1989) argues that "the predominant emphasis of evangelicalism is *doctrine*. It is 'right' doctrine that self-defined evangelicals look for when they 'check out' a person's Christian credentials" (pp. 4–5). Kellstedt proposed a set of doctrinal beliefs which can be used to identify evangelicals: belief in the divinity of Christ; acceptance of Christ as the only way to attain eternal life or salvation; belief in an inerrant Bible; and a commitment to spreading the Gospel. Kellstedt argued that these criteria are not sufficient to identify evangelicals, because some people will profess these four beliefs, then indicate in answers to other questions little psychological investment in religion, or take other doctrinal positions greatly at odds with evangelical doctrine. Instead, those who meet these criteria must be further winnowed to include only those with a strong commitment to religious values.

Few surveys contain measures of these four doctrinal items, however, so researchers doing secondary analysis of survey data must be content with more modest criteria. Since 1980, ANES surveys have contained variants of two items that can be used to identify evangelicals: items on the interpretation of the Bible, and an item asking whether a respondent is born-again. These items are included in other surveys as well, although the wording of the questions varies (Smidt 1989).

There is little controversy over the central role of beliefs about the Bible in identifying evangelicals, but there is some dispute over the level of authoritativeness on which all evangelicals will agree. Fundamentalists generally believe that the Bible is literally true, but many evangelicals reject this position. Most evangelicals would accept a position that the Bible contains no errors, although others believe that it contains some errors in history or science, but is inerrant in teaching spiritual matters.

There is also some dispute over the use of a born-again experience as a criterion for evangelicalism. Kellstedt (1989) suggested that the born-again item is too narrow, for some evangelicals accept Christ without labeling that experience "being born again." However, Smidt and Kellstedt (1987) reported that the born-again item is useful in identifying evangelicals. I classify as evangelicals those who pass a doctrinal test that combines a Bible item and a born-again item. Recognizing the limitations of these items, I posit that those who believe that the Bible is at least inerrant, and who claim a born-again experience, are doctrinal evangelicals and that those who do not meet this test are not. To the extent that this definition rejects some true evangelicals who take slightly different doctrinal positions and accepts other "suspect" evangelicals, the relationships in the data will be slightly attenuated. The relationships I find between evangelical doctrine and support for the Christian Right are conservative estimates.

A doctrinal definition has the advantage of allowing the identification of those who attend nonevangelical denominations, but who profess evangelical beliefs. It can be used to identify Catholic evangelicals as well, although some researchers would exclude Catholics by definition (e.g., Hunter 1983). In this book, I include Catholics who meet the doctrinal tenets of evangelicalism in my analysis of evangelicals. Recently, Welch and Leege (1991) have argued that evangelical devotionalism among American Catholics is accompanied by many of the political attitudes associated with Protestant evangelicalism. By comparing Catholic and Protestant evangelicals, I am able to determine the differences between these two groups.

There are some limits to this type of definition, however. Doctrinal items are uncommon in surveys prior to 1980, and the wording of questions has varied widely. Moreover, it is difficult with these core doctrinal items to distinguish among fundamentalists, pentecostals, and other evangelicals, although additional doctrinal questions (e.g., questions about the gifts of the Spirit) could do so.

The final operational strategy is to ask the respondents whether they consider themselves evangelicals, fundamentalists, pentecostals, or charismatics. This self-identification approach has become increasingly common in recent years (Wilcox 1986a; Cook and Wilcox 1990; Beatty and Walter 1988; Smidt 1988a; Green and Guth 1988). Self-identification has the advantage of selecting those who consider themselves to be evangelicals, but there are unexplored pitfalls to this approach. First, it is possible, and indeed common, for respondents to select more than one identity (Wilcox 1986a; Cook and Wilcox 1990; Green and Guth 1988). How does one classify someone who identifies as an evangelical and a pentecostal, but not as a fundamentalist? Interviews with elites in the Ohio Moral Majority who called themselves both evangelicals and fundamentalists suggested that they labeled their belief in a literal Bible fundamentalist, but considered themselves evangelicals. This suggests that different religious identities may take on different meanings for some respondents. With other populations and other combinations of religious identities, entirely different interpretations are possible.

Second, it is not always clear what respondents mean when they classify themselves as evangelicals, fundamentalists, or charismatics. Although all of the respondents who selected one of these identities in my Ohio Moral Majority survey and most of those who responded to my survey of blacks in Washington, D.C., would have met a doctrinal test, what are we to do with respondents who call themselves charismatics but do not meet doctrinal tests? How do we classify a self-identified fundamentalist who believes that the Bible contains errors?

Jelen (1991a), for example, reports that for some the identity evangelical merely means "proclaimer of the Gospel." He found that some liberal, mainline clergy identified themselves as evangelicals in this sense of the word, although they would not accept the doctrinal tenets of evangelicalism. He also reported unusual interpretations of the identity charismatic, and he found one church in which all members accepted the label pentecostal, but emphatically denied that they were charismatics. Jelen's results suggest the need for further research into what respondents mean when they use certain religious labels.

These three types of operational definitions often identify somewhat different sets of people, who may vary in their religious and political characteristics (Wilcox 1986b; Kellstedt 1989). Whenever possible, it is desirable to have multiple definitions, and to investigate the joint impact of denomination, doctrine, and religious identity. In this chapter and throughout the book, I use each of these three definitions at various points and employ more than one when available. For example, in examining the later ANES surveys, I will be able to use both denominational and doctrinal tests. In other data, I will be able to use all three.

The data for this chapter come from the 1988 ANES, conducted by the Survey Research Center at the Center for Political Studies, University of Michigan, and from the Evangelical Voter Survey, conducted in 1983 by Lance Tarrance and Associates. The latter survey questioned one thousand evangelicals, a much larger number than included in national samples. To have been classified as an evangelical for this survey, the respondent must have agreed that Christ was a real man and the Son of God, and either reported a born-again experience or a personal conversion experience related to Christ. For both surveys, scales have been constructed to measure political values, affect, and attitudes.[2]

---

2. In this and all subsequent chapters, scales were constructed from items identified by factor analysis and cluster analysis. Except where indicated, all scales exhibit acceptable levels of reliability. For more details of scale construction, contact the author.

WHO ARE THE EVANGELICAL CHRISTIANS?

The conventional stereotype of an evangelical is a rural, poorly educated, working class, aging southerner. The 1988 ANES contains items
that allow us to identify those who attend evangelical denominations,
those who hold evangelical doctrinal beliefs, and those who meet both
or neither criteria. From these items, a demographic portrait of white
evangelicals can be obtained. The details are presented in table 3.1.

TABLE 3.1
Demographic Portrait of White Evangelicals (1988 ANES)

	Nonevangelical (%)	Denominational Evangelical (%)	Doctrinal Evangelical (%)	Both (%)
Education				
Less than high school	16	26	23	31
At least some college	50	26	38	34
Income				
Less than $15K	26	30	41	35
$50K and more	19	15	10	8
Occupation				
Blue collar	44	50	41	46
Retired	17	11	17	17
Housewife (women)	19	26	29	24
Identify with working class	45	59	49	61
Region				
South	20	75	32	68
Midwest	31	17	39	17
Sex				
Female	51	52	68	64
Rural Born	25	44	47	49
Age				
Under 35	32	32	29	29
65 +	19	13	21	20
Religion				
Attend church almost weekly	32	25	44	54
Watch religious T.V. or listen to religious radio	18	35	48	54
Pray at least daily	44	46	83	81
Religion very important	22	30	61	70
Born-again	10	29	100	100
Bible inerrant	27	47	100	100

There is some truth to this stereotype, although, like most simplified mental pictures, it is overstated. Doctrinal and denominational white evangelicals have significantly lower levels of education, income, and occupational prestige than other whites. Those who attend evangelical churches are more likely to live in the South, although doctrinal evangelicals who attend nonevangelical churches more frequently live in the Midwest. Each group of evangelicals is more likely than other whites to be born in a rural area, and there is a disproportionately large number of women in each group. Only the age component of the typical stereotype is false, with evangelicals having approximately the same age distribution as other whites. At the same time, note that nearly one-third of evangelicals have attended some college and that many are relatively wealthy and identify with the middle class.

There are some demographic differences among the three groups of evangelicals identified by these two definitions. Denominational evangelicals are wealthier but less well educated than doctrinal evangelicals. This seeming anomaly is explained by the higher proportion of elderly widows among doctrinal evangelicals: when labor-force status is held constant, doctrinal evangelicals are wealthier, and the educational differences are somewhat reduced. (For a similar result with data from the 1980 ANES, see Wilcox 1986b.)

There are important religious differences as well. Compared with doctrinal evangelicals, those who attend evangelical denominations but who do not hold evangelical doctrinal beliefs are generally less strongly attached to religious beliefs and institutions. They are less likely to attend church regularly, to pray daily, to watch religious television or listen to religious radio programs, and to report that religion is important to their lives.

There are differences in the denominational affiliations of these three sets of evangelicals. Not surprisingly, those who attend pentecostal churches are disproportionately found among those who hold evangelical doctrinal beliefs.[3] Those doctrinal evangelicals who do not attend evangelical churches are scattered among mainline Protestant churches (especially Presbyterians, Lutherans, and United Methodists) and among American Baptists, Catholics, and nondenominational Protestant churches.

---

3. Somewhat surprisingly, those who attended fundamentalist Baptist churches in the 1988 survey were not disproportionately found among those who met the doctrinal criteria. However, in the 1980 and 1984 data fundamentalist Baptists generally met the doctrinal test.

THE POLITICAL ATTITUDES OF EVANGELICALS

The same data allow us to examine the political beliefs and values of
evangelicals and to compare them to those of other whites. The details
of this analysis are presented in table 3.2. The scales measuring issues
and values have been normalized, so the values indicate deviation from
the mean for whites. In general, all three sets of evangelicals are more

TABLE 3.2
Political Values and Beliefs of White Evangelicals (1988 ANES)

	Nonevangelical	Denominational Evangelical	Doctrinal Evangelical	Both
Values				
Moral traditionalism	−.14	−.16	.45**	.59**
Equality	−.07	.04	.05	.31**
Patriotism	−.10	.02	.30**	.34**
Anticommunism	−.14	.28**	.29**	.42**
Issue Attitudes				
Racial policy	−.04	.19**	−.04	.13**
Social issues	−.15	.13**	.38**	.43**
Death penalty	−.03	.18**	−.08	.20**
Economic issues	−.02	.16**	.04	.17**
Taxes	−.03	.30**	.00	−.08
Strong defense	−.08	.21**	.10**	.18**
Negotiate with Soviet Union	−.09	.01	.25**	.31**
Isolationism	.00	−.02	−.06	−.11
Distrust government	−.03	.22**	.00	−.04
Spending Priorities				
Poor	−.02	.10	−.05	.11
Elderly	.05	−.04	−.05	−.15**
Liberal programs	−.12	.06*	.09**	.34**
Reagan defense	−.04	−.01	.26**	−.03
Relative Group Affect				
Middle America	70°	67°*	70°	71°
Minorities	45°	38°**	44°	41°**
Establishment	60°	62°	63°*	64°**
Liberals	53°	51°*	51°*	48°**
Right	42°	46°*	61°**	64°**

Note: Mean value on each scale or item for each group. Items normalized by subtracting
mean and dividing by standard deviation. All items and scales recoded, so higher values
indicate more conservative positions. All tests of significance are between group in
question and whites who meet *neither* definition of evangelicalism.
$*p \leq .05$
$**p \leq .01$

conservative than other whites, although there are interesting differences among the three sets.

On many issues, doctrine is clearly more important than denominational affiliation. It is doctrinal evangelicals who report greater levels of moral traditionalism and patriotism, and who are more conservative on social issues, spending for Reagan war policies (Contras and the Strategic Defense Initiative, or Star Wars), and negotiations with the Soviets. They are also warmer toward groups of the Right (the Moral Majority, antiabortionists, and Christian fundamentalists).

Denominational evangelicals are distinct in their conservatism on economic issues, taxes, spending programs for the poor, support for a strong defense, and the death penalty. Moreover, denominational evangelicals show some evidence of prejudice, with lower affect toward minorities and more conservative positions on racial issues. They were cooler than other respondents toward all four minority groups—blacks, Hispanics, illegal aliens, and gays and lesbians. Their somewhat cooler affect toward Middle America is due to their cooler feelings toward Jews and Catholics, who are included in the Middle America scale.

Finally, the two measures of evangelicalism interact on anticommunism, equality values, spending for programs for the elderly, and isolationism. On each of these issues, those who meet *both* definitions of evangelicalism differ from those who meet one or none.

Of course, these different subsets of evangelicals differ from one another and from other Americans on demographic variables that we know are important predictors of attitudes. It is possible that educational and regional differences explain the apparent hostility of white denominational evangelicals toward blacks. To determine the independent effects of evangelicalism, I have removed the effects of education, income, region, rural birth, age, and gender from the attitudes of white respondents. The results of the analysis of covariance are presented in table 3.3. The figures in this table can be interpreted as the mean value on each item and scale, holding constant the control variables. The values are adjusted to reflect population means—so the figures represent the likely mean for each religious group if all white respondents had the level of education, income, and other demographic variables that is the mean for white respondents.

The data in table 3.3 suggest that although demographic variables explain some of the differences among the three groups of evangelicals, and between them and nonevangelical whites, most of the differences remain. What can we make of these differences? We might think of denomination as a sociological attachment, frequently inherited through childhood socialization, and doctrine as a cognitive set of be-

TABLE 3.3
Political Values and Beliefs of White Evangelicals
(1988 ANES, Demographic Variables Held Constant)

	Nonevangelical	Denominational Evangelical	Doctrinal Evangelical	Both
Values				
Moral traditionalism	−.23	−.12	.41**	.60**
Equality	−.06	−.04	.06	.27**
Patriotism	−.09	.03	.34**	.28**
Anticommunism	−.05	.21**	.31**	.33**
Issue Attitudes				
Racial policy	−.01	.14*	−.03	.09
Social issues	−.08	.06*	.37**	.37**
Death penalty	.02	.12	−.04	.15
Economic issues	−.09	.08*	.14**	.18**
Taxes	.00	.26*	.06	−.08
Strong defense	−.05	.15**	.13**	.14**
Negotiate with Soviet Union	−.00	−.14*	.29**	.24**
Isolationism	.00	−.02	−.06	−.11
Distrust government	.03	.14	−.01	−.05
Spending Priorities				
Poor	−.03	.03	.00	.08
Elderly	−.01	−.01	−.03	−.17
Liberal programs	−.11	−.01	.08**	.28**
Reagan defense	−.03	.02	.27**	−.00
Relative Group Affect				
Middle America	13°	12°*	11°	12°
Minorities	−12°	−18°**	−15°	−18°
Establishment	4°	7°	4°*	5°*
Liberals	−4°	−5°*	−9°**	−11°**
Right	−15°	−9°*	2°**	5°**

Note: Mean value on each scale or item for each group. Items normalized by subtracting mean and dividing by standard deviation. All issue scales and items, high scores indicate more conservative positions. All tests of significance are between group in question and whites who meet *neither* definition of evangelicalism. Control variables include education, income, age, gender, region, and rural birth.
*$p \leq .05$
**$p \leq .01$

liefs, sometimes acquired later in life. First, it seems that certain types of attitudes are rooted in sociological attachments—symbolic racism (racial attitudes, minority affect, and attitudes toward the death penalty) is influenced by denominational attachments, as are trust in government and opposition to taxes. The cognitive effects of doctrine are felt on values and attitudes closely related to religion—moral traditionalism and social issues, as well as patriotism and support for spending on Reagan's defense policies. The interaction between doctrine and denomination may represent the results of a long tradition of exposure to a consistent doctrinal message. This interaction is strongest on issues such as spending priorities and equality values.

Guth et al. (1988) have suggested that part of the differences between these different groups of evangelicals may be due to the inclusion of denominational evangelicals with only nominal attachments to their religion. Such respondents may only be voicing an inherited denominational attachment in response to the question of church preference and are therefore suspect evangelicals. This argument gains some weight by inspection of the religiosity of those who meet only the denominational definition: approximately one-fifth never attend church and think that religion is not important in their lives.

To determine if the differences among those evangelicals identified by these definitions is due to differences in religious attachment, I examined the attitudes of whites who attended church regularly (nearly once a week, or more often). The results suggest that the differences between denominational and doctrinal evangelicals persist. In some cases, the differences are magnified: those denominational evangelicals who attend church regularly and do not profess evangelical doctrine are slightly *cooler* toward blacks than those who do not attend, even less trusting of government, more opposed to spending on the poor, and are even more opposed to increased taxation.

POLICY DIFFERENCES AMONG EVANGELICALS

Although the data in tables 3.2 and 3.3 suggest that evangelicals are generally more conservative than other whites, they are not a homogeneous lot. There is disagreement among evangelicals on all social and political issues. As noted in chapter 1, some evangelicals were active in the McGovern campaign in 1972, and others are active feminists (Wilcox 1989a; Wilcox and Cook 1989). Table 3.4 presents the beliefs of different issue groups among white evangelicals. These issue groups were formed using cluster analysis.

The best solution was a four-cluster one, which accounted for over one-half of the variation in the issue scales. One cluster contained consistent conservatives, and a second contained consistent liberals. The third cluster contained economic conservatives—relatively liberal on moral and social issues, and in favor of negotiations with the Soviet Union, decreased defense spending, and pulling back from international commitments, but conservative on economic issues. The final

TABLE 3.4
Issue Groups among White Evangelicals (1988 ANES)

	Conservatives	Liberals	Economic Conservatives	Economic Moderates
Values				
Moral traditionalism	1.03	.02	−.08	.44
Equality	.35	−.05	.03	.27
Patriotism	.22	.15	.31	.35
Anticommunism	.38	.11	.44	.55
Issue Attitudes				
Racial policy	.05	−.05	.05	.20
Social issues	.61	.05	.03	.46
Death penalty	.18	−.07	.10	.25
Economic issues	.49	−.13	.35	.05
Taxes	.08	−.07	−.08	−.11
Strong defense	.32	−.01	.10	.28
Negotiate with Soviet Union	.57	.00	−.12	.25
Isolationism	.27	−.21	−.10	.10
Distrust government	.27	−.05	.07	.03
Spending Priorities				
Poor	.26	−.24	.45	.11
Elderly	.08	−.08	−.29	−.15
Liberal programs	.68	.01	.25	.00
Reagan defense	.12	−.07	−.54	.28
Relative Group Affect				
Middle America	11°	8°	18°	14°
Minorities	−18°	−11°	−15°	−24°
Establishment	3°	1°	14°	9°
Liberals	−18°	1°	−6°	−12°
Right	25°	−8°	−38°	2°

Note: Mean scores on each scale and mean affect toward each group. Scales are normalized and expressed in terms of standard deviations from the white mean. High scores indicate more conservative positions. Affect is relative to individual mean across all social and political groups. High scores indicate warmth toward groups.

cluster contained evangelicals who were conservative on most issues, very conservative on racial issues, but moderate on economic issues.

The liberal cluster of evangelicals were more liberal than non-evangelical whites on a range of issues, including moral traditionalism, and were relatively moderate on social issues. The economic conservatives cluster was moderate on moral and social issues, strongly in favor of reduced defense measures, and strongly antagonistic toward the Right. Finally, the economic moderates were not significantly different from other whites in many of their economic attitudes. In short, evangelicals are not a monolithic conservative bloc, as they are sometimes portrayed in media accounts.

Who are the evangelicals who compose these issue clusters? The conservative cluster of evangelicals came disproportionately from fundamentalist and pentecostal churches, and it was the most likely of the four clusters to meet both criteria for evangelicalism. It was also the group with the highest rate of church attendance, of viewing religious television or listening to religious radio, and of personal prayer. They were the best educated, most female, least southern, and most Republican of the clusters. The liberal cluster was somewhat younger than other evangelicals, somewhat better educated, and more Democratic. They were the wealthiest cluster.

One-half of the economic conservatives belonged to evangelical denominations, but did not hold evangelical doctrinal beliefs. They were the least religious on all measures of attachment, doctrine, and practice. They were older and less well educated and were the most Democratic, southern, and male cluster. Finally, the economic moderates were also in the middle on most demographic variables, although they were the most likely to be born in a rural area.

EXPLAINING THE ATTITUDES OF EVANGELICALS: THE ROLE OF RELIGION

Although evangelicals are a relatively heterogeneous group, they encompass a range of opinion on most political issues. Of course, we expect demographic and political factors to explain the attitudes of evangelicals much as they do for nonevangelicals, but it seems also likely that religious differences may account for a sizable proportion of the differences in these attitudes. Many evangelicals report that religion has a strong impact on their political thinking, and, even among those who do not admit to such a cognitive connection, the correlation between religious variables and political attitudes is often sizable. The 1988 ANES survey does not contain a sufficient range of religious items to allow us to examine the role of religious variables on the political attitudes of evangelicals. For this analysis, data from the Evangelical Voter Study is more useful. This analysis is limited to white evangelicals, and later in this chapter I examine racial differences in these relationships.

These data provide a unique opportunity to study the impact of religious variables on the political attitudes of evangelicals. The richness of religious measures has seldom been equaled in survey research. In addition, a variety of items measured attitudes toward social issues, foreign policy, and educational policy—all items of great salience to evangelicals.

THEORETICAL EXPECTATIONS

Numerous religious variables have been found to influence political attitudes of evangelicals and others. Previous research has demonstrated that denominational affiliation has an independent effect on partisanship and political attitudes. Kellstedt (1988) reported that, even among evangelicals, denominational differences have a substantial impact on variation in support for the Moral Majority platform. In particular, Kellstedt found that those who attended fundamentalist churches were more conservative than those who attended other evangelical or mainstream Protestant churches. Those affiliated with pentecostal churches were even more conservative, a finding echoed by Wilcox and Jelen (1990), who reported that evangelicals in general are less tolerant than other whites and that pentecostals are the least tolerant. The distinction among pentecostal, fundamentalist, and other evangelicals is not the only denomination distinction that scholars have made (see, for example, Hunter 1981).

At least two explanations have been offered for why denomination affects political beliefs. Knoke (1976) argued that denominational differences reflect longstanding social cleavages. Ethnic, economic, and historical differences are associated with religious affiliation, which helps maintain the political effects of these cleavages long after assimilation. Beatty and Walker (n.d.) offer a second explanation. They reported that the social and political messages delivered from the pulpit differ substantially. Frequent attendance may reinforce the effects of denomination, both by exposing the individual to more frequent political messages from the pulpit and by increasing the interactions with like-minded members of the denomination. Indeed, Ammerman (1987) has reported that, for many frequent attenders of fundamentalist churches, other members of the congregation serve as the only source of regular social interaction. In this way, the effects of the denomination are intensified. Wald (1986) reported results that support this interpretation. He found that frequency of attendance, as well as commitment to the denomination, served to magnify the effects of denomination differences. Wald et al. (1988) have suggested that there are even important differences between individual congregations and that congregations might be thought of as political communities—molding and reinforcing the political views of their members. Gilbert (1989) has reported that church discussion partners can influence political choice, providing one mechanism for congregation-level effects.

Religious doctrine has also been shown to influence political beliefs. For example, Wilcox and Jelen (1990) reported that doctrinal orthodoxy was a major source of the greater intolerance exhibited by those who attended pentecostal, fundamentalist, and evangelical churches. The evangelicals in the Evangelical Voter Study share a common theological commitment to personal salvation and the importance of the Scriptures as a source of spiritual knowledge. However, some important theological differences exist among them. Although all respondents believe in personal salvation, not all reported having a born-again experience. Moreover, there was significant variation in the interpretation of the Scriptures. Although many thought that the Genesis Creation story was the literal truth, others viewed it only as the inerrant Word of God, not meant to be taken literally.

How can religious doctrine take on political meaning? Why would a literal interpretation of the Scriptures predispose evangelicals toward more conservative politics? Certainly there are many passages of the Scriptures that can be read as advocating conservative policies. The Old Testament had a quite long list of capital crimes (including disrespect for parents), which were generally punished by stoning. Such passages might be seen as advocating capital punishment. Similarly, the plethora of passages suggesting that men are the head of the household, as Christ is head of the church, can be read as undermining feminist positions. The fate of Sodom and Gomorrah can be read as proscribing homosexual conduct. Such conservative readings of the Scriptures vary from era to era: conservatives in the 1800s quoted the Scriptures to justify a continuation of slavery. In each case alternative readings of these Scriptures are possible, but those who take the Bible literally generally eschew creative interpretations and are culturally inclined to conservative readings of it.

Yet the Scriptures are silent about equal pay for equal work, bussing to achieve school integration, and even abortion, though applicable passages can be found by those seeking to support their views. Moreover, many passages may be read as advocating liberal economic policies, and the New Testament is full of class-based attacks on the rich (Roelofs 1988). Although the camels could indeed crawl with some difficulty through the "eye of the needle" in entering walled cities, the New Testament indicates that the rich will have some problems in entering the Kingdom. Why then does belief in biblical authority translate into conservative politics in the United States?

Religious doctrine takes on political meaning as religious and political elites provide interpretations to the faithful. Although black pentecostal and fundamentalist churches have tended to interpret the Bible's economic message as one of liberation, white churches in these traditions have generally focused on those verses and passages that support more conservative readings. Pastors who preach politics, televangelists, and other religious and political figures have provided conservative interpretations of the Bible for many years, and it seems likely that this political/religious message has taken hold.

Another religious variable that can influence the attitudes of evangelicals is religious identity. Over the past few years the importance of an individual's identification with political and social groups has been rediscovered. Miller et al. (1978) reported the importance of identification as a cornerstone in the development of group consciousness. Conover (1984) and Conover and Feldman (1984) reported that group identification has a strong influence on political perceptions, values, and beliefs. A consensus seems to have emerged that group consciousness is an important part of group mobilization and that group identification is an important prerequisite for group consciousness.

During the past decade, religious and political elites have attempted to develop a politicized group consciousness among evangelical and fundamentalist Christians. Televangelists have told their audiences that evangelicals and their allies have sufficient votes to run the country, and organizations such as the Moral Majority have attempted to mobilize the evangelical community by making evangelicals aware of their common political and social concerns.

To date this effort has been primarily directed at the fundamentalist wing of the evangelical community. Both the Moral Majority and the Christian Voice have couched their appeals in fundamentalist language, although the Robertson campaign may have furthered the development of a politicized pentecostal and charismatic identification. However, at the time of this survey the fundamentalists would be most likely among evangelicals to have developed a coherent political identity.

The role of elites in forming politicized religious identities is important. Those who hold fundamentalist doctrinal beliefs (e.g., literal interpretation of the Bible) may not identify as fundamentalists unless religious or political elites help them label themselves. Elsewhere (Wilcox 1989b), I have reported that although those from fundamentalist denominations are more likely than other evangelicals to have a fundamentalist identity, those who do not attend such churches but who hold fundamentalist doctrinal beliefs are likely to identify as fundamentalists only if they frequently watch televangelists, or perceive a strong connection between religion and politics. Fundamentalist churches often freely adopt the fundamentalist label, but those who do not attend these churches do not know that their beliefs qualify as fundamentalist unless political or religious elites tell them. Televangelists and political groups such as the Moral Majority have attempted to broaden the sense of religious identity and to give it political meaning. Falwell tells his listeners that fundamentalists have a common political interest in certain policy issues. In this way he attempts to mold a religious identity into a political one.

Religiosity has also been shown to predict political attitudes. Those who frequently attend church services are more frequently exposed to the social and political messages from the pastor, as well as more frequently interact with like-minded congregationists. It seems likely, then, that frequency of church attendance should matter most among those respondents whose pastor preaches politics, or who attend fundamentalist or pentecostal churches. Frequency of church attendance may increase the probability of exposure to activists who seek to mobilize evangelicals into active opposition to abortion (Himmelstein 1986).

Research into cognitive structuring (e.g., Graber 1984) has suggested that there is substantial individual variation in the connections among different cognitive domains. For some individuals, religious and political attitudes may be strongly connected. For others, these areas seem quite separate. Shupe and Stacey (1983) reported that support for the Moral Majority was significantly higher among those who perceived strong links between these two domains. Among evangelicals who associate religious and political beliefs, religion may act as a source of constraint. Andersen (1988) suggested that Bible stories serve as scripts to constrain the attitudes and beliefs of some women. These women tested new issues against scriptural teachings, enabling them to integrate unfamiliar political issues into existing cognitive frameworks. Evangelicals who perceive strong associations between their religious and political cognitions should be more conservative than others.

Finally, religious elites may shape the beliefs of their followers. Some pastors and televangelists emphasize the political implications of their message. Those who frequently watch televangelists may be more conservative than other evangelicals, and those whose pastor preaches politics from the pulpit might likewise be expected to be more conservative.

RELIGIOUS CHARACTERISTICS OF EVANGELICALS

Although white evangelicals are more homogeneous in their religious orientations than the general public, there was considerable variation on each of these religious measures. Nearly one in five evangelicals in this survey attended Catholic churches, and more than one in three attended mainline Protestant denominations. Slightly more than one-half were born-again, and approximately 40 percent believed the biblical story of Creation was literally true, with an almost equal number who believed that the story was inerrant, but not literally true. Slightly more than one in four were *both* born-again and accepted a literal view of the Bible.

Approximately one in five labeled themselves as fundamentalists. Fewer than one-half of self-identified fundamentalists either attended a fundamentalist church or held fundamentalist doctrinal views. Among those that both attended fundamentalist churches and held fundamentalist doctrinal views, 37 percent identified themselves as fundamentalists. These results suggest that the phenomenon of religious identification deserves more careful scrutiny.

Approximately one-fourth of evangelicals attended churches in which the pastor promoted a political message in some manner. Two-thirds attended church at least once a week, and one in five attended more often. This public religiosity is matched by a personal commitment to religion: fully 80 percent found religion very important in their lives. Their frequent exposure to sermons from the pulpit was echoed in their viewing of televangelists. More than one-fourth watched at least one televised religious program each week, and more than one-half of all evangelicals were favorably inclined toward televangelists.

Finally, one-third of white evangelicals reported strong connections between their religious beliefs and their political beliefs and behaviors. This extended to elections as well, with 60 percent reporting that religion would have some impact on their vote in 1984, and 11 percent reporting that it would have a strong impact.

RELIGIOUS DETERMINANTS OF POLITICAL ATTITUDES: BIVARIATE ANALYSIS

Denomination

For this study, Kellstedt's (1988) classification scheme for denomination has been adopted. Table 3.5 presents the effect of denomination on the attitudes of white evangelicals. For all three issue scales, pentecostals are the most conservative. Those who attend fundamentalist churches are slightly more conservative than those who attend other evangelical denominations, who are in turn more conservative than those evangeli-

TABLE 3.5
Denomination, Doctrine, and Religious Identity
(Evangelical Voter Survey)

	Women's Issues	Foreign Policy	Education	N
Denomination				
Mainline Protestant	2.6	3.0	3.8	324
Evangelical	2.9**	3.2*	4.0	185
Fundamentalist	3.1**	3.4**	4.0*	121
Pentecostal	3.6**	3.7**	4.2*	27
Catholic	2.8	2.7*	4.2**	182
Doctrine				
Born-again, literal	3.1	3.3	4.0	194
Other	2.7**	3.1*	3.8*	378
Religious Identity				
Fundamentalist	2.9	3.0	4.0	442
Nonfundamentalist	2.8	3.4**	3.8*	130

Note: Mean score on each scale for each group, in which higher scores indicate more conservative positions. Statistical test is one-way analysis of variance, except for denomination, dummy variable regression was employed, with mainline Protestants excluded from the equation.
$*p \leq .05$
$**p \leq .01$

cals who attend mainline Protestant churches. Catholic evangelicals are significantly more liberal on foreign-policy attitudes than Protestant evangelicals, but are among the most conservative on education issues. Catholic evangelicals were quite moderate on the women's issues scale, and if abortion were excluded from that scale they would be more liberal than Protestants. Catholic evangelicals were more conservative than any group except the pentecostals on abortion, but were more liberal on other issues, including birth-control information and government aid for abortions for the poor.

Doctrine

The born-again and Bible items used in this study were combined into a dichotomous measure of doctrine. Those who were born-again and who accepted a literal interpretation of the Scriptures were coded as 1; all others were coded as 0. Note that this differs from the measure of evangelical doctrine discussed above. The current measure is best conceived as tapping fundamentalist doctrine.

There were clear denomination differences in scores on the doctrine scale, with those who attend fundamentalist and pentecostal churches more likely to accept both elements. Nevertheless, the bivariate correlations were fairly low ($r = .33$ for fundamentalist churches, and .09 for pentecostal churches), thus suggesting that doctrine and denomination are empirically distinct concepts. Scores on the doctrine index were strongly related to political attitudes. Table 3.5 presents the results of the analysis. In each case, those who accept these two doctrinal tenets were significantly more conservative than other evangelicals.

Religious Identity

The data in table 3.5 reveal that those who identify as fundamentalists are more conservative than other evangelicals on each of the issue scales, and the differences are statistically significant for foreign-policy and education issues.

If religious identity is to have a political meaning, the individual must understand the political connotations of his or her identity. Televangelists and some pastors have attempted to elucidate the political implications of a fundamentalist identity to their followers. In addition, those who are already politicized should be more likely to perceive a political connotation to their religious identity. Further analysis (not shown) revealed that among those who frequently watch televangelists, or who perceive a strong connection between their religious and political beliefs, there is a strong relationship between fundamentalist identification and political beliefs, whereas among other white evangelicals the relationship is not statistically significant. This evidence indicates that political and religious elites must interpret religious identity in order for that identity to have political meaning. For further details of this interaction, see Wilcox 1989b.

Frequency of Church Attendance

The data in table 3.6 suggest that attendance makes some difference on all issues, but that the largest differences are for attitudes toward women's issues. Further analysis suggests that this relationship is primarily confined to attitudes on abortion. Separate regression equations were estimated, with each item included in the women's issues scale used as a dependent variable. Attendance was a significant predictor only of attitudes toward abortion. This finding tends to support Himmelstein's (1986) argument that church attendance exposes individuals to solicitations by prolife activists. Attendance is also significantly related to attitudes on foreign-policy issues.

TABLE 3.6
Attendance, Cognitive Structure, and Religious Elites
(Evangelical Voter Survey)

	Women's Issues	Foreign Policy	Education	N
Church Attendance				
More than weekly	3.3	3.3	4.1	131
Weekly	2.8	3.1	3.9	237
Less than weekly	2.5**	3.0*	3.9*	200
Connection: religion and politics				
High	3.3	3.2	4.1	161
Medium	2.9	3.2	3.9	146
Low	2.5**	3.0	3.8*	265
Pastors preach politics				
Yes	2.8	3.1	4.0	176
No	2.8	3.2	3.9	396
Watch Televangelists				
Often	3.1	3.3	4.1	174
Sometimes	2.7	3.1	3.8	340
Seldom or never	2.6**	2.9**	3.7**	58

Note: Mean value for each issue scale for each group. Statistical test is one-way analysis of variance.
$*p \leq .05$
$**p \leq .01$

Cognitive Organization: Connecting Religion and Politics

The data shown in table 3.6 indicate that those evangelicals who perceive a strong connection between religion and politics were indeed more conservative than those who perceived a weaker connection. The relationships were statistically significant for women's issues and education issues.

Religious Elites: Televangelists and Pastors

Table 3.6 suggests that those who watch televangelists are more conservative than other evangelicals, but that those who attend churches in which the pastor preaches politics from the pulpit do not differ significantly from those whose pastor does not do so. The failure of politicized pastors to have an effect on the beliefs of their flock may be somewhat illusory: the survey did not ascertain the content of the political messages that these pastors preached. It is possible that liberal and conservative messages by different pastors have offsetting effects, obscuring the effect of pastors' messages.

MULTIVARIATE RESULTS

The analysis above suggests that there are strong bivariate relationships between religious and political variables among white evangelicals. To sort out the independent effects of these religious factors and to hold constant demographic variables, multivariate regression analyses were performed for the three political-attitude scales. In these equations, dummy variables were included for fundamentalist, pentecostal, and other evangelical denominations, as well as for Catholic evangelicals. Included in the analysis but not represented by dummy variables are those evangelicals who attend nonevangelical Protestant churches. Therefore, the coefficients for denomination should be interpreted as indicating a direction relative to those evangelicals who attend mainstream Protestant churches.

Tests for interaction among several of the variables were conducted, but none achieved the traditional level of statistical significance with this relatively small sample. The results presented below do not include these interactions, although it should be noted that the interactions between doctrine and televangelists, and between fundamentalist identity and televangelists, were both nearly statistically significant. This suggests that the role of elites in providing political interpretations for religious doctrine and identity remains to be further explored.

The results are presented in table 3.7. The equations account for a fair portion of the variation in attitudes on women's issues and foreign policy, but only a modest proportion of the variation in attitudes on educational policy. The relatively small R^2 (.08) in the education-policy equation is partly due to the relatively high level of homogeneity among white evangelicals on these issues: there is less variance to explain in this equation.

Attitudes on women's issues are influenced by the cognitive connection between religion and politics, by frequency of church attendance, by personal religiosity, and by denomination (with pentecostals and Catholics more conservative than mainstream Protestants). Demographic and political variables are also important, with gender, income, age, partisanship, and ideology all significant predictors. Further analysis suggests that the impact of the cognitive connection scale is primarily restricted to women, who may be cross-pressured between life circumstances and religious doctrine. An additional regression equa-

TABLE 3.7
Religious, Demographic, and Political Variables
(Evangelical Voter Survey, Multivariate Results)

	Women's Issues	Foreign Policy	Education
Demographics			
Age	.12**	−.00	−.01
Sex	−.08*	.03	−.08*
Income	−.08*	.14**	.02
Education	−.03	−.02	−.08*
South	−.05	.10**	.03
Political Variables			
Partisanship	.08*	.18**	−.00
Ideology	.15**	.07*	−.09*
Religion			
Fundamentalist denomination	.05	.11*	.02
Pentecostal denomination	.10**	.10*	.01
Evangelical denomination	.04	.04	.01
Catholic	.08*	−.02	.18**
Doctrine	.04	.04	.01
Fundamentalist identification	−.05	.08*	.08*
Attendance	.16**	.00	−.01
Personal religiosity	.12**	.04	.17**
Connection between religion and politics	.14**	.01	.00
Pastor preaches politics	.00	.08*	−.08*
Watch televangelists	.03	.08*	.10**
N	749	749	749
R^2	.22	.12	.08

Note: Entries are standardized regression coefficients (betas).
*$p \leq .05$
**$p \leq .01$

tion included an interaction term between gender and the connection between religion and politics. In that equation (not shown), the interaction term was statistically significant, but the connection between religion and politics was not. Those women who do not perceive a strong connection between religion and politics are free to take relatively more feminist positions, whereas those that do connect these two domains are more constrained. Once again the main impact of church attendance is on attitudes toward abortion. Separate regression equations were estimated for each of the separate items that composed the women's issues scale, and attendance was a significant predictor of abortion attitudes, but not other women's issues.

Foreign-policy attitudes are influenced by denomination (with

both fundamentalists and pentecostals more conservative than mainline Protestants), fundamentalist identification, and exposure to televangelists and to pastors who preach politics. The relationship between
televangelists and foreign-policy attitudes may surprise some, but
foreign-policy concerns are frequently voiced in these broadcasts. In
addition, partisanship and ideology are important predictors of the
foreign-policy attitudes of evangelicals, as are income and region.

Finally, the strongest religious predictors of education-issue positions are televangelists, personal religiosity, and fundamentalist identification. The failure of any of the Protestant denominational dummy
variables to achieve significance in this particular equation is somewhat
surprising, given the strong connection between denomination and the
founding of independent religious schools. The strong effects of
Catholicism are easily explained by the tradition of Catholic schools. In
addition, those evangelicals with higher levels of education and income
are less conservative on education issues, as are women. These latter
relationships were strongest with the tuition tax credits item, suggesting that those with stronger commitment to education may be less
supportive of separate religious schools.

RELIGION AND POLITICAL ATTITUDES
AMONG WHITE EVANGELICALS:
SOME ADDITIONAL EVIDENCE

In 1989, the ANES Pilot Study contained an additional set of religious
items. This pilot survey involved reinterviewing over four hundred of
the same individuals who responded to the 1988 ANES survey, so it is
possible to link the answers to these religious items to the political items
in the 1988 survey. Two sets of items were of particular interest. First,
Protestant respondents were asked whether they considered themselves fundamentalists, evangelicals, or charismatics. Catholics were
asked if they considered themselves charismatics. Second, all respondents who attended church were asked if their pastor ever mentioned a
series of political issues.

The number of white evangelicals in this pilot study is too small for
multivariate analysis. Religious identity was associated with more conservative positions on most political issues, particularly social issues,
foreign-policy issues, and political values. Those who identified as fundamentalists, evangelicals, *and* charismatics were generally slightly
more conservative than those who adopted any other combination of
identities, and those who identified only as charismatics were generally
more liberal than those who identified with other combinations of

groups. Among the small number of Catholics in the survey, charismatics were generally more conservative than noncharismatics.

Those who attended churches where ministers preached on a variety of political themes were the most conservative, and this was particularly true for those respondents who attended churches that they considered fundamentalist or conservative.

BLACK EVANGELICALS

Although most research on support for the Christian Right has focused exclusively on whites, there may be a potential constituency for the Christian Right among black Americans. Christian Right elites may have recognized this potential: the *Moral Majority Report* carried a series of articles by black ministers, and Robertson's "700 Club" cohost was black. Nonetheless, Christian Right leaders took positions that could hardly be popular among blacks, including Falwell's highly publicized defense of the South African government.

In the United States, blacks are more likely than whites to hold evangelical religious beliefs, to belong to evangelical denominations, and to show high levels of religiosity. Racial differences on these traits from the 1988 ANES survey are presented in table 3.8. Blacks are substantially more likely than whites to report evangelical doctrinal beliefs, to belong to evangelical, pentecostal, and fundamentalist churches, and to report high levels of personal religiosity. Only on frequency of church attendance are the racial differences small, although blacks are significantly less likely than whites to attend church *in*frequently (not shown).

The greater religiosity of black Americans is not the only reason to expect a black constituency for the Christian Right. Several studies have reported that blacks are more conservative on social issues such as abortion, although racial differences are largely explained by differences in social location and religion (Wilcox 1990c). In the 1988 ANES data, blacks are significantly less supportive of abortion rights than whites, although they are also significantly cooler toward antiabortionists. Blacks are significantly more supportive of school prayer, but also significantly more supportive of legislation to protect gays and lesbians against discrimination. Finally, blacks show significantly higher levels of moral traditionalism than whites. This suggests that there might be a black constituency for certain issues of the Christian Right—especially general moral traditionalism and school prayer, and perhaps a carefully worded appeal on abortion as well. However, blacks are likely to respond negatively to homophobic appeals.

TABLE 3.8
Racial Differences on Religious Attributes

	ANES Data	
	Whites (%)	Blacks (%)
Bible inerrant	46	69**
Born-again	33	51**
Pentecostal denomination	2	5**
Fundamentalist denomination	2	5
Other evangelical denomination	15	32
Attend church almost weekly or more	39	42
Pray daily	27	52**
Watch religious T.V. or listen to religious radio	27	65**
Religion highly salient	33	57
Nonevangelical	67	37
Denominational only	9	21
Doctrine only	14	21
Both	10	21
	Evangelical Voter Data	
Bible literally true	50	42
Born-again	66	56*
Pentecostal denomination	4	3
Fundamentalist denomination	26	14**
Other evangelical denomination	45	22**
Fundamentalist identification	20	20
Attend church weekly	53	66*
Religion highly salient	50	40**
Watch televangelists	57	27**
Pastor preaches politics	49	31**
Strong connection between religion and politics	44	26**

Note: Percentage of each group falling into each category.
*$p \leq .05$
**$p \leq .01$

Also reported in table 3.8 are the racial differences on religious scales and items taken from the Evangelical Voter Study. Again, blacks are more orthodox, and they show higher levels of personal religiosity (but not attendance). They are significantly more likely than whites to watch televangelists, to attend churches in which pastors preach politics, and to report a strong connection between their religious and political views.

Do black evangelicals differ from other blacks in a manner similar

TABLE 3.9
Religion and Politics among American Blacks

	Nonevangelical	Denominational Evangelical Only	Doctrine Evangelical Only	Both
Values				
Moral traditionalism	−.34	−.35	−.15	.11*
Equality	−.99	−.81	−.82	−1.12
Patriotism	−.94	−.51*	−.46*	−.59
Anticommunism	−.11	−.06	.13	.13
Issue Attitudes				
Racial policy	−.98	−.92	−.79	−.97
Social issues	−.17	.04	.15*	.34**
Death penalty	−.76	−.55	−.54	−.88
Economic issues	−.71	−.63	−.52	−.47
Taxes	−.09	−.41**	−.08	−.30*
Strong defense	−.28	−.02*	−.12	−.32
Negotiate with Soviet Union	−.18	−.45*	−.81**	−.20
Isolationism	−.24	−.41*	−.25	−.32
Distrust government	−.30	−.39	−.25	−.43
Spending Priorities				
Poor	−.99	−1.02	−.69*	−1.14
Elderly	−.45	−.56	−.48	−.63
Liberal programs	−.33	−.30	−.22	−.31
Reagan defense	−.24	−.17	−.31	−.13
Relative Group Affect				
Middle America	10°	9°	11°	12°
Minorities	−6°	−7°	−11°	−8°
Establishment	−1°	−2°	−2°	−3°
Liberals	3°	3°	−3°	−1°
Right	−12°	−9°	−4°	−2°

Note: Mean values for each scale or item for each group. High scores indicate more conservative positions. All tests relative to nonevangelical blacks.
*$p \leq .05$
**$p \leq .01$

to white evangelicals? Table 3.9 presents the breakdown of values and issue scales in the 1988 ANES data by the various religious categories. Because of the small number of cases, relatively large differences are not statistically significant. Blacks in general are more liberal than whites, as evidenced by the predominance of negative scores in table 3.9.[4] Nonetheless, black evangelicals are somewhat more conservative than other blacks.

4. Because all of these scores were standardized relative to the distribution of *white* attitudes, negative scores indicate that the respondents are more liberal than all whites.

TABLE 3.10
Religious Sources of the Political Attitudes of Black Evangelicals

	Women's Issues		Foreign Policy		Education Policy	
Fundamentalist denomination	−.08	(.09**)	−.01	(.13**)	.25**	(.03)
Pentecostal denomination	.13*	(.15**)	.13*	(.08**)	−.06	(.03)
Evangelical denomination	.03	(.05*)	−.08	(.06*)	−.01	(−.02)
Doctrine	.26**	(.16**)	−.10	(.13**)	.09	(.04)
Fundamentalist identification	−.00	(.02)	−.00	(.10**)	−.00	(.06*)
Attendance	.43**	(.28**)	.08	(.07*)	.08	(.08**)
Personal religiosity	.34**	(.28**)	.01	(.05*)	.12	(.15**)
Connection between religion and politics	.17*	(.22**)	.06	(.05*)	.18*	(.08**)
Pastor preaches politics	−.08	(.03)	−.01	(.03)	−.05	(.06*)
Watch televangelists	.06	(.09**)	.10	(.10**)	.22*	(.10**)

Note: Entries are Pearson correlations. High scores indicate more conservative political positions and more orthodox religious attributes.
*$p \leq .05$
**$p \leq .01$

Do religious variables predict the attitudes of black evangelicals in the same way as white ones? Table 3.10 presents the bivariate correlations among the various religious variables in the Evangelical Voter Study and the three political-issue scales. For the purposes of comparison, the comparable white correlations are presented in parentheses. Note that the smaller number of black cases preclude relatively healthy correlations from achieving statistical significance. For this reason, it is interesting to note the relative magnitude of the correlations for blacks and whites. Although a correlation of .08 between church attendance and foreign-policy attitudes is not significant for blacks, a smaller correlation is statistically significant in the much-larger white sample.

Religious attributes are associated with more conservative positions on women's issues among black evangelicals, but there is no real relationship between religion and foreign-policy views. Other research (Cook and Wilcox 1990) suggests that religious variables are not associated with attitudes toward economic issues among blacks, after controls for demographic variables.[5]

These results suggest that there may be a constituency for the Christian Right among blacks, who are more likely to hold orthodox doctrinal beliefs and show higher signs of religiosity than whites, and

5. In part this finding is due to the relatively consensual liberalism of black Americans on economic issues.

who are more conservative on social issues. Moreover, religious variables are associated with more conservative positions on social issues
for blacks, although conservative religion does not translate into conservative politics on all issues.

CONCLUSIONS

Evangelicals are considerably more conservative than other citizens on
social issues and moral values. They are more conservative on economic issues as well, despite their lower socioeconomic status. They are
much more patriotic, anti-Communist, and supportive of defense
spending.

Although evangelicals are generally more conservative than other
citizens, there is no conservative consensus among them. Rather, some
evangelicals are consistently liberal, some consistently conservative,
and some vary across issue areas. In short, there are political differences among evangelicals, much as there are among other citizens.

These variations in the political attitudes of evangelicals are explained in part by religious differences among them. Fundamentalists
and pentecostals are more conservative, as are those who hold orthodox doctrine, attend church regularly, and watch televangelists. Religious variables are somewhat more important than demographic and
political variables in explaining the variation in evangelical political
attitudes.

All of this evidence indicates that, although there should be a
strong evangelical constituency for the Christian Right, not all evangelicals will be supportive. Moreover, religious differences may affect
the level of support for the Christian Right among evangelicals.

There may be a black constituency for the Christian Right as well.
Blacks are more likely than whites to hold orthodox doctrinal views, to
attend evangelical, pentecostal, and fundamentalist churches, and to
find religion highly salient to their lives and their politics. They are also
more conservative than whites on some issues on the Christian Right
agenda. Moreover, religious variables affect black attitudes on social
issues much the same as they do white attitudes.

CHAPTER 4

The Old Fundamentalist Right: The Christian Anti-Communism Crusade

During the 1950s and early 1960s, a number of fundamentalist groups flourished on the political Right. These groups took up the theme that the fundamentalist Right of the 1920s had belatedly adopted: anticommunism. Like the secular right-wing groups of the period, Christian Right groups of the 1950s and 1960s focused their attentions on the dangers of domestic communism.

The roots of the Christian Right in this period can be traced to the renewal of evangelical enthusiasm and fundamentalist reaction in the mid-1940s. The American Council of Christian Churches (ACCC), headed by the Reverend Carl McIntire, took up the anti-Communist theme with the rise of Senator Joseph McCarthy. The news media attended to McIntire and his colleagues, who used this heightened interest to air charges of Communist influence in the mainstream Protestant denominations. After McCarthy's fall, McIntire helped several of his protégés establish their own anti-Communist organizations. Among them was the Australian physician Fred Schwarz, who formed the Christian Anti-Communism Crusade. Schwarz used the radio to spread his message and distributed newsletters and other printed matter, but the particular specialty of the Crusade was the traveling School of Anti-Communism (Wolfinger et al. 1969). These schools were organized in various communities, and they involved weekend workshops on the dangers of domestic communism and speeches by various anti-Communist figures.

The Crusade was only one of a set of organizations which attempted to mobilize fundamentalists into anti-Communist activity.

Groups such as the Christian Crusade, the Church League of America, and the Twentieth Century Reformation also were involved in spreading the message. It is unclear how typical Crusade supporters or activists were of the Christian Right of this period, although the Crusade was the best known of the fundamentalist groups of this era.

Schwarz began his career deeply rooted in the fundamentalist Right, but gradually began to deemphasize the religious aspects of his Crusade. Eventually he came to reject the labels fundamentalist and conservative (Clabaugh 1974), but he continued to give support to fundamentalist doctrine while attempting to gain support among mainstream conservative Protestants (Jorstad 1970). Moreover, throughout the 1950s and 1960s, many of the spokesmen for the Crusade proudly accepted the fundamentalist label.

The Crusade grew rapidly during the 1950s, nearly doubling its revenues every year (Clabaugh 1974). Its essential message was that domestic and international communism was a threat to American security. The Crusade focused more on international issues than on domestic ones, although Schwarz did decry the expanded role of government as part of the Communist effort to undermine the United States. The Crusade accordingly opposed Medicare, sex education in schools, and other liberal programs.

The Crusade reached its pinnacle (measured by receipts) in 1961, but did not experience a serious decline in popularity until after the 1964 election. During that election, the Christian Right shed its separatist tendencies and allied itself wholeheartedly with the Goldwater campaign. Goldwater was a favorite of the Christian Right for several reasons. He had regularly taken positions in the Senate which were consistent with those of the Christian Right, and he had been a supporter of McCarthy. Goldwater also had the support of the secular Right: the John Birch Society endorsed him early in the campaign. The Christian and secular Right of this period composed more than one-half of the early supporters of Goldwater (McEvoy 1971), although, as he gathered momentum, his increasing support among mainstream conservatives reduced the importance of the Right to his coalition.

The Goldwater campaign was a mixed blessing for these organizations. As Goldwater won the Republican nomination, the organizations of the Christian Right saw an increase in recruits and contributions, but his devastating defeat led to a sharp decline in support and in media exposure. By 1968, the Crusade's receipts were less than one-half of their 1961 total. Although the Crusade still existed in 1991, its influence had long since waned.

The 1964 election presents the best opportunity to study supporters of the fundamentalist Right of this period. National attention to the prominence of these organizations in the Goldwater coalition raised them to a level of visibility which they had not achieved before and would not receive again. Not until the formation of the Moral Majority in the late 1970s would an organization of the Christian Right again so capture the attention of the national media.

The data on support of the Crusade in 1964 come from the American National Election Study (ANES) conducted by the Center for Political Studies at the University of Michigan. The study contained two questions about the Crusade. First, respondents were asked whether they had heard of the organization. Those who were familiar with the Crusade were then asked to rate it on an imaginary feeling thermometer, in which 0° represented extreme coolness and 100° represented extreme warmth. Similar feeling-thermometer questions were asked of a range of political and social groups.

One of the difficulties with feeling-thermometer items in surveys is that different people may use the same score to indicate different feelings. Some people assign most groups positive scores. For these people, a score of 60° may be the lowest score they assign, and this score may indicate extreme disapproval of the group. Others assign mostly low scores. For these people, a score of 60° may represent extreme warmth. One solution to this problem is to adjust the feeling-thermometer scores according to individual response patterns. In this chapter and throughout this book, the average feeling-thermometer score that each individual has assigned to all groups is used to determine the way that individual responds to feeling-thermometer items. Supporters of Christian Right groups are those who rate the group at least 10° warmer than their average score for all other groups in society. For more details, see Wilcox (1987c) and Wilcox et al. (1989).

AWARENESS OF THE CRUSADE

Most surveys in the 1980s suggested that a sizable proportion of the public was aware of Christian Right organizations such as the Moral Majority and figures such as Jerry Falwell and Pat Robertson. Awareness of the Crusade was much more limited. Only 25 percent of white respondents were familiar with the Crusade.

Table 4.1 presents information on the factors that are associated with awareness of the Crusade. Awareness was significantly higher among those who attended evangelical, fundamentalist, or pentecostal denominations, among those who believed that the Bible is the inspired word of God, and among those who attended churches in which elections were discussed. Those who attended church regularly were no more likely to have heard of the Crusade than those who attended less

TABLE 4.1
White Awareness of the Christian Anti-Communism Crusade (Bivariate Analysis, Percentage)

Denomination	
Evangelical/Fundamentalist/ Pentecostal	31**
Other	24
Bible Interpretation	
Inerrant	28*
Other	23
Politics in Sermons	
Yes	33**
No	25
Attend Church	
Regularly	24
Other	24
Region	
South and West	31**
Other	21
Political Information	
High	33**
Low	19
Involvement in Campaign	
High	29**
Low	20
Education	
Some college +	32**
Other	23
Strength of Partisanship	
Strong	30*
Other	23
Strength of Ideology	
Strong	28*
Other	22

Note: Percentage of each group indicating awareness of the Crusade. All tests one-way analysis of variance.
$*p \leq .05$
$**p \leq .01$

frequently, but among those who attended fundamentalist, evangelical, or pentecostal churches, frequency of attendance was a predictor of awareness of the Crusade. These results suggest that church networks were a source of information about the Crusade.

In addition, awareness of the Crusade was also a function of levels of general political information. Those who knew the most about politics were more likely to have heard of the Crusade, as were those with at least some college education, with regular exposure to multiple media sources, and with strong partisan or ideological attachments.

Finally, the Crusade was more visible in two regions of the country. In both the South and the West, nearly one-third of whites were aware of the Crusade, while in the rest of the country, the figure was closer to one-fifth.

While each of these variables is associated with awareness of the Crusade in bivariate analysis, multivariate analysis is needed to sort out the sources of knowledge of the Crusade. Table 4.2 includes maximum-likelihood estimates from multivariate probit analysis. (The results in table 4.2 are best understood by examining the magnitude of the T value. Larger values indicate that the coefficient is less likely to be due solely to chance and plays a larger role in explaining who was aware of the Crusade.)

The multivariate results show that church networks were one important source of information about the Crusade and that those citizens who paid attention to politics were also more likely to know of the group. Those who believed the Bible was the inerrant word of God,

TABLE 4.2
White Awareness of the Christian Anti-Communism Crusade (Multivariate Probit Analysis)

	MLE	T
Religious Variables		
Frequently attend funda- mentalist churches	.24	1.69*
Bible interpretation	.24	2.53**
Pastor preaches politics	.03	.75
Political Exposure		
Electoral information	.00	.03
Education	.10	1.52
Involvement in campaign	.01	.31
Media exposure	.11	2.03*
Strength of partisanship	.06	1.05
Strength of ideology	.01	2.30*
Reside in South or West	.19	1.96*

Note: Maximum likelihood estimates and T values from probit analysis.
$*p \leq .05$
$*p \leq .01$

as well as those who frequently attended an evangelical, fundamentalist, or pentecostal church, were significantly more likely to have heard of the Crusade. Those who garnered political information from a variety of media were significantly more likely to have heard of the Crusade, as were those with strong ideological views (of the Left or Right) and those who lived in the South or West.

SUPPORT FOR THE CRUSADE

Only sixty-three white respondents can be termed Crusade supporters, and they constituted approximately 5.1 percent of the white population. However, among those who were aware of the Crusade, a more substantial 20 percent actually supported it. Because awareness of the Crusade was higher among those predisposed to support it (by religion and region), we cannot extrapolate that 20 percent of the white population would have supported the Crusade had all been aware of it. At the end of this section, an estimate of likely support among those who were unaware of the organization is computed.

Personality Explanations

Although the 1964 ANES did not contain any items tapping the authoritarian personality, a number of items measured personality variables. From these items I have constructed measures of strong-mindedness, personal competence, distrust of people, and nostalgia. There is some mixed support for a personality explanation here. Supporters of the Crusade scored significantly higher than nonsupporters on the strong-mindedness scale, but were no more nostalgic, did not differ from nonsupporters in their evaluations of their own personal competence, and were not significantly less trusting of others.

Alienation Explanations

There are no good measures of alienation in the 1964 survey, but it is possible to test the explanation indirectly. Supporters of the Crusade were slightly more likely than other whites to believe that the government was not responsive to citizen needs, slightly more cynical, and felt slightly less politically efficacious. However, each of these relationships fell short of statistical significance.

Crusaders did not behave like alienated, isolated individuals. Their level of political involvement was significantly higher than that of nonsupporters, and their activity in electoral politics was also significantly higher. Therefore, alienation explanations find little support in these data.

Social Status Explanations

Although the 1964 survey did not contain items that are ideally suited to testing the social status explanations, the data do allow a number of direct and indirect tests. Table 4.3 also contains information on the status location, consistency, and anxiety of Crusade supporters. Crusaders resembled nonsupporters in education, income, and occupational prestige. These three socioeconomic status indicators allow six possible inconsistencies in social status. Crusaders were significantly more likely than other whites to display two types of status inconsistency: educational attainment far in excess of income or occupational status.[1] However, these are not the sorts of status inconsistency generally theorized to lead to right-wing support, because individuals with this combination of status locators should welcome, not fear, social change. Moreover, Crusaders were *less* likely than other whites to display other types of status inconsistency.

Available measures of status anxiety are more tenuous. Crusaders were slightly, but not significantly, more likely than other whites to report that the heads of their households had a lower level of occupational prestige than did their fathers. Supporters of the Crusade were slightly, but not significantly, *more* satisfied than other whites with their personal economic position, as well as more optimistic about their future economic prospects. On these grounds, Crusaders do not seem particularly worried that their status (or at least their economic position) is declining.

On the other hand, Crusaders were more likely than nonsupporters to report a great deal of interest in social class, and they were somewhat less likely than nonsupporters to feel close to their own social class. Moreover, Crusaders were significantly more likely than nonsupporters to exaggerate their social class. Among those whites in the bottom one-third on education, occupation, or income, Crusaders were significantly more likely than nonsupporters to consider themselves middle class.

1. I tested for the effects of status inconsistency in three ways. First, I regressed each status locator on the other two and used the residuals as a measure of status inconsistency. Second, I trichotomized education, occupational prestige of the head of household, and family income. Those in the top third on one location and the bottom third on any other were classified as inconsistent. Third, I used these trichotomous measures, but classified as inconsistent those who were not in the same level of all three status indicators. The results of these three tests were very similar. In this chapter and throughout the book, I use the second test.

TABLE 4.3
Support for the Christian Anti-Communism Crusade
(Bivariate Analysis)

	Supporters	Nonsupporters	Nonaware	Correlation
Personality Explanations				
Strong-minded	7.3*	5.9	6.6	.10
Personal competence	3.7	3.6	3.6	.04
Distrust people	7.8	7.4	7.5	.30
Nostalgia	4.2	4.2	4.4	−.01
Alienation Explanations				
Government unresponsive	9.4	9.1	9.2	.03
Political cynicism	10.3	9.2	9.9	.03
Efficacy	2.9	2.7	2.6	.05
Political involvement	5.6*	4.8	5.0	.10
Electoral activities	1.4*	0.7	0.7	.19
Social Status Explanations				
Education > income	9%*	2%	3%	.09
Education > occupation	33%*	20%	20%	.08
Feels close to class	51%*	55%	56%	−.08
Labels self middle class when in bottom third on				
Income	47%**	24%	30%	.14
Education	36%	20%	21%	.10
Occupation	74%	68%	63%	.07
Occupational status < father's	25%	20%	20%	.02
Satisfied with income	49%	45%	48%	.01
Optimistic about future	51%*	44%	40%	.08
Symbolic Politics Explanations				
Old order	78	76	79	.03
Left	49**	55	54	−.18
East	63	64	64	−.03
Blacks	41	42	46	−.00
Communists	2**	10	8	−.21
Black Muslims	8**	14	12	−.13
John Birch Society	44**	30	31	.21
Ku Klux Klan	14	17	16	−.05
Jews	62	63	59	−.03
Catholics	66*	62	67	.07
Religious Value Explanations				
Evangelical denomination	29%	21%	25%	.01
Bible inerrant	61%**	49%	54%	.11
Pastors preach politics	17%	11%	15%	.04
Attend church regularly	46%	45%	44%	.02

(*continued*)

Table 4.3 (*continued*)

	Supporters	Nonsupporters	Nonaware	Correlation
Political Explanations				
Republican	38%	32%	36%	.02
Populist	16%*	10%	9%	.11
Mean Scores—Issues				
Aid to education	3.9*	3.5	3.5	.10
Federal government power	3.7**	2.9	3.1	.16
Medicare	3.5**	2.6	2.7	.18
Government help ensure living standard	3.5	3.5	3.4	.02
School prayer	6.6*	6.2	6.1	.09
Fair employment—blacks	3.3	3.1	3.3	.05
School integration	3.1	3.1	3.1	−.01
Residential desegregation	3.5	3.3	3.4	.07
Foreign Aid	2.2	2.2	2.4	−.06
Negotiate with Communists	1.8	1.5	1.7	.06
Trade with Communists	3.8*	3.3	3.4	.11
Get Communists out of Cuba	3.3	3.2	2.9	.09
Leave UN if China admitted	3.4*	2.9	2.8	.15
Invade Vietnam	4.4**	3.6	3.7	.24
Ideology				
Ideological affect	20°**	5°	4°	.18
Geographic Explanations				
South	33%	26%	30%	.02
West	24%	16%	19%	.07
Born in rural area or small town	62%	58%	61%	.04
Born in large city	24%	29%	36%	−.03
Moved in past 2 years	28%	26%	23%	.01

Note: Significance tests were conducted by analysis of variance, using only those who were familiar with the Crusade.
*$p \leq .05$
**$p \leq .01$

There is mixed evidence in these data for social status explanations for support for the fundamentalist Right. On the one hand, Crusaders were generally well educated and confident of their economic future. They are unlikely candidates for economic displacement. However, the social status explanation does not center on economic status, but on social status. Although Crusaders were financially secure, they were more likely than other whites to think about social class, to feel distant from their social class, and to exaggerate their social class status.

Symbolic Politics Explanations

Conover and Gray (1981) proposed a technique for examining the impact of symbolic politics on support for the Right. Because those on symbolic crusades are thought to see the world in terms of groups that are friendly to their values and those that are hostile, they should have strong affect toward different sets of social groups. Symbolic politics occurs when issues or causes come to symbolize broader, affectively charged issues. Generally, these broader issues have been described as group conflicts over lifestyles. If the Crusade served as a symbol of larger conflict, support should have been linked to differences in affect for sets of political groups. Conover and Gray used factor analysis to identify those social and political groups that are perceived as allies by the general public, then constructed scales that measured affect toward those groups. If supporters of the Right differ significantly from others in the population in their affect toward different sets of social and political actors, then they may indeed be involved in a symbolic crusade.

Factor analysis suggested that in 1964 the public identified five sets of groups from those included in the survey. The first set represents the Old Order—farmers, southerners, the military, and Protestants. The second set comprises groups of the Left—liberals, Democrats, labor unions, and the Americans for Democratic Action. The third set represents eastern interests that are often attacked by populist movements. These include easterners, big business, Catholics, and Jews. The fourth set represents blacks and includes the National Association for the Advancement of Colored People (NAACP), the Congress on Racial Equality (CORE), and blacks. The final set represents radicals: the Ku Klux Klan, Black Muslims, the American Communist party, and the John Birch Society. Because supporters of the Crusade might be expected to be much warmer toward the John Birch Society and possibly the Ku Klux Klan than toward Communists and Black Muslims, and because race is inextricably intertwined with affect toward the Klan and the Black Muslims, table 4.3 presents separately affect toward the four groups. In addition, because support for the Christian Right has been linked to religious intolerance (Lipset and Raab 1978), table 4.3 presents the mean scores for affect toward Jews and Catholics.

Predictably, Crusaders are warmer than other whites toward groups of the radical Right (especially the Birchers) and cooler toward groups of the radical Left, especially Communists. However, Crusaders are not significantly cooler toward the eastern elite or significantly more supportive of the Old Order. In addition, Crusaders were not cooler than other whites toward blacks. Indeed, although they were slightly cooler than other whites who had heard of the Crusade toward CORE and NAACP, they were slightly warmer toward blacks. Moreover, Crusaders were slightly, though not significantly, cooler toward the Klan. Finally, they were significantly warmer than other whites who knew of the Crusade toward Catholics and not cooler toward Jews.

These results do not support a symbolic politics explanation. Although Crusaders are somewhat warmer than other whites toward the John Birch Society and cooler toward Communists, they do not see the political world as a conflict between the Old Order and an eastern elite. However, supporters of the Crusade were more likely to view the eastern elite as part of the American Left. Among supporters, the correlation between these two scales was .21, significantly higher than the correlation of .01 for other whites. Nonetheless, supporters of the Crusade did not see the eastern elite as associated with Communists. The correlation between affect for Communists and for the eastern elite was only .01.

Moreover, support for the Crusade was not fed by anti-Catholicism, anti-Semitism, or racism. Although racism and religious prejudice are among the most frequently discussed attitudes in the symbolic politics literature, supporters of the Crusade were, if anything, slightly warmer than other whites who knew of the Crusade toward these groups. This lack of racism and prejudice among supporters of the Crusade also provides additional evidence against certain personality explanations of support which posit projection of feelings of inadequacy onto out-groups.

Religious Explanations

Table 4.3 also presents the differences between Crusaders and nonsupporters on a number of religious variables. Not surprisingly, the Crusade drew support disproportionately from fundamentalist, pentecostal, or evangelical churches. There are too few supporters in these data to separate those who attend churches of these three evangelical traditions. Although the survey did not contain a born-again item, support was higher among people who believed that the Bible is the inerrant word of God. Supporters were more likely to attend churches in which electoral politics were discussed from the pulpit. Support was not higher among regular church attenders, although it was highest among those who regularly attended evangelical, fundamentalist, or pentecostal churches.

These relationships are not surprising; indeed, the most surprising thing is their weakness. Although religion was clearly part of the appeal of the Crusade, a sizable proportion of Crusaders attended church infrequently, believed that the Bible was not even the inspired word of God, and were not associated with evangelical denominations.

Political Explanations

Table 4.3 presents the political attitudes of Crusaders, the nonsupporters, and those who had no knowledge of the Crusade. Despite the association of the Crusade with the Goldwater campaign and the historic connection between support for the Right and partisanship, Crusaders were only slightly, and not significantly, more Republican than nonsupporters. However, support for the Crusade was strongly associated with ideology. Although the 1964 survey contained no measure of ideological self-placement, I have constructed a measure that is the difference in feeling-thermometer scores for conservatives and liberals. The difference in affect for conservatives and liberals is 20° for supporters of the Crusade, four times that of nonsupporters.

Crusade supporters were more conservative than other whites in the survey on almost all issues in the survey, but on domestic issues this difference was statistically significant on only three items: Medicare, school prayer, and the role of the federal government. The Crusade had taken positions on these three issues, arguing that Medicare was a first step toward communism, that school prayer was essential to protect children from communism, and that the federal government was infiltrated by Communists.

More surprising is the finding that Crusaders were not significantly less likely than other whites to oppose talks with Communists or to favor or oppose foreign aid. However, Crusaders were significantly more likely to oppose trade with Communist nations and to favor military action to oppose communism.

Those who described McCarthy's crusade frequently noted its populist appeals. McCarthy's attacks on communism were also attacks on the eastern elite and on big government. To determine if populism was a source of support for the Crusade, a measure of populism was constructed. Those who were relatively cool toward big business *and* labor unions, and who also thought that the federal government was too powerful, were classified as populists. Supporters of the Crusade were more likely than other whites to be classified as populists.

There is evidence that political attitudes contributed to support for the Crusade, then, but the relationships are surprisingly weak. Crusaders were significantly more conservative than other whites on only a few issues, primarily confined to communism in its foreign manifestations, and to those domestic issues that Crusaders associated with creeping communism.

Geographic Explanations: Region, Ruralism, and Mobility

The geographic explanations discussed in chapter 2 include some that posit that support is the result of political socialization and some that see support as the result of social strain. If support is strongest among those who were raised in regions of the country where conservative values predominate, then support is likely due to socialization. Similarly, if support is highest among those raised in rural areas, socialization is the most likely explanation. However, if support is highest among those who have recently moved, especially those who have moved from rural areas to urban ones, then support may be due to social dislocation.

Support for the Crusade came disproportionately from regions of the country where conservative values were strongest: the South and the West. Supporters were slightly more likely than the rest of the public to have been born in a rural community, as well as less likely to have been born in a large city. Crusade supporters were not more likely to have moved in the last two years, nor were they more likely to have moved from a rural area to a large city, or from the South to other regions. None of these relationships achieved conventional levels of statistical significance.

EXPLAINING SUPPORT FOR THE CRUSADE: MULTIVARIATE RESULTS

Although many of these variables are significant predictors of support for the Crusade, multivariate analysis is needed to assess the independent contribution of each variable to support. As before, a multivariate probit equation was estimated, with each of the independent variables discussed above included in the equation. The results are shown in table 4.4.

Two sets of results are presented. The full model contains all variables hypothesized to affect support. Some items have been combined into scales. This model tests the independent influence of each of these variables on support for the Crusade, holding constant all other independent variables.

Although the full model is the most complete test of the explanations of support for the Crusade, the inclusion of so many independent variables results in a substantial loss of cases due to missing data. Accordingly, a series of successive probit models were estimated, in each instance including in the model only those independent variables that displayed coefficients that approached statistical significance in the

TABLE 4.4
Support for the Christian Anti-Communism Crusade (Probit Analysis)

	Full Model		Parsimonious Model	
	MLE	*T*	*MLE*	*T*
Personality				
Strong-minded	−.16	−1.07		
Distrust others	−.13	−1.11		
Nostalgia	−.22	−1.38		
Alienation				
Government not responsive	.06	.40		
Cynicism	−.08	−.45		
Efficacy	−.07	−.48		
Involvement	−.05	−.41		
Social Status				
Status inconsistency/anxiety	.04	.23		
Education	.85	3.04**	.35	2.66**
Income	−.23	−1.36**		
Occupation	.54	2.18		
Symbolic Politics, Affect				
Old order	.00	.30		
Left	−.01	−.69		
East	−.02	−1.99*	−.01	−2.38**
Communists	−.05	−2.07**	−.03	−3.07**
Ku Klux Klan	−.02	−1.07[a]		
Religion				
Conservative denomination	.15	.35		
Catholic	−.61	−1.38		
Interpretation of Bible	.35	1.69	.38	2.31**
Pastors preach politics	.13	1.12		
Attendance	.13	.89		
Political Attitudes				
Partisanship	.28	2.49**		
Ideology	.00	.60		
Government role	.29	1.91[a]		
Race issues	−.22	−1.26		
Military response to communism	.22	1.78[a]		
School prayer	.27	1.97*		
Populism	−1.42	−2.51		
Geography				
South	.13	.34		
West	.57	1.43		
Moved recently	−.04	−.09		
Rural-born	.00	.72		

(*continued*)

TABLE 4.4 (*continued*)

	Full Model		Parsimonious Model	
	MLE	*T*	*MLE*	*T*
Other Demographics				
Age	.00	.45		
Sex	.92	2.64**	.36	1.96*
Intercept	−.39	6.89**	−.49	7.90**
N	157		281	

Note: Entries are maximum likelihood estimates from probit analysis and corresponding *T* values.
ᵃ$p \le .10$
*$p \le .05$
**$p \le .01$

previous iteration. The resulting model is parsimonious and includes only statistically significant predictors.

The results suggest that support for the Crusade is linked to education, negative affect toward Communists and the eastern establishment, belief in the inerrancy of the Bible, and gender (with women more supportive). Support is also associated in the complete model with high levels of occupational prestige, Republican partisanship, support for school prayer, support for military action to combat international communism, and support for a reduced role for the federal government.

Support for the Crusade, then, was the result of a congruity between the religious and political beliefs of potential supporters and the public positions of the Crusade, and not of personality disorders, status anxiety, or alienation. Support was emphatically not linked to racism. Crusaders were less conservative than white nonsupporters on race issues and were cooler toward the Klan.

One surprising result from this table is that Crusade supporters were better educated and had higher occupational prestige than nonsupporters. These relationships run counter to the conventional wisdom that the Crusade attracted lower SES fundamentalists. (Although Wolfinger et al. [1969] reported that those who attended a Crusade rally in California were well educated, their research team surveyed activists, not mass supporters. Political activists in almost all organizations are better educated than nonactivists.) Crusade supporters were better educated primarily because education was associated with greater knowledge about the organization. Indeed, education was also associated with opposition to the Crusade, with less well-educated respondents taking a middle position. An additional equation was estimated, with an index of political information as an additional independent variable. In this equation, education was no longer a predictor of support for the Crusade, although occupation remained statistically significant. Holding constant all other variables, the Crusade attracted a significant following among businessmen.

The most surprising aspect of these results, however, is the generally weak relationships, particularly for the religious and political variables.

THE CRUSADE AND THE JOHN BIRCH SOCIETY

Of the secular Right organizations active during the late 1950s and early 1960s, none attracted as much attention as the John Birch Society. Founded in 1958 by Robert Welch, it was the premier right-wing group of the period. The message of the society combined an antistatist emphasis on the reduction of the size of the federal government with an elaborate conspiracy theory. The conspiracy theory in turn combined an account of a century-old conspiracy by the Illuminati (a short-lived offshoot of the Masons in the sixteenth century) and a more contemporary conspiracy by Communists and "fellow travelers" to undermine American society (Lipset and Raab 1978). Most of the leaders of both political parties were charged with collusion with this conspiracy.

Although Welch bemoaned Communist influence in the mainstream Protestant denominations, he made few explicitly religious appeals. Nevertheless, there was considerable support for the John Birch Society among Catholic clergy, who served as a vehicle for recruitment into the organization (Gargan 1961). Although much of the fundamentalist Right took a vehemently anti-Catholic position, the Birchers steered clear of religious bigotry (Lipset and Raab 1978). Most research suggests that a sizable portion of the membership of the John Birch Society was Catholic (Grupp 1968; Stone 1968). Welch claimed that fully 40 percent of the national membership was Catholic, a figure that researchers failed to confirm. The society seems to have tapped into the historical right-wing Catholic sentiment embodied in the 1930s by Father Charles Coughlin and again in the 1950s by Senator McCarthy. Some researchers argued that the society also had strong appeal for Protestant fundamentalists (Stone 1968), though others disputed this claim (Lipset and Raab 1978).

Unlike the Crusade, the John Birch Society was organized into local chapters, which held regular meetings, generally focusing on a discussion of political matters (taken from Welch's *Bulletin*, a monthly publication). Members were given assignments that often consisted of writing letters to various officials and newspapers (Broyles 1966). The large number of letters written by John Birch Society members enabled several researchers to identify a set of activists in the organization to study (Rohter 1969; McNall 1969).

The message of the John Birch Society differed in subtle ways from that of the Crusade. Both emphasized the dangers of domestic and foreign communism and preached against an increase in federal government. However, the Birchers emphasized more heavily the nature of the domestic Communist conspiracy. In addition, the John Birch Society took a much more explicitly antistatist position. Finally, the society did not emphasize a religious component to its message, which was in marked contrast to the Crusade, especially in its early years.

The 1964 ANES contained a feeling-thermometer item for the John Birch Society. Using an operational definition identical to that for the Crusade, sixty-seven supporters of the society were identified. Thus, the support for the society was roughly 5 percent of the white population, a percentage almost identical to that of the Crusade. However, awareness of the John Birch Society was much higher than that for the Crusade. Although only one in four whites had heard of the Crusade, more than four in five were aware of the John Birch Society. Of those who had heard of the society, only 6 percent supported the group.

Of the sixty-seven John Birch Society supporters in the 1964 ANES, thirteen also supported the Crusade. In most respects, these double supporters resembled the other supporters of the John Birch Society more fully than they did the other supporters of the Crusade. Those Crusaders who also supported the John Birch Society were significantly *less* likely to believe in the inerrancy of the Bible, to belong to an evangelical denomination, and were slightly less likely to attend church regularly. For this reason, I refer to this group as the secular segment. More importantly, these secular supporters were significantly more conservative than other Crusaders. The other, more religious segment, was actually more liberal than other whites on economic issues. These differences are reflected in the government-role scale in table 4.5, which compares the secular supporters (i.e., those who also supported the John Birch Society) and religious supporters of the Crusade.

These data explain the generally weak relationships between religious and political variables and support for the Crusade. It appears that the Crusade attracted two groups of supporters. One group was

TABLE 4.5
Secular and Religious Supporters of the Christian
Anti-Communism Crusade

	Secular	Religious	Other Whites
Evangelical denomination	15%	32%	21%
Bible inerrant	33%	66%	50%
Attend church regularly	40%	48%	44%
Republican	67%	32%	33%
Ideological affect	58°	7°	5°
Federal government role	4.5	3.4	3.2
Race issues	4.5	3.4	3.4
Foreign policy	2.9	1.8	2.0
N	21	53	250

Note: Mean positions for each group or percentage of each group falling into each category. Secular supporters are those who also supported the John Birch Society.

motivated by religious concerns. These supporters were disproportionately of fundamentalist, evangelical, and pentecostal denominations, attended church frequently, and believed the Bible to be the
inspired word of God. They were politically moderate, except for their
dislike of Communists. The second, somewhat smaller group of supporters were considerably more secular. They may have been drawn to
the Crusade through their involvement in other organizations of the
political Right, including the John Birch Society. These supporters did
not share either the religious involvement or the political moderation
of the first set of supporters.

What factors led individuals to support one of these groups, or to
support both? To answer this question, a multivariate discriminant
analysis was conducted, and the results are presented in table 4.6. The
coefficients are total-structure coefficients and are interpreted as correlations between the underlying discriminant function and the independent variable. The analysis does a good job of predicting those who
supported the two right-wing groups, particularly those who supported the John Birch Society.

Those variables with high scores on function 1 distinguish between
those who supported neither group and those who supported the John
Birch Society (especially those who also supported the Crusade). Those
individuals who were strong conservatives, who strongly disliked the
Left, who wanted a limited government role, who opposed racial integration, who disliked the symbols of the eastern establishment, who
were nostalgic for an idealized past, who believed that the government

TABLE 4.6
Support for the Christian Anti-Communism Crusade and the John Birch Society (Discriminant Analysis)

	Function 1[a]	Function 2[a]	Function 3[a]
Affect for Left	−.47		
Ideology	.44		
Limit government role	.36		
Cynicism	.31		
Conservative on race issues	.28		
Nostalgia	.20		
Affect—East	−.20		
Government not responsive	.20		
Affect—Ku Klux Klan	.30	.38	
Education		−.31	.22
Southern residence		.24	.20
Occupational prestige		−.23	
Catholic		−.21	
Military response to communism		.21	
Affect—Communists			−.36
Gender			.28
Interpretation of Bible			.23
School prayer			.20
Evangelical denomination			.20
Political involvement			−.21
Moved			−.20
Percentage of groups classified correctly	76		
Percentage of nonsupporters classified correctly	74		
Percentage who supported Crusade only	72		
Percentage who supported John Birch Society only	100		
Percentage who supported both	100		

Canonical Discriminant Functions Evaluated at Group Means

	Function 1	Function 2	Function 3
Neither	−.42	.04	−.28
Crusade	−.01	−.42	.96
John Birch Society	2.00	2.49	−.35
Both	3.60	−1.33	−.63

[a]Correlations with discriminant function. Only correlations ≥ .20 shown.

was generally nonresponsive to citizen demands, and who were cynical about the functioning of society were more likely than other respondents to support the John Birch Society, and especially both groups. These individuals were also more likely to live in the West and to be well educated.

Those variables with strong loadings on the second function distinguish between those who supported only the John Birch Society and those who also supported the Crusade. Those variables with high positive scores are associated with exclusive support for the John Birch Society, and those with high negative scores are associated with support for both groups. Those who supported the John Birch Society but not the Crusade were markedly warmer toward the Klan, were less well educated, had less occupational status, were more likely to live in the South, were more likely to be Catholic, and were less supportive of a muscular foreign policy to oppose communism.

Finally, the third function discriminates between those who supported only the Crusade and all others, especially those who supported the John Birch Society. Although this function narrowly misses the conventional requirements of statistical significance, it is included for heuristic purposes. Those who supported only the Crusade were more negative toward Communists, more likely to be women, more likely to believe that the Bible is the inerrant word of God, more likely to support school prayer and to attend evangelical, fundamentalist, or pentecostal churches, and less involved in politics.

DISCUSSION: SOURCES OF SUPPORT FOR THE RIGHT

The results above clarify the generally weak relationships between religious and political variables and support for the Crusade. There were two distinct sets of supporters of the Crusade—one motivated largely by religion and not particularly conservative, and the other motivated primarily by political conservatism and not particularly religious. The Crusade was able to attract secular support by its focus on communism. During the 1960s, Schwarz increasingly deemphasized the religious connection and increasingly emphasized the dangers of communism. This tactic may have cost him some support from the fundamentalist Right, but it gained support among more secular anti-Communists.

These data suggest that supporters of the John Birch Society fit the nonrational theories of right-wing support much better than supporters of the Crusade. The Birchers were alienated from government and showed evidence of racism. Elsewhere, I have reported that supporters of the John Birch Society showed evidence of social dislocation, status anxiety and inconsistency, and distrust of others (Wilcox 1988d). Given the elaborate conspiracy theories preached by the Birchers (e.g., that a centuries-old offshoot of the Masons had controlled human history), psychological and other nonrational theories seem relevant. However, these theories do not fit supporters of the Crusade, who were generally motivated by strong negative affect toward Communists.

THE CONSEQUENCES OF SUPPORT FOR THE CHRISTIAN RIGHT: ELECTORAL BEHAVIOR

One of the claims of the New Christian Right in the 1980s is to have mobilized previously apolitical evangelicals, fundamentalists, and pentecostals into political action. The Christian Right leaders of the 1960s made similar claims for their efforts on behalf of Goldwater. The evidence from these data is inconclusive. Crusaders were more active in the electoral arena than nonsupporters, and these differences were statistically significant after controls for education, age, age squared, occupation, and strength of ideology and partisanship. It is impossible from these data to determine whether this indicates mobilization by the Crusade, or whether the Crusade appealed to extremely active ideologues. I suspect the latter.

The Crusade endorsed the presidential candidacy of Goldwater and worked hard to elect him. Schwarz claimed to have helped Goldwater win the nomination, and McEvoy (1971) found that supporters of the Old Right constituted a considerable proportion of Goldwater's early supporters.

Supporters of the Crusade did vote for Goldwater in significantly larger numbers than did the general population. More than one-half of Crusade supporters voted for Goldwater, while fewer than 40 percent of nonsupporters cast a Republican vote for president in 1964. Among the religious supporters, only four in ten voted for Goldwater, while, among the small number of secular supporters, the Goldwater vote was twice as high. Nonetheless, it is striking that nearly one-half of white Crusade supporters voted for Johnson, despite Schwarz's enthusiastic endorsement of Goldwater. Table 4.7 presents the details of this analysis.

It is possible that the endorsement by the Crusade swayed the votes of some of its supporters, but it is also possible that others with the same demographic profile, partisan and ideological positions, and political attitudes also supported Goldwater in equal numbers. To determine the effects of the Crusade endorsement, I have successively removed the effects of demographic variables, partisanship, ideology, and political attitudes from vote decisions.

TABLE 4.7
Vote Choice and the Christian
Anti-Communism Crusade

	Nonsupporters (%)	Supporters (%)
Voted for Goldwater	39	53*
Control demographics	42	51[a]
Also control party and ideology	44	48
Also control political attitudes	49	49

[a]$p \leq .10$
*$p \leq .05$

The results from the analysis of covariance suggest that although Crusaders were slightly more likely to have voted for Goldwater than white nonsupporters with a similar demographic profile, this difference was primarily due to partisanship, ideology, and, especially, political attitudes. To determine the factors that led to a Goldwater vote, I estimated a probit equation for vote choice. The results (not presented) suggest that partisanship, ideology, attitudes toward the role of government, race, and military means to combat foreign communism were the strongest predictors of a Goldwater vote and that support for the Crusade was *not* a significant predictor with these other variables controlled. This suggests that the Crusade did not bring new votes to Goldwater, although Crusaders did contribute 9 percent of his final votes.

BLACK SUPPORT FOR THE CRUSADE

Most studies of the Christian Right have focused on white support, in part for convenience and in part because its organizations are thought to appeal primarily to whites. However, blacks are more likely than whites to attend conservative churches, to believe the Bible is the inerrant word of God, to report a born-again experience, and to engage in private and public religious worship. Moreover, a significant proportion of blacks are conservative on social issues such as school prayer, abortion, and crime. It seems quite possible that blacks could support the Christian Right in numbers that rival those for whites.

The 1964 survey contained an oversample of black Americans, resulting in over four hundred respondents. Approximately 29 percent of black respondents were familiar with the Crusade, and 5 percent of all black respondents can be classified as supporters. Black supporters constituted 23 percent of those blacks who were familiar with the organization. Each of these figures is nearly identical to that for whites.

Because only twenty blacks can be termed supporters of the Crusade, multivariate analysis is problematic. To examine the sources of support for the Crusade among blacks, I have computed bivariate correlations among demographic, religious, and political variables. Table 4.8 compares these correlations for blacks and whites.

The correlations are remarkably similar. Black support, like white support, was higher among those who believed that the Bible is the inerrant word of God, among those who supported prayer in schools, and among those who disliked Communists. Neither ideological affect nor support for aggressive military action to combat communism is associated with support for the Crusade among blacks, although both are strongly correlated with support among whites.

The failure of ideology to predict support for the Crusade among blacks is interesting, for political attitudes do predict support. The rhetoric of the 1964 election involved a good deal of ideological positioning, with Goldwater repeatedly calling himself a conservative. Goldwater opposed many desegregation efforts and linked this opposition to his conservatism, which may have made that ideology less attractive to blacks. Indeed, only one black (out of more than four hundred) in the entire 1964 survey reported voting for Goldwater, and only 6 percent identified themselves as Republicans.

TABLE 4.8
Racial Differences in Determinants of Support for the Christian Anti-Communism Crusade

	Whites	Blacks
Education	.14*	.13*
Sex	.08	−.03
Bible interpretation	.08*	.14*
Church attendance	.04	.06
Partisanship	.02	−.09
Ideology	.17**	−.03
Government role	.17**	.18*
School prayer	.09*	.16*
Military response to communism	.17**	.03
Negotiate with Communists	.12*	.03
Affect—Communists	−.21**	−.36**
Affect—East	−.03	.04
Political information	.08*	.15*

Note: Entries are Pearson product moment correlations between support for the Crusade and the variable indicated.
*$p \leq .05$
**$p \leq .01$

The failure of black supporters of the Crusade to favor a more muscular foreign policy to contain communism may be related to the strong likelihood that military action would disproportionately result in deaths of blacks (as the Vietnam War was to demonstrate a few years later) and would draw funds from the War on Poverty. However, there are too few cases of black supporters of the Crusade to investigate this explanation.

What is clear from these data is that support among blacks is *not* an artifact of the methods of the survey or of general black support for any organization with "Christian" in its name. It was not less well-educated blacks or those who knew little about politics who supported the Crusade, but rather those who shared its focus on religion and communism.

POTENTIAL SUPPORT FOR THE CRUSADE

The Crusade lacked the media attention of the Moral Majority two decades later, and the majority of the public was unaware of the Crusade. As noted above, although only 5 percent of whites supported the Crusade, fully 20 percent *of those who knew of the crusade* were relatively warm toward it. We cannot extrapolate from this that, if the entire population knew of the Crusade, it would have commanded the support of one-fifth of the public, because knowledge of the Crusade was highest among those predisposed to support it.

It is possible to estimate the potential support for the Crusade from the results of the probit analysis presented in table 4.4. The maximum-likelihood estimates from that table can be transformed into probabilities, and these can be used in conjunction with information about those in the public who were unaware of the Crusade in order to estimate likely support.[2] These computations suggest that, had the entire public known of the Crusade, it would have had the support of approximately 10 percent of the white population—roughly that of the Moral Majority some twenty years later.

CONCLUSIONS

Although Wolfinger and his colleagues were doubtlessly correct in labeling the Crusade as a right-wing organization, its supporters were

2. Probit equations can, after some computations, produce estimated probabilities that the dependent variable will have a value of 1. In this case, I have rounded all cases with a value of .51 or greater to 1 and considered these cases to be likely supporters of the Crusade.

not consistently conservative. Indeed, those who were attracted to the Crusade for its religious message were on many issues more liberal than other whites. In this way, the Crusade differed substantially from the New Christian Right in the 1980s. However, the anti-Communist message of the Crusade did allow it to attract a core of relatively more secular supporters, who were strongly conservative.

Support for the Crusade does not appear to have been related to social or psychological strain. It was not associated with racism, anti-Semitism, or anti-Catholicism. Instead, support is best understood in terms of political and religious values and attitudes. Support for the Crusade is the rational result of politically active individuals backing organizations that reflect their political, religious, and cultural views—in the same way that we conceive of support for any other political group.

CHAPTER 5

Support for the Fundamentalist
Right in the 1980s:
The Moral Majority

The fundamentalist Right in the 1980s achieved a degree of notoriety which far surpassed that of the Christian Anti-Communism Crusade in the 1960s. The Christian Right of the 1970s and 1980s was a series of organizations which shared an overlapping set of leaders (Johnson and Bullock 1986). Almost all of these groups catered primarily to fundamentalists, although a few had a constituency among pentecostals as well (Guth 1983b). Although most national attention was focused on the large, national organizations, many local organizations were also active. The lack of scholarly research on these local organizations constitutes a major gap in our understanding of the Christian Right.

Of the several organizations that claimed the Christian Right banner, two were especially prominent. Christian Voice, formed in 1978 from California-based antigay, antipornography, and antiabortion groups, was active in electoral politics. It claimed a membership of over two hundred thousand and a budget in excess of $3 million. Its Political Action Committee (PAC) contributed to a variety of conservative Republican candidates (Wilcox 1988b), and its publications rated the voting records of members of Congress. This Morality Scorecard attracted widespread attention when it became known that some ordained ministers had scored 0 and that members convicted in the Abscam sting operation or censured for affairs with teen-aged pages had scored a perfect 100.

Far more visible was the Moral Majority. Founded in 1978 by Reverend Jerry Falwell, a Baptist Bible Fellowship pastor from Lynchburg, Virginia, the Moral Majority claimed a national membership of over four million, with over two million active donors (Johnson and Bullock 1986). The Moral Majority used the existing network of Baptist Bible Fellowship pastors to start state-level organizations, although few of these thrived. Whereas the Christian Voice claimed a constituency among the pentecostal Assemblies of God churches in the Southwest, as well as from fundamentalist Baptist congregations (Guth 1983a), the Moral Majority centered its organizational efforts around fundamentalist churches, principally the Bible Baptist Fellowship (Liebman 1983).

When Reagan won in 1980 with surprising ease, sweeping into office a set of conservative though sometimes inexperienced Republican senators, the media needed an easy explanation. Most polls a week before the election had showed a virtual dead heat, but Reagan's victory margin was sizable. Falwell was a telegenic figure with an easy answer—he claimed that the Moral Majority and other Christian Right organizations had mobilized previously apolitical fundamentalists and other evangelicals into electoral action.

Falwell retained a media visibility throughout the next few years, and this attention made the Moral Majority better known than competing organizations of the New Christian Right, and much better known than the fundamentalist organizations of the 1950s. The media attention was generally critical, and Falwell began to show up on lists of leading unpopular national figures. The greater attention to the Moral Majority doubtlessly crystallized public opinion in a way that the Crusade had not: those predisposed to support the Moral Majority were likely to have heard of the organization, but so were those predisposed to oppose it.

This chapter examines public support for the Moral Majority. First, I test the various theories described in chapter 2 for support for the Right. Second, I explore the political impact of the Moral Majority on turnout and vote choice. Third, I examine the different bases of support for the Moral Majority and the other major movement that was frequently called rightist during this period—the right-to-life movement. Next, I examine the religious bases of support for the Moral Majority among white evangelicals. Finally, I explore the possibility of a black constituency for the Moral Majority.

THE DATA

The data for this part of the chapter come from the 1980 and 1984 American National Election Studies (ANES) surveys and the 1987 ANES Pilot Study. Respondents were asked in 1980, 1984, and 1987 to rate "evangelical political groups like the Moral Majority" on a feeling thermometer. A similar item asked respondents in 1984 to rate "anti-abortion activists." As before, these feeling thermometers have been adjusted for individual differences in response patterns.

Each of the three ANES surveys contained a series of items which measured political attitudes and values. Some of these items have been combined into scales. From the 1984 data, scales were constructed to measure attitudes toward racial policy (affirmative action, guaranteed jobs, busing, and whether civil-rights leaders were pushing too hard), foreign policy (Central America, defense spending, and détente), and social issues (women's roles, abortion, and school prayer). Additional scales measured support for spending on social programs (schools, Social Security, food stamps, Medicare, government jobs for the unemployed, and assistance to blacks), and for conservative programs (defense, science, dealing with crime).

TESTING EXPLANATIONS FOR SUPPORT FOR THE RIGHT

The Moral Majority never had the support of a majority of Americans; indeed, it was never even a sizable minority. In both the 1980 and 1984 surveys, slightly over 10 percent of whites supported the Moral Majority. In contrast, opposition to the group was widespread. If we define as opponents those who were at least 10° cooler toward the Moral Majority than toward other groups, between one-half and two-thirds of whites opposed the Christian Right during this period.

I focus my analysis on the 1984 data because this was the last large national survey in which the Moral Majority was used as an explicit referent. When items in the 1980 or 1987 surveys allow a different look at the question, or when results differ from those of 1980 and 1987, I also present results from these surveys.

Personality Explanations

None of the recent ANES surveys contains items that allow a direct test of personality explanations for support for the Christian Right. However, one indirect test is possible. One of the personality traits hypothesized to be common among right-wing activists and supporters is dogmatism, which has a concomitant cognitive style of simplism. Rightists are posited to see the world in black and white instead of shades of gray. Moreover, some personality theories suggest that rightists are predisposed to see the social and political world as a struggle between the opposing armies of good and evil. To see if supporters of the Moral

Majority see the world in simpler terms than other whites, I performed separate factor analyses for supporters and other whites on the feeling thermometers for social groups. If supporters saw the world in terms of two opposing sets of groups, then the factor analysis for supporters should produce a maximum of three factors: those groups sympathetic toward the Moral Majority, those who oppose it, and those that are not involved in the conflict. The results do not support a personality explanation—supporters did not see the social and political group universe as composed of two opposing coalitions, nor did they see fewer differences among social groups than did nonsupporters. However, some interesting differences in factor structures did appear.

For white nonsupporters, four factors emerged. The first factor, which I call Middle America, consisted of women, the middle class, the poor, whites, and older citizens. Weaker, second loadings on this factor included blacks, Hispanics, and Catholics. The second factor, which I call Minorities, consisted of blacks, Hispanics, gays and lesbians, and civil-rights leaders. The third factor, which I call the Right, included conservatives, big business, the military, antiabortion activists, and the Supreme Court. In a separate analysis that included affect toward the Moral Majority, nonsupporters perceived the Christian Right as part of the Right. The final factor, the Left, consisted of labor unions, liberals, black militants, welfare recipients, and the women's liberation movement.

For Moral Majority supporters, the factor structure was somewhat different. The Middle America factor emerged, but without the secondary loadings for blacks and Hispanics. Catholics appeared in the Minority factor. In a separate analysis that included the Moral Majority, the Christian Right loaded on the Middle America factor. However, the most important difference was in the Left factor. For supporters of the Moral Majority, this factor split, with a Mainstream Liberal factor including labor unions, liberals, and the Supreme Court, and a factor including groups that constitute the out-groups of the New Right: black militants, the women's liberation movement, and gays and lesbians.

The factor structure for supporters and other whites suggests important differences in the way that Moral Majority supporters perceive the social and political world. For supporters of the Moral Majority, racial minorities are not part of Middle America, and Catholics are a minority group. The Supreme Court is still perceived as liberal, and the Left is composed of moderate and radical elements. Gays and lesbians are part of the radical left, not a minority group.[1] The Moral Majority is part of Middle America, not part of the Right.

1. Interviews with activists in the Ohio Moral Majority suggested that the elites were worried that gays might achieve minority status and be protected by civil-rights legislation. This finding suggests that Moral Majority supporters may share this apprehension.

Alienation

Table 5.1 presents the results of tests of the alienation hypothesis. Once again, there are no direct measures of alienation, although indirect tests are possible. Scales were constructed to measure attachments to groups, cynicism, efficacy, and distance from government policy. There is no evidence that supporters of the Moral Majority are currently lacking in group ties. There is no difference between supporters and other whites in the average warmth felt toward social groups, or in the number of groups with which they report feeling close.

One variant of the alienation hypothesis, however, emphasizes alienation from government. In this explanation, support is seen as coming from those who feel disenfranchised, who are cynical about government, who believe that they can make little difference in government policy, and who feel that government does not represent their needs. There is mixed support for this sort of political alienation explanation. New Christian Right supporters are no more cynical than other whites, nor do they feel less efficacious. However, they are somewhat less active in the electoral arena and feel more distance from government policy. Although supporters are themselves more conservative than other whites, their perception of the government position on issues is significantly more liberal. This means that the distance between their own position and the perceived position of the government is quite high. This policy alienation is somewhat surprising in 1984.[2] Most respondents tended to associate the position of the federal government with that of the president, but Moral Majority supporters perceive a greater gap between government policy and the position of Reagan. These results are supportive of a policy-alienation explanation of Moral Majority support. A similar test with the 1980 data showed even more distinctive differences.

The 1980 data also allowed two other tests of alienation from government. First, a series of feeling-thermometer items asked respondents to rate the federal government, federal workers, the Supreme Court, and the Congress. Supporters of the Moral Majority were significantly cooler toward government than other whites, although these scores do not indicate a hostility toward government. Second, a series of items asked respondents to rate the job being done by government institutions. Supporters of the Moral Majority rated the federal, state, and local governments, the presidency, the Congress, and the Supreme Court significantly less favorably than did other whites.

This policy alienation is very different from the alienation posited

2. Although this same policy alienation was found in Moral Majority supporters in 1980, the high correlation between the perceived position of the president and the perceived position of the government made this finding in 1984 intuitively unlikely.

TABLE 5.1
Support for the Moral Majority (Bivariate Analysis)

	Supporters	Other Whites	Correlation
Alienation Explanations			
Social Group Attachment			
Average affect for social groups	58°	58°	.00
Number of group identifications	9	8	.04
Political Involvement			
Turnout	68%	68%	.00
Other electoral activities	1.6	1.8	−.03
Interest in campaign	2.1	2.2	−.02
Sees difference between parties	68%	69%	−.01
Efficacy	3.0	3.1	−.04
Cynicism	3.8	3.7	.00
Perceived Position of Federal Government			
Helps women	3.9	4.3	−.10**
Central America	3.0	3.3	−.09**
Détente	4.6	4.5	.01
Defense spending	5.2	5.0	−.05*
Government services	4.1	4.5	−.10**
Minority aid	3.6	3.9	−.06*
Guaranteed job	4.2	4.6	−.09**

	Supporters	Other Whites	Percentage of Supporters
Social Status Explanations			
Status Inconsistency Scores			
Income > education	31	20	17**
Status Anxiety			
Identifies as middle class if:			
Bottom third in education	42	35	18*
Bottom third in occupation	41	34	18*
Bottom third in income	33	40	10
Feels Close to Own Class			
Middle	52	54	12
Working	66	66	11
Better off than last year	52	47	13
Income > inflation	20	17	14
Better off next year	40	40	12
Generational Occupational Mobility			
Upward	31	34	11
Downward	25	23	13

	Supporters	Other Whites	Correlation
Symbolic Politics Explanations (Affect for Social Groups)			
Middle America			
Women	72°	75°	−.06*
Middle class	73°	73°	−.02
Poor people	72°	71°	.02
Whites	76°	75°	.03
Older people	80°	78°	.05*

(continued)

TABLE 5.1 (*continued*)

	Supporters	Other Whites	Correlation
Minorities			
Blacks	59°	63°	−.08**
Hispanics	58°	59°	−.03
Civil-rights leaders	43°	53°	−.15**
Catholics	63°	63°	−.00
The Right			
Conservatives	66°	60°	.11**
Big business	57°	51°	.10**
Military	73°	68°	.09**
Anti-abortion activists	63°	48°	.18**
Mainstream Liberals			
Labor unions	48°	54°	−.07**
Liberals	47°	56°	−.16**
Out-groups of New Right			
Black militants	26°	31°	−.07**
Women's liberation movement	44°	58°	−.20**
Gays/lesbians	15°	32°	−.21**

Religious Explanations			Percentage of Supporters
Doctrine			
Born-again	64	29	27**
Bible inerrant	76	42	21**
Both	52	16	32**
Denomination			
Fundamentalist	3	1	29*
Pentecostal	3	1	29*
Southern Baptist	11	7	18*
Other evangelicals	18	36	23**
Catholic	18	31	8**
Religiosity			
Attend services weekly	47	21	22**
Religion important	92	73	14**
Religion—great deal of guidance	72	40	23**
Political Explanations			
Republican partisanship	59	43	16**
Ideological self-placement	5.6	4.5	45**
Social Issues			
Women's equality	3.8	2.7	40**
Government help for women	4.4	3.9	19**
Abortion	4.6	3.1	33**
School prayer	4.4	3.0	17**
Foreign-policy issues			
Central America	4.0	3.4	20**
Détente	4.8	4.0	31**
Defense spending	4.6	3.9	20**

(*continued*)

TABLE 5.1 (*continued*)

	Supporters	Other Whites	Correlation
Domestic Issues			
Government services	4.4	4.1	20**
Minority aid	4.7	4.2	17**
Guaranteed job	4.7	4.3	19**
Busing	6.2	6.0	12
Civil rights too fast	6.0	5.5	19**
Equality values	2.6	2.3	30**
Gender-equality values	3.0	3.7	29**
Geographic Explanations			
Region			
Born South	34	25	19
Live South	34	30	15
Either	40	31	19*
Rural birth	40	32	15*
Moved in past 2 years	12	13	12
Own home	77	71	13
Moved from region of birth	18	20	11
Rural birth to urban now	13	14	11
N	187	1434	

Note: Final column reports either bivariate Pearson's correlation between scale or percentage of group which supports the Moral Majority.
*$p \leq .05$
**$p \leq .01$

by mass-society theorists. The latter type of alienation was thought to be found among individuals who lacked community attachments and who were easily mobilized by groups out of the mainstream, political or not, right-wing or not. In contrast, policy alienation can be a very rational response to governmental policy that is at odds with a citizen's preferences.

Social Status Explanations

Supporters of the Moral Majority were somewhat more likely to have failed to finish high school than were other whites and were more likely to hold lower-status occupations (not shown). The negative relationship between education and support for the Moral Majority increased between 1980 and 1984, as information about the group became widely distributed. However, there was little difference between supporters and other whites on family income.

In order to test the status-inconsistency explanation, two sets of measures of status inconsistency were computed.[3] Supporters are significantly more likely to display one type of status inconsistency: income greater than occupational prestige. This type of status inconsistency is not particularly consonant with theories of support for the Right, although those who use these explanations have linked all kinds of inconsistency with all types of political attitudes. In addition, New Christian Right supporters were slightly less upwardly mobile than the rest of the white population.

Not only is there no support for a status-inconsistency explanation, but Moral Majority supporters also do not appear to subjectively experience higher levels of status anxiety. Although the available measures are far from perfect, there is no clear pattern of Moral Majority supporters overreporting their social status, nor is there a tendency for working-class supporters of the New Christian Right to feel distanced from others in their social stratum.

Moral Majority supporters are actually slightly less anxious about their income than other whites—they are more likely to feel that they are better off now than a year ago, more likely to feel that their income has risen more than inflation, and slightly less likely to feel that their income will decline next year.

Symbolic Politics Explanations

Once again, the symbolic politics explanation is tested by examining differences in group affect. Symbolic group scales were computed based on the factor structure from the analysis of supporters. Because of the two groups' different perception of the Supreme Court, I have not included it in any scale. However, I list the data for Catholics under the minority factor because anti-Catholicism has been a characteristic of the fundamentalist Right. Not surprisingly, Moral Majority supporters display significantly different affect toward many social and political groups than do other whites. The results yield support for a symbolic politics explanation. Supporters of the Moral Majority were significantly cooler toward minorities, liberal groups, and the Left. They were significantly warmer toward the Right. The strongest correlations are between support and positive affect for antiabortion activ-

---

3. For both measures, education, occupation, and income were recoded into three relatively equal categories. Status inconsistency was then computed from these measures, much as in chapter 4. As in chapter 4, a regression-based measure was also constructed, but the results did not differ from those presented here.

ists, and negative affect toward gays and lesbians and the women's liberation movement. There is no correlation between affect for Catholics and support for the Moral Majority.

These results could be interpreted as indicating that the issue agenda of the New Christian Right symbolizes a larger clash over lifestyle issues and that strong affective ties are linked to these symbols. Alternatively, these results could be seen as evidence of rational political evaluations of the likely supporters and opponents of the issue agenda of the New Christian Right.

Religious Explanations

A fifth set of explanations examines the role of religious values, identifications, and behaviors on support for the Christian Right. Religious variables are clearly related to support for the New Christian Right. Supporters of the Moral Majority are more likely than other whites to attend fundamentalist, pentecostal, and evangelical denominations, although the majority of supporters come from outside these religious denominations. Support is significantly lower among Catholics, although, among those who meet the criteria for doctrinal evangelicalism, nearly one-fourth support the Moral Majority.

Support is higher among doctrinal evangelicals—those who were born-again and who believed the Bible to be at least inerrant. Among Protestants who meet this doctrinal test, fully one-third support the Moral Majority. Finally, supporters of the New Christian Right have higher levels of religiosity, as measured by religious salience and frequency of church attendance.

Political Explanations

A sixth set of explanations posits a connection between political attitudes and identifications and support for the Right. These explanations are rational ones, in which support is seen as the result of the perception that the group articulates a political position that is similar to that of the supporter. The explanations find strong support in this data. As expected, there is a strong relationship between partisanship and support for the Moral Majority. Although there were no items in the survey to determine whether these supporters were recent converts to the Republican party, other studies (Guth and Green 1987c) suggest that they are primarily lifelong GOP stalwarts.

In addition, there is a strong relationship between ideological self-identification and support. Supporters are also conservative on individual-issue items. With the single exception of school busing to achieve racial integration,[4] Moral Majority supporters are significantly more conservative on all items in the survey, including attitudes toward social issues, defense spending, foreign policy, government spending, and aid to minorities.

This conservatism is mirrored in measures of values, such as equality, opportunity, and moral traditionalism. New Christian Right supporters were significantly less likely than other whites to score high on a scale measuring these values. New Christian Right supporters were also significantly less supportive of gender-equality values. In the 1987 pilot survey data, there was a strong correlation between support for the Moral Majority and support for moral traditionalism.

Geographic Theories

One set of explanations of support for right-wing groups suggests that support is associated with certain geographic variables. Supporters of the Moral Majority are more likely to be born in and currently living in the South. In addition, they are more likely to have been born in a rural area and to currently live in a rural environment. Both these geographic explanations are rational ones, positing a congruence of values and beliefs between regional residence and support for the Right.

There is no support, however, for the social-dislocation theory. Supporters of the New Christian Right are no more likely than other respondents to have moved in the past few years, are actually more likely to own their own home, and are slightly less likely to have moved from the region of their birth or have gone from an rural upbringing to an urban lifestyle.

MULTIVARIATE ANALYSIS

Bivariate analysis revealed some evidence for all of the traditional explanations for support of the Right. However, to assess the independent effects of these variables, a multivariate probit equation was estimated. For this analysis, several of the measures presented above were combined to form scales. Successive equations were reestimated until the most parsimonious equation was produced. Both sets of results are presented.

Table 5.2 presents the results of the analysis. Rational explanations

---

4. The busing item was so skewed that statistical significance was nearly impossible. Nearly all whites opposed bussing, regardless of their level of support for the Moral Majority.

TABLE 5.2
Testing Explanations of Support for the Moral Majority (Probit Analysis)

	Full Equation		Parsimonious Equation	
	MLE	T	MLE	T
Alienation				
Cynicism	.01	.07		
Efficacy	.09	.76		
Policy distance	.18	1.07		
Social Status				
Status inconsistency/anxiety	.35	1.68[a]		
Education	−.14	−2.01*	−.06	−1.98*
Income	−.00	−.03		
Occupation	.01	.04		
Symbolic Politics, Affect				
Middle America	−.02	−1.90[a]		
Liberals	−.01	−1.37		
Left	−.02	−1.68[a]	−.01	−3.89**
Minorities	−.01	−.87		
Right	.02	1.98*	.01	2.34*
Religion				
Fundamentalist denomination	1.58	1.78[a]		
Pentecostal denomination	−.09	−.10		
Southern Baptist	.61	1.42		
Other evangelical denomination	.12	.20		
Catholic	−.23	−.66		
Evangelical doctrine	.67	2.12*	.68	5.95**
Attendance	.16	1.68[a]	.08	2.00*
Religious salience	.54	2.80*		
Political Attitudes				
Partisanship	.12	1.76[a]	.06	2.17*
Ideology	.18	1.72[a]		
Racial attitudes	−.10	−.60		
Foreign policy	.29	1.98*		
Social issues	.35	2.11*	.10	2.59*
Spending on social programs	−.37	−.98		
Equality values·	.24	.47		
Gender equality	.30	2.50*	.13	2.57*
Geography				
South	−.51	−1.63		
Moved recently	−.46	−1.29		
Rural-born	−.26	−.95		
Other Demographics				
Age	−.02	−1.98*		
Sex	−.50	−1.98*	−.27	−2.40*
	N = 379		N = 1061	

(continued)

TABLE 5.2 (*continued*)

Note: Maximum likelihood estimates from probit analysis. Parsimonious equation created by successively eliminating the variable with the lowest T value and reestimating the equation.

$^a p \leq .10$
$^* p \leq .05$
$^{**} p \leq .01$

dominate nonrational ones in the results. In the inclusive equation, personal religiosity, evangelical doctrine, gender-equality values, and attitudes toward social issues are among the strongest predictors. Among the nonrational explanations, only a dummy variable that captured status inconsistency and anxiety even approached statistical significance.

In the parsimonious equation, evangelical doctrine is by far the strongest predictor. Frequency of church attendance is the only other religious variable to achieve statistical significance. Partisanship, attitudes toward women's issues, and gender-equality values are significant political predictors. Support for the Moral Majority is predicted by negative affect toward leftist groups and positive affect toward other rightist groups. Finally, supporters were significantly less well educated and significantly more likely to be male.

Although these results are not surprising, they do indicate that nonrational explanations based on social dislocation, alienation, and status inconsistency are less important than values and attitudes.[5] Moral Majority supporters are doctrinal evangelicals and fundamentalists with high levels of religiosity, who hold conservative positions on social issues and are cool toward the symbols of the Left and warm toward those of the Right.

THE MORAL MAJORITY AND THE RIGHT-TO-LIFE MOVEMENT

In chapter 4, we saw significant differences in the bases of support for the Crusade and another visible right-wing organization of the time, the John Birch Society. During the 1980s, no secular, non-candidate-oriented group attracted the visibility of the John Birch Society. However, one set of political groups did attract a great deal of support. The right-to-life movement was thought by some to be part of the Christian Right itself.

---

5. Because the survey did not contain personality measures, this explanation was not tested in the probit analysis.

It is unclear, however, that the prolife movement can be considered a right-wing movement. Although many prolife activists were consistently conservative and opposed gender equality more broadly than merely opposing abortion (Luker 1984), many of the same Catholic bishops who condemned abortion advocated greater spending on the poor, decreased spending on the military, an abolition of the death penalty, and the elimination of sexism in society. Some of the prominent spokespersons for the prolife movement would otherwise be termed liberals, and some prolife organizations (e.g., Just Life) took liberal positions on a range of related issues. The ideological diversity of prolife elites was mirrored among prolife activists: Fried (1988) reported that some prolife activists took generally feminist positions on nonreproductive issues. In short, although some of the prolife movement's support doubtless came from the Right, some may also have come from otherwise liberal forces.

How do supporters of the Moral Majority differ from supporters of the prolife movement? Table 5.3 presents the results of a discriminant analysis. All of the independent variables from table 5.2 were included in this analysis, although only those with a correlation of at least .20 with one of the functions is included in the table. The first function distinguishes between those who support the Moral Majority (and especially those who also support the prolife movement) and those who support neither organization (and, to a lesser extent, those who support only the prolife movement). The second discriminates between those who support the Moral Majority and those who support the prolife movement, and the final function distinguishes between those who support both organizations and those who support only one.

Those who support the Moral Majority are more likely than others to hold evangelical doctrine, to find religion highly salient, to attend church frequently, to be cool toward leftist and liberal groups, to be conservative on women's issues and gender-equality values, to hold conservative positions on racial issues, foreign policy, and spending on social services, and to be conservatives and Republicans. These results confirm those of the probit analysis discussed above. However, note that these variables not only distinguish Moral Majority supporters from other whites but also discriminate between those who support the Moral Majority and those who support *only* the prolife movement.

Those who support the prolife movement are distinguished from those who support only the Moral Majority by their relatively liberal positions on women's issues and on gender and societal equality, support for spending for social programs, liberal positions on racial issues, relative warmth toward minorities, and gender.

Finally, those who support both organizations are distinguished

TABLE 5.3
Support for the Moral Majority and the Prolife Movement
(Discriminant Analysis)

	Function 1[a]	Function 2[a]	Function 3[a]
Evangelical doctrine	.58		.34
Affect—Left	−.48		
Women's issues	.42	.21	
Gender-equality values	.38	.22	
Salience of religion	.36		
Foreign policy	.31		
Ideology	.31		
Affect—liberals	−.27		
Republican	.24		
Spending on social programs	−.21	20	
Racial policy	.20	.20	
Minority affect		.52	
Church attendance	.42	−.42	
Equality values		.35	
Female		.26	
Catholic			−.35
Income			.33
School prayer	.31		−.39
Evangelical denomination			−.36

Canonical Discriminant Functions Evaluated at Group Means

	Function 1	Function 2	Function 3
Support neither	−.43	−.04	.17
Support Moral Majority	.92	1.23	−.48
Support prolife	.05	−.51	−.49
Support both	2.90	−.25	.78
Percentage Predicted Correctly			
Support neither	61		
Support Moral Majority	65		
Support Prolife	59		
Support both	93		
Total	62		

[a]Correlations with discriminant function. Only correlations ≥ .20 shown.

from those who support only one by their higher levels of income and education, as well as their decreased likelihood of being Catholics or belonging to nonfundamentalist, nonpentecostal evangelical churches.

Taken together, these results suggest that the prolife movement attracted two sets of supporters: strongly conservative supporters who also supported the Moral Majority, and more moderate supporters who did not. This more moderate group was distinguished by its equality values, which were manifested in attitudes toward gender issues and on racial issues.

To get a different perspective on what distinguished those Moral Majority supporters who also supported the prolife movement from those who did not, I estimated a probit equation (not shown). Moral Majority supporters who also supported the prolife movement were more likely to come from accommodating evangelical (not fundamentalist, pentecostal, or Southern Baptist) denominations, to hold evangelical doctrine, to identify themselves as conservatives, and to attend church frequently. This latter relationship provides additional confirmation of Himmelstein's (1986) argument that prolife groups recruit through church networks and therefore attract those who attend church most often. In addition, support for the prolife movement was significantly related to affect toward Catholics. Although passive supporters of the Moral Majority in general were not cooler than other whites toward Catholics, those who were cool toward them were less likely to be willing to support the prolife cause. This hesitancy to support the prolife movement suggests that religious intolerance may be a limiting factor in forming a broad Christian Right coalition.

RELIGION AND SUPPORT FOR THE MORAL MAJORITY AMONG WHITE EVANGELICALS

Because evangelicals are the target constituency of the New Christian Right, they constitute an excellent population among whom to examine the religious bases of support for the New Christian Right. The data from the Evangelical Voter Study provide us with an opportunity to more closely examine the religious sources for support among white evangelicals.

I expect support to be stronger among those who accept a fundamentalist religious doctrine (born-again status and a literal interpretation of the Bible).[6] Support is stronger among those who hold evangelical doctrinal beliefs, and fundamentalist doctrine should be an even

---

6. Although the born-again item is one of the possible screening questions, respondents were classified as evangelicals if they believed in the need for personal salvation, but did not report a born-again experience. Although born-again status does not distinguish evangelicals from fundamentalists, Ammerman (1987) reports that the first question the pastor of the fundamentalist church asked her when she proposed the research was, "Are you born again?" The born-again experience is central to fundamentalist doctrine.

stronger predictor because of the Moral Majority's connection to fundamentalist Baptist churches.

Moreover, I anticipate that support will be higher among those frequently exposed to televangelists. Tamney and Johnson (1983) reported that televangelists had a strong influence on support for the Christian Right among citizens of Muncie, Indiana. Because Falwell, head of the Moral Majority, is a televangelist, and because many other televangelists endorse much of the Moral Majority platform, a connection between viewing televangelists and support for the Moral Majority seems likely.

Because the Moral Majority spans the interstitial zone between religion and politics, it seems likely that support will be higher among those who perceive a strong connection between their religious and political beliefs, and among those who attend churches in which the minister preaches politics. Shupe and Stacey (1983, 1984) found support for the Christian Right highest among those who perceived a strong connection between religion and politics, and Beatty and Walter (n.d.) reported that the political messages of ministers are an important influence on the political attitudes of their congregations.

It seems likely that support will be highest among those with the highest levels of religiosity. Wilcox (1987c, 1989e) and Sigelman et al. (1988) reported that religiosity is a strong predictor of support for the Christian Right in the general public. Moreover, Himmelstein (1986) argued that the strong connection he found between frequency of church attendance and support for the prolife movement is due to more frequent exposure to political messages from congregants (and, presumably, pastors). Wald (1986) confirms the connection between frequent church attendance and political attitudes in the general public.

Support may also be higher among those who attend churches in which politics is frequently preached. Guth (1989) reported that support for the Moral Majority among Southern Baptist preachers grew dramatically in the 1980s. The preaching of political messages by these and other supportive pastors may increase support among the flock. Unfortunately, the survey contains no measure of the *content* of these political messages.

Support should also be directly related to political attitudes and identifications. Wilcox (1987c) and Sigelman et al. (1987) reported that support in the general public was highest among Republicans (a finding that is common to most studies of right-wing organizations). Most studies have found strong correlations between conservatism on social issues and support, and some have reported that conservatism on economic and foreign-policy issues is also a good predictor of support.

Buell and Sigelman (1985) found that attitudes on school prayer, abortion, and defense spending were the strongest predictors of Moral Majority support, and Wilcox (1987c), using somewhat different methods, added partisanship, attitudes toward feminism, and trust in government to the list. Shupe and Stacey (1983, 1984) found that Texas supporters were more conservative than other white Texans on social and educational issues.

THE DATA

The data for this section come from a national survey of evangelicals. Once again, I limit the analysis to whites, although the sources of support among black evangelicals will be described later in this chapter.

The questionnaire contained two items that are useful in identifying supporters of the Moral Majority. Respondents were asked to evaluate the Moral Majority and Falwell. From these two items, a scale of Moral Majority support was constructed.[7] Evangelical supporters of the Moral Majority numbered 204, fully 24 percent of white evangelicals and 37 percent of those white evangelicals who had sufficient information to evaluate the organization. In the following analysis, those with insufficient knowledge of the Moral Majority to rate it are excluded.

DEMOGRAPHIC AND RELIGIOUS VARIABLES

Among evangelicals, there are few significant bivariate relationships between demographic variables and support for the Moral Majority. Table 5.4 presents the results of the analysis. Moral Majority support is highest among southern and less well-educated evangelicals. There is no bivariate relationship between support and income, age, or sex.

Predictably, however, there are significant religious differences

---

7. The combined scale had greater variation than either of the items that went into it. The two items were highly correlated ($r = .56$). Close inspection revealed that three predictor variables had different effects on the two component items: although women, southerners, and older respondents were warmer to Falwell, they were not more likely to support the Moral Majority.

In defining supporters of the Moral Majority, those respondents who supported nearly every group listed in the survey were recoded as nonsupporters. Previous studies (Wilcox 1987c) have demonstrated that group-support items are vulnerable to positivity-response sets. Detailed analysis suggested that those removed from the supporter category did not fit the demographic or attitudinal profiles of other supporters.

TABLE 5.4
Predictors of Support among Evangelicals (Evangelical Voter Study)

	Pearson's r	MLE	T
Demographic Variables			
Age	−.01	.00	.04
Education	−.16**	−.12	−1.98*
Income	−.03	−.02	−.36
Gender	−.03	.03	.37
Southern residence	.11**	.27	2.09*
Religious Variables			
Fundamentalist identification	.16**	.47	3.36**
Fundamentalist doctrine	.10**	.30	1.99*
Religion in politics	.28**	.20	2.54*
Pastors preach politics	.01	.01	.54
Private religiosity	.15**	.05	.50
Attendance	.14**	.04	.36
Fundamentalist denomination	.10*	.26	1.32
Pentecostal denomination	.09*	−.31	−.94
Other evangelical denomination	.09*	.21	1.31
Affect for Catholics	−.12**	.02	.10
Political Variables			
Partisanship	.11**	.08	1.99*
Ideological identification	.11**	.11	1.99*
Women's issues	.19**	.15	2.24*
Foreign policy	.23**	.20	3.40**
Educational policy	.12**	.03	.52
		N = 504	

Note: Pearson's correlation coefficients and maximum likelihood estimates and *T* values from probit analysis.
*$p \le .05$
**$p \le .01$

between Moral Majority supporters and other evangelicals. Support was highest among fundamentalist, pentecostal, and other evangelical denominations and was lowest among Lutherans and Catholics. Supporters were significantly more likely than other evangelicals to hold fundamentalist doctrinal beliefs (i.e., to be born-again, to literally interpret Genesis). Support was higher among those who identified themselves as fundamentalists, among those who reported that religion was extremely important in their lives, and among those who attended church frequently.

As expected, Moral Majority supporters scored significantly higher on a scale measuring the connection between their religious beliefs and their political attitudes and behaviors. However, their scores on a scale measuring the activity of their pastor in politics were no different from other evangelicals. Moral Majority supporters are not heavy viewers of televangelists (over one-half watch them "hardly ever" or "never"), but they spend significantly more time tuned in than other evangelicals. Moreover, they hold a significantly more favorable opinion of religious television programs than do other evangelicals. These data were gathered before the series of scandals which befell televangelists in 1988. However, supporters of the New Christian Right in 1989 were more likely than nonsupporters to watch televangelists.

Moral Majority supporters were significantly more negative toward the Catholic church than other evangelicals. This anti-Catholicism is consistent with a long tradition among fundamentalist groups (Lipset and Raab 1978), although it was not a predictor of support for the Crusade.

The demographic and religious patterns of evangelical support for the Moral Majority holds few surprises. Supporters are less well educated and southern and are highly religious fundamentalists who perceive a strong connection between their religious and political beliefs and who are more likely than other evangelicals to watch televangelists.

POLITICAL VARIABLES

Moral Majority supporters were significantly more likely than were other evangelicals to report Republican voting and registration, and they were also significantly more likely to call themselves conservatives.

The dataset contained a number of items which measured the attitudes of respondents on political issues. Factor analysis of these variables produced three scales: women's issues (abortion, ERA, birth-control education, and government aid to poor women for abortions), foreign-policy issues (El Salvador, defense spending, and a nuclear-weapons freeze), and education issues (school prayer, tuition tax credits). Moral Majority supporters were significantly more conservative than other evangelicals on all three scales.

As expected, then, Moral Majority supporters are also different from other evangelicals on a series of political issues, including partisanship, ideological self-identification, and issue positions. To sort out the independent impact of demographic and political variables, multivariate analysis is needed.

MULTIVARIATE ANALYSIS

To ascertain the direct and indirect impacts of these variables on Moral Majority support, a probit equation was estimated, with a dichotomous support–not support version of the dependent variable. Support for the Moral Majority is explained largely by religious and political variables. Two demographic variables are significant predictors: supporters are more likely than others to come from the South and to be less well educated.

Religious variables are stronger predictors. Those who identify themselves as fundamentalists or who hold fundamentalist religious doctrine are more likely to support the Moral Majority, as are those who watch religious television and who have strong connections between their religious and political beliefs.

Supporters are more likely than other evangelicals to be Republicans, to consider themselves conservatives, and to hold conservative positions on foreign policy and women's issues. It may seem surprising that foreign-policy attitudes are among the strongest predictors of support. In the next chapter, we shall see that foreign-policy concerns were central to the founding of the Ohio Moral Majority and that anticommunism was a strong force among the members of that organization.

The Moral Majority commanded the support of nearly 40 percent of those evangelicals who knew enough about the organization to evaluate it, but only around 25 percent of all evangelicals. Although this level of support was not the monolith originally portrayed by media accounts, it was a sizable percentage of the target constituency. The level of support among those with high scores (in the top one-third of the sample) on all predictor variables from the probit analysis was substantially higher—78 percent. Among the 45 percent of white evangelicals who scored high on at least six of the eight predictors, support was approximately 50 percent.

Support dropped precipitously among those with high scores on three or fewer of the significant predictors. This result suggests that the practical limit to Moral Majority support among evangelicals may have been roughly 60 percent.

ELECTORAL MOBILIZATION

Falwell claimed to have registered millions of fundamentalists and evangelicals and mobilized them into political action. Some limited evidence in the ANES data supports this claim. Table 5.5 presents the

TABLE 5.5
New Christian Right and Political Mobilization

	Supporters (%)	Nonsupporters (%)
Validated Vote, 1984	68	68
Self-Report—Participation		
Voted 1984	75	77
Voted 1980	79	74
Voted (Recall) 1976	86	88
Voted in 1980, When:		
Voted in no or some past elections	44	32
Voted in most or all past elections	91	90
Did not vote in 1976, though over 18	39	28
Turnout, 1984, Adjusted for Demographic Characteristics	78	73
Turnout, 1980, Adjusted for Demographic Characteristics	79	75
Turnout, 1980, Adjusted for Demographics and Vote History	78	74
Voted Reagan 1980	84	53**
Voted Reagan 1984	81	62**
Voted Republican—House 1980	72	47**
Voted Republican—House 1984	54	47
Democrats for Reagan 1980	52	26*
Democrats for Reagan 1984	24	25
Voted Reagan 1980—Newly mobilized	70	46
Democrats who voted Republican—House 1980	37	27*
Democrats who voted Republican—House 1984	22	24
1980 Survey		
Republicans with Democratic parents		
Mother	38	18
Father	41	19
Both	38	16
Recalled vote—Ford	59	45
Voted Carter in 1976, Reagan in 1980	21	15
Voted for same party in past	33	44*
Reasons for Republican Partisanship		
Lifelong member	38	56*
Parent's partisanship	38	47
Usually support	48	63*
Issue stands	71	63

*$p \leq .05$
**$p \leq .01$

raw turnout rates for Moral Majority supporters and other whites in the 1980 and 1984 elections. For the 1984 election, the table includes both validated self-reported turnout and turnout validated by the Center for Political Studies. In the elections, supporters did not vote at significantly higher rates than the rest of the population. In 1984, reported turnout declined slightly among supporters and increased slightly among nonsupporters.

In the 1980 election, however, there is some evidence that hints at mobilization. Among those who had seldom or never voted in the past, and among those who had not voted in 1976, Moral Majority supporters voted at a higher rate. Moreover, when turnout rates are adjusted for demographic variables (education, income, age, age squared, and region), Moral Majority supporters voted at rates higher than predicted. Although none of these relationships attained conventional standards of statistical significance, they hint that more sensitive measures (e.g., large surveys in states where the Moral Majority made an effort at registration) might find evidence of mobilization.

There is also evidence that the Moral Majority produced changes in vote choice among its followers. Moral Majority supporters were more likely than other whites to vote for Reagan in both 1980 and 1984, and they were more likely to vote for Republican House candidates in 1980. However, given the Republican partisanship of these supporters, such voting is not surprising. More importantly, white Democratic supporters were more likely than white Democratic nonsupporters to cross partisan lines to vote for Republican candidates in 1980.

More than one-fifth of Moral Majority supporters switched from Carter in 1976 to Reagan in 1980, while only one-sixth of nonsupporters reported that switch. In 1980, more than one-half of Democratic Moral Majority supporters voted for Reagan, compared with 24 percent of other whites. This pattern of partisan defection was mirrored in vote choice for House election. However, during the 1984 election, the evidence of vote change disappears. Democratic Moral Majority supporters are no more likely than other white Democrats to defect to Reagan: for both groups the defection rate is about 25 percent. What this 1984 pattern means substantively is unclear. It is possible that those Moral Majority supporters who voted for Reagan in 1980 against the pull of their partisanship are among those who did not vote in 1984, or perhaps they had changed their partisanship to Republican by that election. There were few Democratic Moral Majority supporters in either survey, so it is also possible that the differences were partially due to sampling error.

There is some evidence that Moral Majority supporters have been converted to Republicanism at some point in their lives in greater numbers than nonsupporters. Moral Majority supporters were significantly less likely in 1980 to report having always voted for the same party, and they were more likely to be Republicans with Democratic parents. They also reported different reasons than nonsupporters for their partisanship. Supporters were significantly less likely to say that they were lifetime Republicans or usually supported the Republican party. They were somewhat more likely to say they supported the Republican party because of its issue stands.

In short, there is evidence that the Moral Majority *may* have mobilized new voters and perhaps changed the direction of their votes. The questions left unanswered by these data are whether the changes reported by supporters are due to the Moral Majority's influence and when the mobilization occurred. Without longitudinal data, it is impossible to determine when Moral Majority supporters switched their partisanship and when Democratic supporters began defecting to Republican candidates.

It is also difficult to determine whether the Moral Majority is responsible for the increased turnout of supporters in the 1980 election. Elsewhere (Wilcox 1989c), I reported that the turnout of white evangelicals increased in 1976 with the candidacy of Carter, a born-again Southern Baptist. The continued candidacy of Carter, coupled with the candidacy of a popular conservative candidate (Reagan), may have had as much to do with mobilizing supporters of the Moral Majority as the organization itself. Supporters were significantly more likely than others to rate both candidates warmly (not shown) in 1980.

BLACKS AND THE MORAL MAJORITY

Although nearly all of the research on support for the Moral Majority has focused on whites, it had a sizable black constituency. Among black respondents to the 1984 ANES, fully 13 percent met the criteria for support, a figure slightly higher than for whites. Among black evangelicals in the Evangelical Voter Study, nearly one-third of those who knew enough about the Moral Majority to rate it were supporters, although more than 40 percent could not rate the organization.

The correlates of black support for the Moral Majority resembled those of whites. Once again the small number of black respondents (missing data reduces the N to 158) makes multivariate analysis suspect. In table 5.6, black correlates of support are presented. At the top of the table are the correlates of support among black evangelicals in the Evangelical Voter Study. White correlations are reported earlier in table 5.4. At the bottom of table 5.6, the correlates of black support in

TABLE 5.6
Black Support for the Moral Majority (Correlates)

	Evangelical Voter Study, 1983
Fundamentalist denomination	.01
Pentecostal denomination	.11
Other evangelical denomination	.08
Catholic	−.11
Fundamentalist identification	.04
Fundamentalist doctrine	.14*
Connection between religion and politics	.15*
Watch televangelists	.03
Pastors preach politics	.30**
Attendance	.13
Personal religiosity	−.12
Women's issues	−.02
Foreign policy	.13*
Educational issues	.08
Partisanship	.05
Ideology	.07

	American National Election Study, 1984	
Fundamentalist denomination	−.08	(.06**)
Pentecostal denomination	.11*	(.06*)
Southern Baptist	.08	(.05*)
Other evangelical denomination	−.04	(.07**)
Catholic	−.04	(−.10**)
Evangelical doctrine	.12*	(.32**)
Religious salience	−.01	(.21**)
Attendance	.08	(.16**)
Partisanship	−.09	(.12**)
Ideology	.07	(.20**)
Social issues	.18**	(.27**)
Foreign policy	.16*	(.17**)
Equality values	.14*	(.13**)
Gender-equality values	.04	(.20**)
Affect—Left	−.03	(−.22**)
Affect—Right	.14*	(.12**)
N	158	

Note: Entries are Pearson product moment correlations. White correlations are in parentheses.
*$p \le .05$
**$p \le .01$

the ANES data are presented, with white correlations in parentheses. Once again, the smaller number of cases in the black sample require a larger correlation to achieve statistical significance. For this reason, it is useful to compare the magnitude of the correlations even when they are not statistically significant.

The sources of support for the Christian Right differ from those of whites, but the main predictors remain the same. Conservative religious doctrine and conservative positions on social and foreign-policy issues are significant predictors among blacks and whites, as is the subjective connection between religion and politics, as well as affect for other right-wing groups. In the Evangelical Voter Study data, blacks who attended churches in which pastors preach politics were more likely to support the Moral Majority.

Black supporters were not as consistently conservative as white supporters, however. For example, there was no relationship between affect for the Left and support among blacks, and the correlation between ideological self-placement and support was modest and not statistically significant. In many ways, black support for the Moral Majority resembled white support for the Crusade—support was tied to support for a narrow conception of the Moral Majority agenda, but was not linked to a consistent ideological position.

CONCLUSIONS

Although the Moral Majority was never a majority, it had the support of a fairly sizable portion of the white evangelical community, as well as of black evangelicals. Once again support for the Christian Right is best understood as the rational result of a set of religious and political values and beliefs. Evangelical doctrine, partisanship, and conservative positions on social issues and gender equality were the strongest predictors of support, and there was no evidence that support is explained by social or psychological strain. Among evangelicals, support was most strongly linked to fundamentalist identification and doctrine, to a connection between religion and politics, and to partisanship, ideology, and conservative attitudes toward women's issues and foreign policy. Supporters were somewhat less well educated than the rest of the public and more likely to be female. One finding not highlighted above that will become important in later chapters is that, in both sets of multivariate analyses, those who attended pentecostal churches were slightly more *negative* toward the Moral Majority than were mainline Protestants.

Unlike the Crusade, the Moral Majority attracted a fairly homogeneous set of religious and political conservatives. Supporters differed from those who supported the prolife movement in their opposition to gender equality, their conservative position on other women's issues, their opposition to social-program spending, and their cooler affect toward minorities.

There is mixed evidence concerning the possible mobilization of previously apolitical evangelicals and fundamentalists by the Moral Majority. Although supporters did not turn out at a significantly higher rate than nonsupporters, there are hints in the data that they voted more often than others with a similar demographic and participatory background. Moreover, although the vote choice of the Moral Majority supporters is fully consistent with their partisanship, there is some evidence that they have changed their partisanship at some point in their life.

CHAPTER 6

Activists in the Fundamentalist Right: The Crusade and the Moral Majority

The literature on right-wing movements has frequently mixed studies of mass support and activists, without noting the important differences between them. Indeed, studies of activists in right-wing causes have been cited to demonstrate that support for the Right came from high-status individuals. Such conclusions are misleading because one of the most firmly established findings in political science and sociology is that activists in political and social organizations have higher levels of education, occupational prestige, and income than the general public.

It is more difficult to study activists than mass publics because it is difficult to obtain a list of activists from which to draw a sample. Moreover, activists in right-wing causes may distrust academics: in several studies (including those upon which this chapter is based) large majorities of activists believed that colleges and universities were pervaded by Communists. Wolfinger et al. (1969) reported that the college students who distributed the questionnaires for their study of the Christian Anti-Communism Crusade were routinely accused of being dupes of Communist professors.

This chapter examines activists in the Crusade and the Moral Majority. The data come mainly from two state and local surveys of activists. The first was conducted by Wolfinger et al. in 1962, at the San Francisco Bay Region School of Anti-Communism. Students distributed questionnaires and self-addressed, stamped return envelopes to participants. Thirty-nine percent of the surveys were returned. Additional, in-person interviews were conducted. The survey produced a total of 308 activists in the Crusade, although there is no way to determine how representative the respondents were of all activists. Wolf-inger et al. have graciously made their data available to the academic community, and I have reanalyzed it for much of the discussion below.

Data on the Moral Majority come from my own mail survey of members of the Ohio Moral Majority, conducted in 1982. Mail surveys were sent to the entire membership of the organization. Although Columbus newspapers had printed claims by the state chairman that there were 20,000 members, the actual lists contained 285 names. Of the 260 surveys mailed to valid addresses, 149 were returned, for a response rate of 57 percent. Although there were no significant differences between those who answered the first and second wave of the survey, it is still possible that those who responded differed in some way from those who did not.

The Ohio Moral Majority membership list was composed of individuals who had done one or more of the following: signed a petition at a statewide rally, joined a local chapter, written to the state chairman, requested a copy of the monthly newsletter, or sent a contribution to the organization.

In my study of the Ohio Moral Majority, I interviewed state and county officials, as well as members and supporters of the organization, and attended state and county meetings. Insights from these interviews are used to help interpret the data from the mail survey.

In addition, I supplement these data with occasional discussion of published data from two other surveys. The first, conducted by Koeppen in 1962, was a survey of Crusade activists in the Bay Area, which was similar to that conducted by Wolfinger et al. The second, conducted by Georgianna in 1983, was a mail survey of the members and leaders of the Indiana Moral Majority. The Indiana chapter was the largest in the Midwest and had nearly ten times the membership of the Ohio chapter.

It should be noted again that the Crusade and the Moral Majority were only two of many Christian Right groups active during the 1960s and 1980s. It is possible that surveys of the membership of other groups would tell a somewhat different story. However, there are remarkable continuities between activists in the Crusade and the Moral Majority, which suggest that these two groups may be representative of a broader type of Christian Right activist.

Those who I have called activists in this chapter vary in their level of involvement in Christian Right organizations. Students of interest groups frequently distinguish between members and activists, and, in that sense of the term *activist,* most of the respondents to these surveys are not activists. Scholars who study political behavior frequently use this term to refer to a citizen who participates in politics to an extent that distinguishes him or her from an ordinary citizen, and, in this sense of the term, the respondents to these surveys were surely activists. All had spent time at meetings, contributed money, or in some other way been involved with an ideological organization. Only a small minority of citizens are members of political groups. These activists differ in important ways from the passive supporters of the Christian Right described in chapters 4 and 5.

THE CHRISTIAN ANTI-COMMUNISM CRUSADE

Wolfinger et al.'s study of those who attended a rally of the Crusade in the Bay Area found that activists in the Crusade were similar to activists in other political groups. More than one-half had completed college, and nearly 60 percent were members of households headed by professionals, businessmen, managers, or officials. Of those who were professionals, approximately one-third were clergymen. Crusaders were somewhat older than the rest of the Bay Area population and substantially more male: nearly two-thirds of Crusaders were men. Koeppen (1969) studied participants in a later Crusade rally and reported a similar, high socioeconomic-status group of activists.

Contrary to expectations, however, Crusaders did not display high levels of religiosity. Only one-half reported attending church regularly, with nearly one-third attending seldom or never. No single denomination was dominant among Crusaders. Slightly more than one-third attended fundamentalist, Baptist, or nondenominational community churches, but a somewhat larger contingent attended high-status churches, such as Presbyterian and Episcopal ones.

Moreover, Crusader activists were not consistently conservative. Although they were nearly unanimous in accepting the Crusade message of the dangers of domestic communism, nearly 40 percent believed that U.S. membership in the United Nations was a good thing, and approximately one-third supported negotiations with the Soviet Union. On domestic issues, they were even more divided. More than one-half supported federal aid to education and favored racial integration. Despite the opposition of Schwarz to Medicare, nearly four in ten supported it. A small majority believed that Freud should be taught in schools, and more than two-thirds supported the teaching of evolution. This moderation is consistent with the portrait of mass-public supporters of the Crusade in chapter 4.

Crusaders were overwhelmingly Republican (71 percent Republican, 9 percent Democrat), but, despite the ideological congruity that led the Crusade to enthusiastically endorse Goldwater in 1964, only 58 percent of those expressing a preference chose Goldwater over Nixon for the 1964 Republican nomination. Wolfinger et al. reported that, among those who had recently moved to California (and were therefore less influenced by Nixon's native-son status), Goldwater was preferred by two-thirds, a figure that nonetheless points to the relative moderation of Crusaders.

Religion and Political Attitudes

Wolfinger et al.'s survey did not include many religious variables. Respondents were asked their denominational affiliation, their frequency of church attendance, and how they initially heard of the Crusade (some reported that they learned of it in church). These three religious variables are significantly related to political attitudes. Table 6.1 pre-

TABLE 6.1
Correlations between Religion and Political Attitudes in the Christian Anti-Communism Crusade

	Denomination	Attendance	Recruitment
Domestic Issues			
Medicare	−.01	−.22**	−.20**
Aid to education	−.02	−.12*	−.24**
Integration	−.11*	−.24**	−.21**
Labor unions harmful	−.09*	−.19**	−.14**
Big business not harmful	−.13**	−.11*	−.07
Freud not taught	.05	.23**	.07
Darwin not taught	.23**	.37**	.23**
Communist influence in			
Democratic party	.06	.09*	.07
Republican party	.06	.00	.03
Colleges	.00	.04	−.04
Not allow news to criticize	.02	.07	.04
Forbid Communists on T.V.	.09*	.08*	.06
Forbid Socialist papers	−.06	.09*	−.07
Foreign Policy			
Foreign aid	−.05	−.08	−.07
UN	−.03	−.12*	−.24**
Negotiate with Soviet Union	−.05	−.03	.00

Note: All items coded, so high scores indicate more conservative positions and greater religious commitment. Denomination is a dummy variable for fundamentalist churches. Recruitment is a dummy variable with a value of 1 if the respondent learned of the Crusade in church.
*$p \leq .05$
**$p \leq .01$

sents the correlations between these three variables and various political attitudes.

The correlations in table 6.1 confirm and extend Wolfinger et al.'s observation that those who were attracted to the Crusade because of its religious appeal were generally more liberal than their more secular counterparts. This is particularly true on domestic issues that focus on the role of the federal government—the more religious Crusaders are more willing to expand the federal role in Medicare, education, and desegregation. However, they are *less* willing to tolerate the teaching of Darwin or Freud in the schools, suggesting that religious Crusaders were motivated by different issues than their secular counterparts. Religious Crusaders were also slightly less tolerant. In their greater concern for education issues, including the teaching of evolution, religious Crusaders echo the fundamentalist activists of the 1920s.

The Gender Gap in the Old Right

Klatch (1987) notes that few of the studies of activists in the Right discussed the role of women. Indeed, Trow (1957) did not include women in his analysis because he felt that their lack of political knowledge and interest would bias his sample. Lipset (1963a) refers in a footnote to gender differences in tolerance and support for "morality" in politics, which he attributes to women's greater concern with family status. Lipset saw this concern not as the traditional feminine concern for protection of children, but rather as status anxiety and frustration over the prestige of the family unit.

TABLE 6.2
Gender Gap in the Christian
Anti-Communism Crusade

	Men	Women
Communist danger	2.7	3.2**
Domestic communism	4.4	4.5
Government role	4.2	4.3
Economic issues	4.8	4.2**
Education	1.3	2.0**
Tolerance	3.3	3.9**
Foreign policy	3.6	3.6

Note: Mean scores for men and women for each scale. All scales coded, so high scores indicate more conservative positions.
*$p \leq .05$
**$p \leq .01$

There was a sizable gender gap among Crusaders. Table 6.2 presents mean scores for men and women for several scales constructed from the items in table 6.1. Women are significantly less tolerant than men, significantly more worried about domestic communism, significantly less willing to allow Freud and Darwin into the classroom, and significantly more liberal on economic issues. Whereas male Crusaders adopt conservative positions on economic issues and more moderate positions on tolerance and education, women adopt an opposite set of positions.

Explaining the Political Attitudes of Crusaders

These bivariate patterns may be due to other factors. For example, the women in the Crusade may differ from the men because the women were more likely to be recruited to the organization through church networks. To determine whether religion and gender influence the political attitudes of Crusaders after controls for other variables, a series of ordinary least squares (OLS) regression equations were estimated. Included as independent variables were gender, denomination, church attendance, church recruitment, education, income, rural birth, and age. Table 6.3 presents the standardized coefficients (betas) for the three religious variables and for gender. These coefficients are readily interpretable—larger values indicate a greater relationship between the independent and dependent variables.

The more religious Crusaders remain significantly more liberal than their more secular counterparts on the role of the federal govern-

TABLE 6.3
Religion, Gender, and Politcal Attitudes (Regression Results)

	Denomination	Church Attendance	Recruitment	Sex	R^2	N
Communist danger	.01	.13*	.06	.22**	.16	183
Domestic communism	.06	.11	.02	.16*	.07	178
Government role	−.04	−.18*	−.23*	.09	.21	120
Economic issues	−.00	.10	.05	−.16*	.08	180
Education	.09	.38**	.05	.15*	.23	119
Tolerance	−.07	.08	−.03	.20**	.10	179
Foreign policy	−.14*	−.21**	−.14*	.04	.07	172

Note: All scales coded, so high values indicate more conservative positions. Control variables include age, education, income, and rural birth. Cell entries are standardized regression coefficients. R^2 values adjusted for small sample size.
*$p \leq .05$
**$p \leq .01$

ment and on foreign policy, and they are significantly less worried about the dangers of domestic communism. Women were more worried about communism, less tolerant, and more liberal on economic issues. The religious Crusaders and women were more conservative on education issues.

Wolfinger et al. reported that attitudes concerning the dangers of domestic communism were strong predictors of foreign-policy attitudes. It seems reasonable that fear of communism would also be a strong predictor of intolerance. Separate equations were estimated for foreign-policy attitudes and tolerance, including as predictors the demographic variables mentioned above and the two scales measuring attitudes toward communism. The results indicate that gender differences in tolerance are not explained by attitudes toward communism. The more liberal foreign-policy views held by the more religious Crusaders are even more significant after controls for attitudes toward communism.

EXPLAINING ACTIVISM IN THE CRUSADE

It is impossible to directly test various theories of support for the Christian Right with these data. Wolfinger et al.'s data was not based on a random sample of Crusader activists, and there is not a readily comparable control group with which to compare Crusader activists. However, Wolfinger et al. did design their survey to test various theories and compared their activists to white, northern, college-educated respondents to the 1960 American National Election Study. They concluded that Crusaders were not alienated, but were deeply involved in community and political life. Crusaders did not appear to suffer from status anxiety or inconsistency, nor were they likely to be displaced provincials desperate to defend their previous values. Instead, Wolfinger et al. concluded that activism in the Crusade was best explained by Republican identification and anti-Communist beliefs. Again, rational explanations seem to prevail over irrational ones. In sum, activists in the Crusade were predictably concerned about domestic and foreign communism, but these attitudes are the only ones on which a conservative consensus exists. As was the case with the mass-level supporters of the Crusade, Crusade activists were deeply divided on domestic policy. Moreover, those who were attracted to the Crusade by its religious message were more liberal than the secular supporters— again, a pattern mirrored in the mass-level data.

THE OHIO MORAL MAJORITY

The Ohio Moral Majority was formed in 1978, after a group of Baptist Bible Fellowship pastors was shown a film on the dangers of the Soviet military. The film suggested that the United States was far behind the Soviet Union in military might, and the pastors responded by forming a state chapter of the Moral Majority and attempting to build a grass-roots movement. That the issue that motivated the formation of the Ohio chapter was defense spending, rather than abortion, school prayer, or gay rights, may seem surprising. Recall, however, from chapter 5 that foreign-policy attitudes were strong predictors of support for the Moral Majority among white evangelicals. Among the elites of the Ohio chapter, this concern for defense spending seemed to come from a visceral anticommunism.

The original core of the organization recruited other pastors of its denomination and asked them to form county chapters. Although the goal was to establish functioning chapters in all eighty-eight counties in Ohio, at the time of my survey only five county chapters were functioning, although several others existed on paper. Active chapters had monthly meetings in which speakers discussed topics such as abortion, marijuana abuse, homosexuality, and, especially, topics related to education.

The state chapter had an executive board, consisting primarily of Bible Baptist Fellowship ministers. It published a monthly newsletter and held monthly meetings after meetings of the clergy in the state Bible Baptist Fellowship in space owned by the Ohio Christian Schools Association. Although the executive board and county leaders felt deeply about the issue agenda of the Moral Majority, they were unable to spare the time or money to attempt a fuller mobilization. Most were involved with a number of local organizations, were sole pastors of their churches, and were administrators of the Christian schools that their churches sponsored.

Activists in the Moral Majority: Demographic Characteristics

Members of the Moral Majority exhibit social-status characteristics that resemble those of political activists in other organizations. Over one-half had completed college, a figure nearly three times higher than that of other whites in Ohio. The education of members is influenced by the disproportionate number of Baptist preachers, nearly all of whom had graduated from Bible colleges. With ministers excluded, 43 percent of the members of the Ohio Moral Majority had completed college. Georgianna (1989) reported that the membership of the Indiana Moral

Majority was also well educated, although only one-third had college degrees. The membership of the Ohio Moral Majority was likewise disproportionately drawn from upper-status occupations. Nearly one-half had a professional occupation, although with ministers excluded this figure dropped to 21 percent, approximately the same rate as other whites in Ohio.

Almost one-half of all Ohio Moral Majority members attended Baptist churches, primarily the Bible Baptist Fellowship. An additional one-fourth attended other fundamentalist churches. Only 8 percent attended Catholic churches, suggesting that Falwell's claim to attract support among conservative Catholics and Jews may have been exaggerated. The clergy who headed the Ohio Moral Majority were even more anti-Catholic than other fundamentalists. A sermon entitled "Roman Catholic Church: Harlot of Rome" preceded one meeting of the state executive committee. The sermon attacked not only Catholics but also evangelicals, pentecostals, charismatics, and mainline Protestants. With this level of religious intolerance evident, it is not surprising that the membership was mainly restricted to those associated with fundamentalist churches.

Georgianna (1989) reported that membership in the Indiana chapter was even more concentrated in fundamentalist churches, with almost 75 percent associated with independent Baptist churches. This figure suggests that the Indiana chapter relied even more heavily on religious networks to recruit its membership. A county chairman active in the Ohio Moral Majority told me that the Ohio chairman, Reverend Tom Trammel, had been more active in recruiting membership through political networks than had Reverend Gregg Dixon, chairman of the Indiana chapter. Some activists in the Ohio chapter were recruited through right-to-life organizations, Christian school networks, and other local conservative groups. This recruitment strategy may account for the few Catholic members of the Ohio Moral Majority, for Georgianna reports no Catholics among her sample of the Indiana chapter.

An overwhelming majority of Moral Majority members believed the Bible to be literally true and reported a born-again experience. This fundamentalist doctrine is mirrored in their religious identification: 40 percent identified themselves as fundamentalists, 39 percent as both evangelicals and fundamentalists, 9 percent as evangelicals, and only 12 percent rejected both labels. More than four in five attended church services once a week or more. Georgianna (1989) reports similar religious consensus, with the vast majority of members of the Indiana chapter agreeing with a set of conservative doctrinal statements.

In short, the demographic profile of members of the Ohio Moral Majority is that of well-educated fundamentalists with strongly held religious beliefs and high levels of involvement in fundamentalist churches.

Involvement in the Moral Majority

The membership of the Moral Majority came to the organization through a variety of routes. More than one in five heard of the organization during a series of patriotic rallies sponsored in 1978–79 in various parts of Ohio by the national Moral Majority organization. Those who attended these rallies were asked to sign petitions, and those who signed were added to the rolls of the Moral Majority. Another 15 percent were recruited in church, where active pastors discussed the organization in their sermons. Such politicized preaching was not always popular with parishioners: one county chairman reported that his church had split over his involvement in the Moral Majority.

Others heard of the Moral Majority through friends or the media. Because the pastors who formed the Ohio Moral Majority did not hold statewide or even local television ministries, religious television was not a major source of recruitment to the organization. Indeed, only a few members reported viewing substantial amounts of religious television.

Members varied in their level of involvement as well. Approximately one-third of members had attended rallies sponsored by the organization or monthly meetings held by county chapters. Over one-half had signed petitions. Fully one-third had participated in more than one of these three activities. Approximately one-fourth termed their involvement with the Moral Majority "very important" to their lives, and another one-half termed it "somewhat important." Approximately one-fourth thought of the Moral Majority as an unimportant involvement.

Wilson (1973) argued that members of organizations receive either purposive, solidary, or material benefits. Purposive benefits are ideological in nature: members believe they are furthering a political purpose or goal by their group membership. Solidary benefits are those derived from social interactions at potluck dinners and meetings. Material benefits involve tangible benefits such as goods or services. Those who valued their involvement differed in the sources of their satisfaction, but most chose purposive benefits. Nearly one-third wrote that they were restoring the United States' moral standards: "bringing America back to God," as one woman wrote. Others valued their influence on public policy—one man wrote that he was pleased to "join with others to influence legislation." Still others voiced satisfaction in letting their policy voice be heard. One group valued a material benefit: nearly one-fifth reported that their main satisfaction came from the information in the newsletter. Finally, some members valued the solidary benefits. Fully 16 percent echoed a woman who wrote that she most valued "banding together with other patriots."

The Ohio Moral Majority had no evident influence on state legislation during the period before the study. There was a clear relationship between political sophistication and the sources of satisfaction. More politically active and sophisticated respondents valued mostly the expressive, solidary, or informational benefits, while those who were less politically sophisticated were more likely to value the effects they believed they had on legislation.

Other Political Involvement

Falwell often claimed to have mobilized a core of previously apolitical fundamentalists into politics. These newly mobilized voters were not evident in the membership of the Ohio Moral Majority. More than three-fourths of the members reported having voted in all previous elections for which they were eligible, and another 20 percent reported having voted in most previous elections. Only 4 percent of the Ohio Moral Majority membership reported voting in 1980 after having voted in only some previous elections.

Moreover, more than one-half of the Ohio Moral Majority membership reported belonging to other political organizations. Fully one-fifth belonged to three or more political groups. Many belonged to other organizations of the Christian Right, particularly to local or statewide organizations, and others belonged to organizations of the secular Right (including the John Birch Society). Clearly, the membership of the Ohio Moral Majority was composed of political activists, not apolitical Christians recently mobilized into politics.

Political Beliefs

If the members of the Moral Majority differed in their involvement in the organization and the satisfaction they drew from that involvement, they did not differ significantly in their political attitudes. They were overwhelmingly Republican: only 3 percent identified themselves as Democrats. They had voted for Reagan in large numbers—only 2 percent reported voting for Carter in 1980. They remained supportive of Reagan during the recession. At a time when Reagan's national popularity was plummeting to what would be the lowest point of his

TABLE 6.4
Political Attitudes of Ohio Moral Majority Members

	Ohio Moral Majority (%)	National Supporters, 1980 (%)
Social Issues		
ERA	95	62
Abortion	75	72
Society discriminates against women	64	53
Women's role	65	34
Government Role		
Federal government power	92	81
Affirmative action	72	52
Social-service spending	73	53
Foreign and Defense Policy		
Defense spending	81	83
Détente	68	42
Communist Influence in		
Federal government	74	
Colleges and universities	87	
Civil Liberties		
Not allow Communists on T.V.	60	
Remove antireligious books from libraries	18	
N	151	152

Note: Figures indicate percentage of each group selecting conservative options to item. Conservative position on abortion is that it be allowed only to save the mother's life, or never. Items on Communist influence and civil liberties not included in the 1980 National Election Survey.

presidency, 95 percent were satisfied with his job performance, and 45 percent were very satisfied.

Overwhelming percentages of the membership took conservative positions on a variety of political issues. For the purposes of comparison, supporters of the Moral Majority in the 1980 American National Election Study data are included in table 6.4. The Ohio Moral Majority membership is considerably more conservative than mass-level supporters and is considerably more homogeneous. This homogeneity was surprisingly strong on women's issues. Almost all members of the Ohio Moral Majority opposed the ERA, although over one-third of Moral Majority supporters favored it. The membership remained supportive of the Reagan military buildup, although by 1982 the national consensus had evaporated after a stream of articles about expensive toilet seats, coffee makers, and hammers, which the military had labeled "multi-directional, multi-purpose impact devices" in order to justify their high prices. The support for increased defense spending among activists in the Ohio Moral Majority in 1982 rivaled that among passive supporters two years earlier, when a national consensus for increased defense expenditures was evident in many polls.

Georgianna (1989) reported substantial consensus among members of the Indiana Moral Majority on the ERA, abortion, homosexuality, school prayer, school busing, the teaching of Creationism, defense spending, a nuclear freeze, and a balanced budget, but less consensus on racial integration and negotiations with the Soviets.

Moral Majority members shared the suspicion of domestic communism which earlier Christian Right movements had voiced. Nearly all respondents believed that Communists had a lot of influence in colleges and universities, and nearly three-fourths believed that they had strong influence in the federal government. Fewer than one-third believed that Communists should be allowed to speak on radio and television. However, the membership was not overwhelmingly intolerant. Less than 20 percent believed that antireligious books should be removed from libraries, and several respondents wrote long notes on the dangers of book-burning in the survey's margins in response to a question about this issue.

Religion as a Source of Differences in Political Attitudes

In chapter 3 we saw that religious variables influenced the political attitudes of white evangelicals. This is true also for the members of the Ohio Moral Majority. Despite the relative consensus of these members on political matters, religious variables explain a good deal of the variation in political attitudes. In the Ohio Moral Majority, members and leaders alike pointed to differences between the Bible Baptist Fellowship participants and other members. Table 6.5 shows the attitudinal differences between Baptist members and other ones. Denominational differences were large, with members of various independent Baptist churches more conservative than other Moral Majority members on every item. These differences were statistically significant on three sets of issues: gender issues, defense spending, and attitudes toward communism.

Nearly all of the Moral Majority members attended church every week. Differences between those who attended weekly and other Moral Majority members are presented in table 6.6. Although there is little variation in the frequency of attendance, it is a significant predictor of attitudes on abortion. This provides additional confirmation of Him-

TABLE 6.5
Denominational Affiliation and Political Attitudes
of Ohio Moral Majority Members

	Baptists	Others
Social Issues		
ERA	2.95	2.84
Abortion	2.24	1.79**
Society discriminates against women	2.61	2.24**
Women's role	5.36	4.41**
Government Role		
Federal government power	2.94	2.87
Affirmative action	5.46	5.28
Social-service spending	5.51	5.22
Foreign and Defense Policy		
Defense spending	5.84	5.15**
Détente	5.28	5.26
Communist Influence in		
Federal government	2.77	2.44**
Colleges and universities	2.91	2.69**
Civil Liberties		
Not allow Communists on T.V.	2.49	2.13**
Remove antireligious books from libraries	1.57	1.51

Note: Mean values on each scale for each group. High scores indicate more conservative positions.
*$p \le .05$
**$p \le .01$

melstein's claim that frequent attendance at conservative churches exposes individuals to mobilization by right-to-life groups. Himmelstein argued that this exposure in turn increases opposition to legal abortion. Those members of the Ohio Moral Majority who attended church weekly were significantly more likely than others to belong to right-to-life groups.

There was also a statistically significant-interaction effect between denomination and attendance. Those Baptists who attended church weekly were more conservative than those who did not, particularly on attitudes toward the proper role of government, but frequency of attendance had little impact on the attitudes of other members of the Moral Majority. This may have been due to the frequency of political messages by the Bible Baptist Fellowship pastors, who confirmed in private interviews that they frequently discussed politics from the pulpit.

TABLE 6.6
Frequency of Church Attendance and Attitudes
of Ohio Moral Majority Members

	Every Week	Less Than Every Week
Social Issues		
ERA	2.93	2.80
Abortion	2.45	1.88**
Society discriminates against women	2.44	2.41
Women's role	4.97	4.52
Government Role		
Federal government power	2.91	2.93
Affirmative action	5.33	5.73
Social-service spending	5.39	5.41
Foreign and Defense Policy		
Defense spending	5.54	5.25
Détente	5.50	5.25
Communist Influence in		
Federal government	2.60	2.61
Colleges and universities	2.82	2.75
Civil Liberties		
Not allow Communists on T.V.	2.32	2.28
Remove antireligious books from libraries	1.55	1.50

Note: Entries are mean values for each group on each item. Higher scores indicate more conservative positions.
**$p \leq .01$

Religious identity was also an important source of variation on political attitudes. Nearly all respondents considered themselves to be fundamentalists, but one-half of the fundamentalists also identified themselves as evangelicals. Interviews with some members suggested that those with dual religious identification thought of themselves primarily as evangelicals and used the term *fundamentalist* to describe their beliefs about the Bible. Indeed, those who identified themselves as both fundamentalists and evangelicals were virtually indistinguishable from those who identified themselves as simply evangelicals, with one important exception: the former were more likely to believe that the Bible was literally true. For this reason, those who identified as both evangelicals and fundamentalists have been grouped with those who identified themselves as evangelicals only.

Table 6.7 shows the differences in political attitudes between those who identified themselves as fundamentalists only and those who iden-

TABLE 6.7
Religious Identity and Political Attitudes
of Ohio Moral Majority Members

	Fundamentalists	Evangelicals
Social Issues		
ERA	3.00	2.88**
Abortion	2.34	1.93**
Society discriminates against women	2.68	2.31*
Women's role	5.39	4.72**
Government Role		
Federal government power	2.94	2.88
Affirmative action	5.91	4.91**
Social-service spending	5.70	4.99**
Foreign and Defense Policy		
Defense spending	5.96	5.27*
Détente	5.80	5.15
Communist Influence in		
Federal government	2.82	2.21*
Colleges and universities	2.96	2.79**
Civil Liberties		
Not allow Communists on T.V.	2.52	2.25
Remove antireligious books from libraries	1.48	1.55

Note: Entries are mean values for each group for each item. Higher scores indicate more conservative positions.
$*p \leq .05$
$**p \leq .01$

tified themselves in part as evangelicals. The fundamentalists were more conservative than evangelicals on nearly every item in the survey, and these differences were statistically significant on nine of thirteen issues. The fundamentalists differed from the evangelicals in a number of other ways. Although evangelicals were generally involved in other political organizations, including mainstream political ones, fundamentalists were seldom involved in any organization but the Moral Majority. Those fundamentalists who were involved in other political groups were generally members of other organizations of the Right and were rarely involved in mainstream political organizations.

Finally, members differed in the strength of the connection they perceived between their political and religious beliefs. In table 6.8, the political attitudes of Moral Majority members who reported different levels of connections between these two domains are presented. Those who reported that their political beliefs were strongly influenced by

TABLE 6.8
Connection between Religion and Politics (Cognitive Structuring)

	High	Medium	Low
Social Issues			
ERA	2.96	2.80	2.93
Abortion	2.16	2.11	1.66*
Society discriminates against women	2.44	2.43	2.35
Women's role	5.15	5.10	4.31*
Government Role			
Federal government power	2.93	2.85	2.93
Affirmative action	5.61	5.02	5.40a
Social-service spending	5.55	5.11	5.40
Foreign and Defense Policy			
Defense spending	5.79	5.35	5.30*
Détente	5.90	4.96	4.89**
Communist Influence in			
Federal government	2.77	2.59	2.45*
Colleges and universities	2.96	2.84	2.60*
Civil Liberties			
Not allow Communists on T.V.	2.44	2.38	2.02*
Remove antireligious books from libraries	1.60	1.50	1.26*

Note: Entries are mean scores for those with high, medium, and low scores on the scale measuring the connection between religion and politics. Higher scores indicate more conservative positions.
*$p \leq .05$
**$p \leq .01$ for linear pattern
a$p \leq .05$ for curvilinear pattern

their religious beliefs were generally more conservative than other Moral Majority members. This was particularly true for women. Among Moral Majority women, those who perceived a strong connection between their religious and political beliefs were markedly more traditional in their attitudes toward gender issues than those who separated these two cognitive domains. Those women who think of religion and politics as closely intertwined feel constrained to take positions that are strongly antifeminist. Those women who are able to separate these two domains are able to take more moderate positions.

There was a significant interaction effect with the connection between religion and politics and religious identity. Among fundamentalists, those who perceived a strong connection between religion and politics were more conservative than other fundamentalist members on all issues. However, among evangelicals a strong connection between religion and politics was associated with a more *liberal* position on issues of domestic politics. It seems likely that the doctrine of Social Gospel activism in some evangelical churches is responsible for this result. One evangelical pastor who headed a county organization told me that "the Bible teaches us to care for the sheep—the poor and hungry. We do this through charity, but it is only right for the government to do it too." This pastor was extremely conservative on social issues and on defense spending, but saw a Christian commitment to caring for the downtrodden which included a role for government. Although fundamentalist pastors also voiced a concern for the disadvantaged, they emphatically did *not* see a government role.

MULTIVARIATE RESULTS

Although each of these religious variables is a significant predictor of political attitudes by itself, multivariate analysis is needed to assess the independent impact of these variables and to control the effects of demographic variables. Three scales were constructed from the political attitudes in the survey. The first scale measured attitudes toward big government and included evaluations of the federal government and Congress, attitudes toward spending on social programs, attitudes toward affirmative action, Communist influence on the federal government, and assessments of the power of the federal government.

The second scale tapped attitudes toward social issues. A scale was constructed from evaluations of the U.S. Supreme Court, support for the ERA, as well as attitudes on the role of women, on whether society discriminates against women, and on abortion. Finally, a third scale was constructed to measure attitudes toward communism. This scale included perceptions of domestic Communist strength, free speech for Communists, détente, and defense spending.

Separate OLS regression equations were estimated for each of the three scales. Initial equations were estimated with interaction terms, but none proved statistically significant. The results presented in table 6.9 are from separate equations estimated without interaction terms. The coefficients are again standardized regression coefficients; those values that are farthest from zero are the most important predictors of attitudes. Even after the introduction of controls for partisanship, education, age, and sex, religious variables are significant predictors of political attitudes of the Ohio Moral Majority. Religious identity is the strongest predictor of attitudes toward big government, followed by the connection between religion and politics. Denomination and attendance are among the strongest predictors of social-issue attitudes,

TABLE 6.9
Religion and Political Attitudes of Ohio Moral Majority Members
(Regression Results)

	Big Government	Social Issues	Communism
Denomination	.04	.24*	−.06
Attendance	.13	−.28*	.02
Fundamentalist/evangelical	.29*	−.02	.31*
Connection between religion and politics	.26*	.05	−.21
Party identification	.11	.04	−.10
Education	−.01	.27*	−.22*
Age	.01	.01	−.06
Sex	.10	−.03	.23*
R^2	.21	.19	.31

Note: Entries are standardized regression coefficients.
*$p \leq .05$

and religious identity is the strongest predictor of attitudes toward communism.

These findings make intuitive sense. The lingering tradition of Social Gospel activism among moderate evangelicals produces a strong fundamentalist-evangelical split on attitudes toward big government. The effects of denomination and attendance among the Moral Majority are due to the frequent sermons on gender issues in Baptist churches, in which those who attend frequently are more often exposed to the message. Finally, the importance of religious identity in explaining attitudes toward communism is probably due to the historical connection between fundamentalism and anticommunism. In addition, the more frequent participation of evangelicals in mainstream political organizations might decrease their perception that the federal government is overrun with Communists.

POLITICAL BEHAVIOR OF MORAL MAJORITY MEMBERS

As might be expected of political activists, Moral Majority members were quite active politically. Fully 98 percent reported voting in 1980, and 28 percent said that they had taken part in three or more other electoral activities. Clearly, Moral Majority members were not apolitical, separatist fundamentalists. Georgianna (1989) reported that the level of activism among members of the Indiana Moral Majority made many of the members and leaders uneasy, because it clashed with the traditional fundamentalist doctrine of separation from the secular world. Members of the Ohio Moral Majority, at least, have learned to live with any cognitive dissonance this activism may cause. Moreover, they were not recently mobilized into politics. Fully 96 percent reported that they had voted in most or all past elections (some of those who had not were too young to have voted previously).

When the Moral Majority voted, it voted Republican. More than 98 percent reported voting for Reagan in 1980, and their loyalty did not waver during the recession of 1982.

EXPLAINING MEMBERSHIP IN THE OHIO MORAL MAJORITY

Although my survey was not designed to test theories for activism in the Moral Majority, the survey results, combined with insights from in-depth interviews with county leaders and activists, offer some possible explanations. My observations suggest that the resource-mobilization explanation is important to an understanding of the members of the Ohio Moral Majority. Early in my research, the state chairman claimed that there were twenty thousand members. But the organization had a mailing list of fewer than three hundred names. The state chairman had exaggerated the number because he believed that, based on the attendance at statewide rallies, there were at least that many potential members in the state.

Whatever the truth to the size of the chairman's estimate, it is clear that the Moral Majority recruited only a fraction of its potential support in Ohio. In general, activists in the Moral Majority seem to have been recruited from a potential pool of conservative Republicans through church networks, particularly that of the Baptist Bible Fellowship. Pastors of that denomination are religious entrepreneurs who establish their own churches with little organizational support (although larger congregations supply resources to fledgling congregations). Those pastors active in the Moral Majority were deeply conservative fundamentalist Christians who recruited some of their parishioners into the organization. In those few county chapters headed by nonfundamentalists, members were recruited through other politically sympathetic organizations, especially local right-to-life groups.

Recruitment is only part of the equation, however. Activists in the Ohio Moral Majority were uniformly conservative in their religious and political beliefs. As before, the evidence points to a rational explanation of activism in the Moral Majority. Those who were active were attracted to the organization because they shared its social and political goals, much as environmentalists join the Sierra Club and liberal feminists join the National Organization of Women.

One of those goals was clearly lifestyle defense. Activists in the Moral Majority were very concerned with education issues. Many of the Baptist pastors active in the organization sponsored Christian schools, and the state chapter shared a core of activists (and its headquarters) with the state Christian schools organization. Education figured prominently in the state newsletter, was discussed frequently at statewide meetings, and was highly salient to activists and other members. Moral Majority members did not necessarily want all children in the state to be educated according to their values (although many would have preferred this, if possible), but they felt strongly that they should be allowed to form their own schools to socialize their children.

Although religious and political conservatism seems the best explanation for activism in the Moral Majority, I did encounter some evidence of status and personality concerns. One county leader told me that "we common people in the middle of the country are sneered at by elites on the East and West Coast. It is time we got some respect." Another told me that he had become involved in the Moral Majority because of his concern with rampant bestiality among high-school students in his county. Although I have no independent evidence to refute his claim, one could make a good case for a personality explanation for his activism.

All social and political groups attract some marginal individuals, however, and these two cases were the exception, not the rule. Interviews with activists in groups of the Left and Center would doubtlessly turn up a few activists who became involved because of status or personality needs. The vast majority of members and leaders with whom I spoke were seemingly well-adjusted, conservative Christians who sought to enforce their social and political values on the larger population.

A final word of caution is in order, however. The data in this chapter come mostly from two small surveys of members and activists in the Christian Right. Other studies are needed to better understand the motivations and goals of activists in the Christian Right.

CHAPTER 7

The Pentecostal/Charismatic Right: Sources of Support for Robertson's Presidential Campaign

As the Moral Majority began to fold its tent, Robertson replaced Falwell as the leading spokesman for the New Christian Right. Robertson was also a televangelist and a longtime competitor of Falwell's. Although the two men shared a common political ideology, there were several important differences between them.

Foremost among these differences was religious doctrine. Whereas Falwell and the Moral Majority were firmly rooted in the fundamentalist, Bible Baptist Fellowship tradition, Robertson was more closely linked with pentecostal and charismatic Christianity. Fundamentalists shared with pentecostals and charismatics a belief in the authority of the Scriptures and in the necessity of personal salvation. Indeed, a list of the major tenets of fundamentalism would find general acceptance among pentecostals, as well as among many charismatics. Pentecostals and charismatics add to this doctrinal core the belief in the gifts of the Holy Spirit. These gifts include glossolalia, which is of primary importance to pentecostals, and prophecy, healing by faith, and other gifts, which charismatics accord equal importance with glossolalia (Smidt 1989).

Fundamentalists discern God's will by studying the Scriptures. Bible study groups play a vital role in fundamentalist churches because it is through the Bible that God reveals himself. Pentecostals and charismatics believe that the Bible is God's revealed word, but also believe in a personal dialogue with God. The Holy Spirit guides their actions. For fundamentalists, knowing God's will involves hard work, but, for charismatics and pentecostals, it is often an ecstatic experience of the Holy Spirit which guides them. Thus one of the main differences between the pentecostals/charismatics on the one hand and the fundamentalists on the other is style. Fundamentalists worship soberly and thoughtfully. Charismatics and pentecostals worship enthusiastically and emotionally.

By the 1980s, the vehement antipentecostal rhetoric of the fundamentalists had been replaced by one of tolerant disapproval. Falwell (1981) noted that although early fundamentalists and evangelicals had rejected pentecostalism and assigned it to the lunatic fringe of American religion, in more recent times the pentecostal and charismatic movements have been accorded a legitimate place among evangelicalism. However, he notes that "fundamentalists, as a group, violently reject the Pentecostal-Charismatic movement because of its emphasis on the doctrine of tongues" (p. 70), although he acknowledges that pentecostalism is surely rooted in evangelical doctrine. Ammerman (1987) reports that in the fundamentalist church of her study, "although the pastor rarely declares that such folk [pentecostals and charismatics] are actually unsaved, he makes it clear that they are allowing Satan to work in their lives and that believers should be careful to avoid them and their mistakes" (p. 81). Robbins (1988) echoes this charge in his analysis of Robertson's use of the Scriptures: "The Bible plays a quite subsidiary role in guiding him. It is little more than an Ouija board for his fingers to fall on. . . . This sort of misuse of Scripture is Satanic" (p. 64). Whether this antagonism of religious elites is shared by the rank and file is not clear. Ammerman goes on to note that the congregants in that fundamentalist church were not as intolerant of pentecostals as the message of their pastor would indicate, but that they did voice a general disapproval of the religious practices of pentecostals.

At one time this antagonism seemed primarily to run exclusively from fundamentalists to pentecostals. Early pentecostals referred to themselves as fundamentalists, and many continue to identify themselves as fundamentalists today (Green and Guth 1988). However, when Falwell temporarily assumed control of the Praise the Lord (PTL) ministries after the fall of Jim and Tammy Bakker, the outpouring of resentment from pentecostals and charismatics suggests that by the 1980s the negative feelings had become mutual. Indeed, Fitzgerald (1990) suggested that Falwell's unsuccessful stint at the PTL was a visible symbol of the antipathy between these two religious groups. She described one highly symbolic manifestation of the stylistic differences discussed above. She noted that when Falwell took over the Bakkers' empire for a short time, he found it politically useful to visit the Bakkers' theme park. One of the drawing points of this park was a very large water slide. Water plays a very important symbolic role for pentecostals, symbolizing the gifts of the Holy Spirit. Fitzgerald noted that although Falwell owns a swimming pool and enjoys swimming, this was not evident in his photographed trip down the water slide.

A memorable photograph of the occasion shows him [Falwell] lying on the chute a few feet from the top, and a few seconds after he has let go. He is wearing what he always wears in public—a black Baptist suit—and his arms are folded over his chest in the manner of a corpse in an open coffin. He is clearly not enjoying himself. In fact, the photograph suggests that he is doing this over his own dead body. . . . The fundamentalist Baptist is plunging into the Pentecostal pool, and it is precisely the waters of the Holy Ghost that separate the Pentecostals most distinctly from their cousins the parchy-dry fundamentalists. So Falwell had to show that he did not enjoy the plunge. (P. 69)

The PTL contributors' rejection of Falwell suggests that the antipathy may now be reciprocal. Jelen (1991a) reports a basic symmetry in negative affect among fundamentalists, pentecostals and charismatics, and evangelicals in his study of Greencastle, Indiana.

In addition to religious conflicts, Robertson also differed from Falwell in background. Whereas Falwell was a television preacher and somewhat new to politics, Robertson was a senator's son, and his television program was more of a religious talk show than a sermon. For several years, he had included a regular discussion of political news on the "700 Club." Moreover, Robertson's style was more inclusive than that of the less-tolerant fundamentalists. His program featured a black cohost, and his guests often included born-again Catholics and others that the fundamentalists might not have welcomed so readily.

It seems likely, then, that the religious sources of Robertson's support differed somewhat from those of the Moral Majority. Although they shared a common political agenda, their religious heritage and style were vastly different. In this chapter and the next, I shall explore the sources of support for Robertson. In this chapter, I focus on support for Robertson during his presidential campaign. Most of the discussion centers on Robertson's support in the South, although I also discuss briefly his support in Iowa and New Hampshire. In chapter 9, I shall explore the sources of lingering Robertson support nationwide.

THE ROBERTSON CAMPAIGN

Robertson delayed the initial announcement of his presidential bid until he had gathered three million signatures on petitions urging him to run. These signatures formed the core of a direct-mail solicitation network that proved quite effective. Many less-affluent contributors joined the "1988 Club" and pledged to donate $19.88 per month. Robertson raised more money than any other Republican candidate in 1987, although the expenses of direct mail drained away most of his funds (Wilcox 1991).

Robertson's campaign got off to a good start, winning the initial balloting in the Michigan caucus-convention process, and placing second in the Iowa caucuses. His campaign made ready use of the network of pentecostal churches and conservative political groups in many states, and that organizational advantage helped Robertson win caucuses in Washington, Hawaii, and Alaska. In many states, his efforts continued after the initial balloting, with Robertson forces capturing (at least temporarily) control of state party machinery in several states, including Arizona, Nevada, Oregon, Washington, Michigan, South Carolina, Georgia, Virginia, Hawaii, and Florida (Hertzke 1989b; Oldfield 1989).

Although Robertson did well in caucus states, he was far less successful in states with primary elections. The reason for this difference is clear: in caucus states, the low levels of turnout allow well-organized candidates with a strong, supportive base to defeat more popular candidates who cannot get their supporters to the polls. Caucuses often require substantial commitments of time from their participants, and few citizens are willing to make the investment. In 1988, fewer than 2 percent of the voting-age population of caucus states participated. In contrast, primary elections require only a few minutes of time once the prospective voter has reached the polls, so turnout in primary states is generally much higher—usually one in six of the voting-age population. As a result, whereas Robertson captured fully 28 percent of the votes in caucus states, his primary election support was closer to 10 percent.

Although Dole won the Republican caucuses in Iowa, Robertson got as much media attention from his second-place finish (Lichter, Amundson, and Noyes 1988). This media attention was not always favorable. Over the next few weeks his campaign suffered a number of setbacks. He placed last in the balloting in New Hampshire, despite heavy spending.[1] In addition, he attracted a good deal of attention for a series of controversial statements which reinforced doubts about his political judgment. Robertson claimed that he knew where hostages were being held in Lebanon (although he had yet to share this information with the administration), that nuclear missiles were stored in secret

---

1. One of Robertson's more publicized expenditures was to send a videotaped message to all registered Republican voters.

caves in Cuba, and that the Bush campaign was responsible for the sex scandal that had embroiled fellow pentecostal televangelist Jimmy Swaggart. Additional publicity surrounded a story that Robertson's wife had been pregnant long before they married. Finally, Robertson was embroiled in a lawsuit against former California congressman Pete McClosky, who claimed that Robertson had bragged that his father had kept him out of the Korean War. Robertson dropped his libel suit against McClosky when it became evident that he would not win an easy legal victory.

Robertson's campaign also suffered from a series of controversies and scandals which befell televangelists in early 1988. The Reverend Oral Roberts claimed that if he did not raise several million dollars by a specific date, God would call him home,[2] and Jim Bakker and Jimmy Swaggart were involved in sex scandals. The Bakker scandal exposed wide rifts among competing televangelists Bakker, Swaggart, and Falwell, when Bakker accused both preachers of plotting to take over his ministry. Although none of these stories involved Robertson directly, they did tarnish the image of television preachers. The timing of the Swaggart scandal was particularly unfortunate for Robertson, coming between the Iowa caucuses and the Super Tuesday primaries.

Robertson staked his credibility on the South Carolina primary a week before Super Tuesday, but Bush defeated him easily. In the southern Super Tuesday primaries, Robertson failed to carry a state or even a congressional district, although he consistently gathered between 10 percent and 20 percent of the Republican primary vote.

THE DATA

The data for this chapter come from several sources. First, support for Robertson among those who intended to vote in the Republican primary election in South Carolina will be examined using a *Washington Post* tracking poll. Second, support for Robertson among the general public in the South will be explored through data from the American National Election Study (ANES) Super Tuesday survey. This telephone survey included a preelection wave conducted between 17 January and 8 March, as well as a postelection wave conducted after the primary. The response rate for the first wave was 59 percent, and the reinterview response rate was 79 percent. The survey included respondents from all states that held primaries on Super Tuesday. For the purposes of this

2. Roberts's claim prompted a good deal of derision in the secular press. The cartoonist Garry Trudeau suggested that Roberts's claim made God out to be a common terrorist—holding hostages for ransom.

analysis, respondents from nonsouthern states have been excluded. Additional analysis on data from exit and tracking polls in Iowa, New Hampshire, and in the South are summarized, but not discussed in detail.

SUPPORT FOR ROBERTSON IN SOUTH CAROLINA

The South Carolina primary took on tremendous political importance for the four remaining Republican candidates, Robertson, Bush, Dole, and Kemp. Held three days before the all-important Super Tuesday primaries, it could provide the victor with important momentum. Kemp's campaign was faltering after poor showings in Iowa and New Hampshire, and he desperately needed a victory to keep his hopes alive. Bush and Dole had split those first two contests, although Dole needed a victory more to reestablish momentum leading into the South, where tracking polls showed a large Bush lead. Finally, Robertson had publicly announced that he would win in South Carolina, where a substantial portion of the citizenry held doctrinally conservative religious views.

The *Washington Post* tracking poll in South Carolina was a random-digit phone survey of households. The survey contained several items that have been combined into dependent variables. First, respondents were asked for which candidate they planned to vote, and undecided respondents were asked toward which candidate they leaned. These two items have been combined into a nominal variable, with those preferring or leaning toward each candidate coded together. In addition, respondents were asked whether they were a strong or a weak supporter of the candidate, and who their second choice would be. Finally, respondents were asked whether they held favorable or unfavorable opinions about the candidate. From these items I have constructed a measure of support for Robertson.[3]

Respondents were asked which issues were most important to them (though their positions on these issues were not ascertained) and which candidate characteristics were most important. Their partisanship and ideology were assessed. Separate items asked how religious

3. These items have been combined into a measure of support for Robertson, as follows: those who held an unfavorable view were coded as 0; those who held a favorable view but who did not further support Robertson were coded as 1; those for whom Robertson was their second choice were coded as 2; those who leaned toward Robertson as their first choice were coded as 3; those who planned to vote for Robertson but who were only weak supporters were coded as 4; and those who were strong supporters and planned to vote for Robertson were coded as 5.

the respondent considered himself or herself, whether he or she was born-again, an evangelical, and/or a charismatic or pentecostal, and whether he or she watched televangelists and was currently or ever had been a member of the 700 Club.[4]

Among those respondents who planned to vote in the Republican primary, approximately 13 percent planned to vote for Robertson, and most of this group strongly supported him. However, many more of South Carolina's likely voters had unfavorable impressions, with fully 61 percent negative toward Robertson.

To explore the sources of Robertson support, I have estimated a regression equation for the Robertson evaluation item, as well as a discriminant analysis equation for the nominal variable on candidate preference. The results are presented in tables 7.1 and 7.2. The regression results suggest that support for Robertson was primarily explained by religion. Those who identified themselves as evangelicals or charismatics and those who frequently watched televangelists or were members of the 700 Club were all significantly more likely to support Robertson. In addition, Robertson supporters were more concerned with social issues, less concerned with foreign-policy issues, more conservative, and younger than other prospective Republican voters.

The discriminant analysis confirms these results, adding religiosity and born-again identity to the list of predictors of Robertson support. These latter two variables were also associated with support for Kemp, although such support was relatively low among those who frequently watched televangelists.

One surprising result from this analysis is that evangelical identity is a somewhat stronger predictor of Robertson support than is charismatic/pentecostal identity. These two religious identities interacted in an additive fashion—those who selected both identities were far more supportive of Robertson than those who selected only one. This result is similar to that reported by Green and Guth (1988), who found that support for Robertson was higher among those who identified with three religious labels: fundamentalist, evangelical, and pen-

4. Unfortunately, Catholic respondents were not asked the born-again item or the evangelical- and charismatic-identification items. This omission creates a problem—because Catholics are missing on these variables, they would be excluded from any multivariate analysis. Therefore, I have performed the regression analysis and discriminant analysis twice: first with Catholics excluded, and second with them included, and assigned scores on these three items. Based on responses to other surveys, I have coded Catholics as having a score of .20 on the born-again item (i.e., that 20 percent of southern Catholics are born-again, a figure taken from the ANES Super Tuesday survey), a score of .14 on the charismatic identification item (a figure derived from responses of Catholics to the *Christianity Today* survey—thanks to Corwin Smidt), and .05 on the evangelical identification item (taken from responses to CBS News Super Tuesday exit polls).

TABLE 7.1
Support for Robertson in South Carolina
(Regression Results)

	Beta
Demographic Variables	
Age	−.11**
Sex	−.02
Education	−.02
Income	−.06
Black	.05
Religious Variables	
Pentecostal/charismatic identification	.14**
Evangelical identification	.15**
Watch televangelists	.17**
Member of 700 Club	.16**
Born-again	.01
Religiosity	.03
Political Variables	
Partisanship	−.01
Ideology	.08*
Economic attitudes	.02
Civil-rights attitudes	.02
Social issues	.24**
Foreign policy	−.12*
N	618
R^2	.33

Note: Entries are standardized regression coefficients
(betas). Political issue scales represent the relative salience
of these issues to vote choice.
*$p \le .05$
**$p \le .01$

tecostal. However, among those who selected only one label, evangelicals were slightly (but not significantly) more likely than charismatics
and pentecostals to support Robertson. Although this relationship is
not statistically significant, in the ANES Super Tuesday survey discussed below, those who attended evangelical churches were not warmer toward Robertson than other whites, whereas those who attended
pentecostal churches most emphatically were. The data do not permit
a detailed exploration of this finding. There is no measure of denominational affiliation in the survey, nor are there any measures of doctrine which would distinguish between pentecostals/charismatics and
evangelicals.[5]

5. I think it likely that those respondents who identified as both evangelicals

TABLE 7.2
Candidate Choice in South Carolina (Discriminant Analysis)

	Function 1 [a]	Function 2 [a]	Function 3 [a]
Social issues	−.60		
Evangelical identification	−.52		
Born-again	−.45		−.21
Charismatic identification	−.45		
Watch televangelists	−.43		.30
Member of 700 Club	−.41		
Religiosity	−.30		−.21
Education		.48	−.29
Foreign policy		−.42	−.34
Civil rights	−.25	−.29	
Economic attitudes		.29	
Age		−.26	
Partisanship			−.49
Ideology			−.44
Sex			.24

$N = 618$

Canonical Discriminant Functions Evaluated at Group Means

	Function 1	Function 2	Function 3
Bush	.26	−.27	−.05
Dole	.36	.40	.27
Kemp	−.03	.68	−.58
Robertson	−1.55	−.02	.08
Percentage correctly classified	49	Modal category	54
Bush	46	Sample probability	54
Dole	39	Sample probability	23
Kemp	59	Sample probability	8
Robertson	69	Sample probability	14

[a]Entries are total structure coefficients, which represent correlations between function and variable. Only correlations of at least .20 are shown. All scales and items are coded, so high scores represent more conservative responses.

and pentecostals/charismatics are pentecostals who express their doctrinal ortho-doxy through their additional identity and that those respondents who identify solely as charismatics/pentecostals are predominately charismatics in mainline Protestant churches. The data permit only an indirect test of this explanation: those who identify as *only* pentecostals or charismatics are significantly less likely than those who identify only as evangelicals or who identify as both to report a born-again experience. This hypothesis would explain the higher level of Robertson support among evangelicals—they were more supportive than mainline Protestant charismatics, but less supportive than pen-tecostals. Unfortunately, there is little data with which to test this theory.

SUPPORT FOR ROBERTSON IN THE SOUTH

The data from the ANES Super Tuesday survey contain several items that can be used to determine support for Robertson. Although the survey contains a measure of vote choice, I have not used this as a dependent variable. Nearly 20 percent of those contacted in the initial wave were not contacted during the postelection follow-up. The turnout rate for the sample was only 43 percent, and the proportion of those voting who cast a Republican ballot was only 42 percent. The net result is that only 231 whites voted in the Republican primary, less than 15 percent of white respondents to the first wave. Although I am interested in Robertson support among Republican primary voters, I am also interested in his support among those who voted in Democratic primaries or who did not vote. I have also not used items that asked respondents which of the candidates they would prefer to win each party's nominations, because preliminary analysis suggests that a few voters used strategic calculations in answering this question.[6] Instead, I base the analysis below on responses to feeling-thermometer items.

Respondents were asked in both the pre- and postelection surveys to rate all candidates on an imaginary-feeling thermometer, ranging from 0° to 100°. From these scores, I have created several dependent variables. I have adjusted these feeling thermometers in two ways: first by subtracting the average score assigned to all other Republican candidates from the Robertson feeling thermometer, and second by subtracting the mean score assigned to all other candidates, both Democrat and Republican. From these variables, I have constructed two other measures, which are the original measures dichotomized into support/nonsupport.[7] In addition, I have constructed a measure that indicates which Republican candidate still in the race was the most positively rated by each respondent.

Several items were included in both waves which asked respondents whether each candidate was decent, intelligent, compassionate, a strong leader, moral, caring, or inspiring. Factor analysis revealed that these items are strongly correlated and load on a single factor. A scale has been constructed from these items, measuring attitudes toward Robertson's character. Inspection of response patterns on items that

6. Specifically, those who were warmer toward a candidate who they believed was not likely to win were somewhat more likely to prefer that the nomination go to their second choice.
    7. As in earlier chapters, I have labeled those who rated Robertson at least 10° warmer than their individual means as supporters, and the rest of the respondents as nonsupporters.

measure candidate character suggested that some individuals rate the character of all candidates highly. I have consequently adjusted the Robertson character scale by subtracting from it the mean scores for identical scales for other Republican candidates.

The survey contained a number of items which measured political issues. Several scales were constructed from these items. Two scales were constructed to measure basic values. The first measured moral traditionalism, while the second measured basic equality values. Scales were constructed to measure attitudes toward current political issues, including foreign policy, economic policy, and social issues. In addition, three scales were constructed from items on spending priorities. Separate scales tapped support for spending on entitlement programs, military programs, and liberal programs, such as Welfare, job training, and environmental protection.

There were no doctrinal items in the survey which would allow separating pentecostals and charismatics from evangelicals and fundamentalists, nor were there any self-identification items. Those who attended pentecostal denominations were identified with a dummy variable (coded as 1 if the respondent attended a pentecostal church, and 0 if he or she did not), as were those who attended fundamentalist Baptist churches and the theologically divided Southern Baptist churches.[8] Both dummy variables identifying fundamentalists and pentecostals were highly skewed, suggesting that the relationships reported below may *understate* the strength of these relationships. The dummy variable for pentecostal denomination also understates the power of that relationship for a second reason. Because charismatic Christians are scattered among the mainline Protestant and Catholic churches, they are not included in the dummy variable for pentecostals. If it were possible to isolate them and combine them with pentecostals, the average level of Robertson support among nonpentecostals/noncharismatics would likely be smaller. Finally, an additional dummy variable was constructed to identify those who attended other evangelical churches.

Because religion and politics are connected in markedly different ways for whites and blacks, and because of the strong effects of partisanship and the Jesse Jackson candidacy on the attitudes of blacks, I examine the attitudes of blacks and whites separately.

---

8. The ANES contains an additional, ambiguous code for "other fundamentalists." The support for Robertson was high among the few respondents in this category. It seems likely that small pentecostal denominations are coded into this category, explaining this relationship.

KNOWLEDGE OF ROBERTSON

One of the most pressing tasks for presidential candidates is to become widely recognized by potential voters. Robertson achieved this goal to a reasonable extent. Among southern whites, nearly 75 percent were willing to assign Robertson a score on the feeling thermometer. Similar percentages were willing to evaluate Robertson's traits, such as intelligence, compassion, and decency. However, a closer look reveals that Robertson was not a well-known figure to most respondents. Approximately 60 percent of white respondents either were unable to label Robertson as a liberal or a conservative, or classified him as a liberal. Of those who were able to apply the ideology scale to Robertson, nearly one in four did not classify him as a conservative.

Respondents were asked how much they knew about each candidate. Slightly over one in four claimed that they knew "quite a lot" about Robertson, and an equal amount knew "a fair amount." Nearly one in four indicated that they knew nothing or almost nothing.

THE EFFECTS OF THE CAMPAIGN:
CHANGING SUPPORT FOR ROBERTSON

Because the first wave of the survey was conducted over several months, it is possible to examine the effects of campaign events on candidate evaluation. The first interviews were conducted prior to the Iowa caucuses, and the final interviews in the first wave occurred just prior to the balloting on Super Tuesday.

Despite the changing fortunes of the Robertson campaign, the relative preference among the four Republican candidates altered little over the course of the campaign. Relative affect for Robertson and evaluations of his character were also relatively constant across time, although there was a slight increase in support after his strong showing in Iowa, as well as a small decline after the spate of negative press. However, the campaign had little effect on candidate preferences.

RELIGION AND ROBERTSON'S SUPPORT

Although Robertson's constituency was composed of clearly doctrinally conservative Protestants, the Bush campaign publicly trumpeted exit-poll results that indicated that Bush defeated Robertson among born-again Christians. It seems likely that the fundamentalist-pentecostal dispute accounts for this result, with Robertson doing better among

TABLE 7.3
Religion and White Support for Robertson (ANES Super Tuesday Survey)

	Support/Republican (%)	Support/All (%)	First Republican (%)
Denomination			
Southern Baptist	21	25	8
Pentecostal	59	59	43
Fundamentalist	14	14	0
Evangelical church	20	23	10
Attend seldom	12	12	4
Attend frequently	23	27	11
Not orthodox doctrine	14	16	5
Orthodox doctrine	29	34	18
Attend frequently *and* orthodox	29	34	14
Other Protestant	16	17	11
Catholic	12	15	11
Catholic evangelical	33	33	17
Born-again	19	32	28
Bible inerrant	30	33	21
Attend church more than weekly	37	44	22
Total	18	18	11

Note: Percentage of white respondents supporting Robertson on each measure. Support/Republican indicates that respondent rated Robertson at least 10° warmer than the average for other Republican candidates. Support/All indicates that respondent rated Robertson at least 10° warmer than average for other white candidates, Democratic and Republican. First Republican indicates that Robertson is rated more warmly than other Republican candidates.

pentecostals, but less well among fundamentalists and "accommodating" evangelicals (Hunter 1983). Table 7.3 presents the relationship between religious variables and various measures of support for Robertson.

Although support was not linked with identification with evangelical, nonpentecostal denominations, it was highly associated with pentecostal churches, slightly higher among Southern Baptists, and much lower among fundamentalist Baptists. Kellstedt (1989) has argued that those seeking to identify evangelicals in survey data should use other measures, such as church attendance and doctrine, to eliminate "suspect" evangelicals. Among those other evangelicals who never or infrequently attended church services, support for Robertson was substantially lower than among the white public. However, among those who attended regularly, and among those who believe in the inerrancy of the Scriptures *and* report a born-again experience, support was substantially higher. But even among those evangelicals who both attend evangelical churches regularly and hold evangelical doctrinal beliefs, support for Robertson was lower than support for Bush. Only among those who attend pentecostal churches does support for Robertson slightly exceed support for Bush. Although Robertson had some appeal to Catholics, his support was lower among them than among other whites. However, among those white Catholics who accepted evangelical doctrinal tenets, Robertson's support was markedly higher.

SUPPORT FOR ROBERTSON:
MULTIVARIATE ANALYSIS

Multivariate analysis is needed to assess the independent impact of religious, political, and demographic variables on support for Robertson. Table 7.4 presents the results of separate regression equations for affect for Robertson relative to all white candidates and relative to Republican candidates, as well as the adjusted measure of evaluations of Robertson's character. The results of these three equations are remarkably consistent and reveal a pattern quite similar to that from the South Carolina survey. To facilitate comparisons across equations, table 7.4 presents the unstandardized regression coefficients, as well as their T values. Unlike the betas presented in other chapters, the unstandardized coefficients should not be compared within an equation. To determine which variables are the most important predictors in each equation, compare the T values. To determine how a given variable (e.g., religious doctrine) affects the three dependent variables, compare the unstandardized coefficients across the equations.

The sources of affect toward Robertson are firmly rooted in religion. Pentecostal denomination and orthodox doctrine are both significant predictors of affect toward Robertson, and Southern Baptists were significantly warmer than other whites, whereas members in fundamentalist Baptist churches were relatively more negative. Recall that the highly skewed nature of these two denominational dummy variables results in coefficients that understate the strength of the relationship. Catholics are significantly cooler toward Robertson relative to all candidates, but the relationship is not significant in the other two equations.

Among basic values, moral traditionalism is a significant predictor of affect, and, among political attitudes, only social issues emerges as a

TABLE 7.4
Affect for Robertson and Evaluations of His Character
(Regression Results)

	Affect/All		Affect/ Republican		Character/ Republican	
	B	T	B	T	B	T
Demographics						
Age	−.08	−1.50	−.05	−.98	−.01**	2.75
Sex	.76	.45	.90	.52	.11a	1.76
Education	−.91	−1.23	−.29	−.39	−.01	−.34
Income	−.49	−.86	−.26	−.45	.03	1.31
Married	−1.11	−.87	−1.20	−.62	.01	.08
Religion						
Southern Baptist	8.96*	2.39	7.23*	1.99	.23a	1.68
Pentecostal denomination	17.31**	3.20	13.33**	3.21	.40*	1.98
Fundamentalist denomination	−20.56	1.69	−21.26a	−1.68	−1.11*	1.97
Other evangelical denomination	−7.76**	−2.14	−6.47*	−1.97	−.14	1.00
Catholic	3.20	−1.40	−4.45*	−1.96	−.00	−.00
Doctrine	9.71**	4.10	11.79	4.99	.24	2.78
Church attendance	.35	.99	.32	.89	.00	.21
Political Attitudes						
Partisanship	.51	1.13	−.61	−1.35	−.02	−1.32
Idological identification	.88	1.32	.19	.29	.03	1.17
Social issues	5.86**	4.42	5.11**	4.91	.20**	5.06
Economic issues	−1.56	−1.52	−1.91	−1.84a	−.03	−.87
Foreign issues	.26	.31	.93	1.06	−.03	−.90
Spending entitlement	−.71	−.61	−.10	−.09	.06	1.30
Spending liberal	−1.62	−1.34	−1.12	−.92	.03	.63
Spending on Reagan defense	1.45a	1.68	.55	.67	.01	.24
Basic Values						
Moral traditionalism	2.52**	2.99	2.63**	3.10	.09*	2.75
Equality	.27	.30	.02	.02	−.03	−.87
Constant	−18.22a	−1.74	−16.42	−1.56	2.41**	5.63
N	787		787		780	
R^2	.27		.21		.16	

Note: Entries are unstandardized regression coefficients and T values for each variable. All scales are coded, so high scores indicate more conservative positions. Affect/All is Robertson affect relative to affect for all other white candidates. Affect/Republican is Robertson affect relative to other Republican candidates. Character/Republican is Robertson character relative to that of other Republican candidates.
[a]$p \leq .10$
*$p \leq .05$
**$p \leq .01$

significant predictor. No other demographic variables, political attitudes, or basic values are related to affect for Robertson.

The relationships in table 7.4 represent the sources of affective response to Robertson. That reaction was largely negative, so the relationships in this table represent the sources of negative as well as positive responses to the Robertson candidacy. Elsewhere (Wilcox 1990b), I have reported that the sources of negative and positive reactions for political groups are not always the same. To determine if this is the case with Robertson, I have estimated a series of three probit equations—two with the dichotomized affect measures of Robertson support relative to all white and Republican candidates, and one with a dichotomized measure of preference for Robertson among all Republican candidates. The results are presented in table 7.5.

The probit results provide further evidence that Robertson's support was strongly tied to religion. Again pentecostal denomination and doctrinal orthodoxy are significantly related to support, and again social-issue positions and moral traditionalism are alone among political attitudes and basic values in predicting support. Although those from fundamentalist denominations remain less supportive toward Robertson, in the probit equations these relationships fall far short of statistical significance. Fundamentalism, then, is associated with the degree of negative affect toward Robertson, but not with actual support. One demographic variable attains significance in these equations. Robertson's support came disproportionately from young southerners.

The relationships in the final equation, estimating preference for Robertson among all Republican candidates, are somewhat weaker. Pentecostal denomination and moral traditionalism fail to achieve conventional standards of statistical significance, although the directions of these relationships are all in the predicted direction. In this equation, evangelicals are somewhat less positive about Robertson's personality.

These results are not surprising and merely confirm the conventional wisdom that Robertson drew heavily from religious conservatives, primarily pentecostals and charismatics, who had traditional moral values and held conservative positions on social issues. What is somewhat surprising is that these are the only variables associated with support for Robertson. Despite his efforts to distance himself from his televangelist past, Robertson was unable to make headway among conservatives who focused on economic or foreign-policy issues.

One other surprising result is that partisanship is not a significant predictor of Robertson affect and support relative to *all* candidates, Democratic and Republican. Support for Robertson relative to all candidates was correlated with partisanship, but only strong Democrats

TABLE 7.5
Support for Robertson (Probit Results)

	Support/All		Support/ Republican		First Republican	
	MLE	*T*	*MLE*	*T*	*MLE*	*T*
Demographics						
Age	−.01ᵃ	−1.80	−.01*	−1.96	−.01*	−2.22
Sex	.00	.02	.04	.30	.07	.48
Education	−.01	−.19	−.00	−.00	−.12	−1.73ᵃ
Income	−.08	−1.61	−.07	−1.43	−.07	−1.16
Married	−.01	−.09	−.05	−.35	.11	.68
Religion						
Southern Baptist	.68*	2.23	.96**	3.07	1.10*	2.18
Pentecostal denomination	1.06**	2.89	1.08**	3.10	.47	1.37
Fundamentalist denomination	−3.33	−.25	−3.23	−.25	−2.33	−.18
Other evangelical denomination	−.55	−1.88	−.72	−2.38	−1.22*	−2.49
Catholic	−.23	−1.24	−.02	−.14	.18	.89
Doctrine	.56**	3.85	.55**	3.64	.56**	3.24
Church attendance	.04	1.52	.01	.40	.00	.03
Political Attitudes						
Partisanship	.04	1.26	.00	.04	−.01	−.18
Ideological identification	.03	.61	.02	.33	.07	1.23
Social issues	.32**	4.10	.25**	3.23	.35**	3.67
Economic issues	.04	.53	.06	.82	−.04	−.45
Foreign issues	.03	.44	.04	.61	.01	.14
Spending on entitlements	−.07	−.87	.01	.11	.05	.54
Spending on liberal programs	−.09	−1.03	.02	.21	−.15	1.50
Spending on Reagan defense	.06	1.02	.01	.09	.03	.53
Basic Values						
Moral traditionalism	.11*	1.85	.15**	2.42	.13ᵃ	1.74
Equality	.02	.34	−.04	−.63	.02	.28
N	788		788		788	

Note: Entries are unstandardized maximum likelihood estimates and *T* values for each variable. All scales are coded, so high scores indicate more conservative positions.
ᵃ$p \leq .10$
*$p \leq .05$
**$p \leq .01$

showed decreased levels of Robertson support. Across the partisan spectrum from weak Democrats to weak Republicans, a constant 16 percent of whites were relatively warm toward Robertson. This provides support for Robertson's claim that he was able to attract religiously conservative Democrats to his campaign.

Although only those who were able to rate Robertson on a feeling thermometer are included in these equations, respondents varied in their degree of knowledge about him. Additional equations were estimated, with knowledge of Robertson included as an additional independent variable. The direction of the relationship was consistently negative, with increased knowledge about Robertson leading to decreased support. However, only in the equation that measured relative evaluations of Robertson's character was this relationship statistically significant. Those white southerners who were most knowledgeable about Robertson were the least likely to rate his character favorably in comparison with other Republican candidates' characters.

THE DETERMINANTS OF CANDIDATE CHOICE: CHOOSING AMONG THE REPUBLICAN CANDIDATES

Although the information in tables 7.4 and 7.5 plainly reveals the sources of support for Robertson, it is not clear from these analyses how these sources differ from those for the other candidates. To examine the sources of support for the four Republican candidates remaining in the race on Super Tuesday, I have used discriminant analysis. Function 1 discriminates between supporters of Robertson and supporters of other candidates (especially Dole and Bush). Function 2 discriminates between supporters of Bush and supporters of other candidates (especially Dole). Finally, function 3 discriminates between supporters of Kemp and supporters of other candidates.

These results confirm the findings in tables 7.4 and 7.5 that the sources of Robertson's support were religious, with religion, conservative position on social issues, and moral traditionalism loading most strongly on the function that distinguishes Robertson supporters. There also were political differences between Robertson's supporters and supporters of other candidates. Robertson's supporters were more conservative, more favorable toward general equality, and less willing to support spending on liberal programs, such as environmental protection and education. They were somewhat less conservative on foreign policy and defense spending than supporters of other Republican candidates, and somewhat more likely to be Democrats.

It is interesting that Robertson's supporters are more supportive of general equality. Robertson ran a campaign that had as a minor theme equality of opportunity, though Kemp sounded this theme louder and more consistently. The most surprising result is that Robertson's supporters were slightly more liberal on foreign policy and defense spending than other Republicans. In bivariate analysis, Robertson's supporters were markedly more conservative than supporters of Bush, Dole, or Kemp on these issues. Note also that Robertson's loading on factor 2 partially counters the correlation on factor 1. We shall see in the next chapter that activists in the Robertson campaign were also more supportive of defense spending and hard-line, anti-Communist foreign policy.

The variables that distinguished between Bush supporters and supporters of other candidates (particularly Dole) were foreign policy, defense spending, economic issues, age, evangelical denomination, sex, and partisanship. Compared with Dole backers, Bush supporters came from those who took more moderate positions on foreign policy and defense spending and more conservative positions on economic issues, from men, from Democrats and Independents, and from members of evangelical churches, not pentecostal ones.

Compared to supporters of other candidates, Kemp supporters were more likely to call themselves conservatives, more supportive of economic programs to benefit the disadvantaged, more likely to voice support for societal equality, more conservative on foreign policy, and less conservative on spending on entitlement programs. They were also somewhat wealthier than supporters of other candidates. This interesting profile of supporters of "equal opportunity Republicanism" shows that citizens responded to the differing messages of these four candidates.

ROBERTSON AND POLITICAL MOBILIZATION

One of the frequent claims of the Moral Majority spokesmen was that they had mobilized previously apolitical fundamentalists and evangelicals into political action. Some observers credited the Moral Majority voter-registration drives, particularly in the South, with widespread success. The Robertson campaign also claimed to have registered and mobilized new voters into politics, and newspaper accounts of Robertson activists, especially in caucus states, appeared to confirm their claims.

The ANES Super Tuesday survey did not contain items that asked respondents about their previous electoral participation. Those white respondents who preferred Robertson to all other candidates did claim to vote at a rate somewhat higher than that of other whites (60 percent versus 55 percent). Because Robertson supporters were comparatively less well educated and younger than other whites, I have adjusted these figures for age, age squared, education, income, and marital status. Adjusting for these covariates increased the reported turnout gap between Robertson supporters and other whites somewhat (62 percent to 54 percent). These data suggest that Robertson's supporters voted more frequently than others who shared their demographic profile.

This provides some tentative support for the claims of his campaign to have mobilized a silent army of previously apolitical supporters.

Analysis of the results of network exit polls, however, suggests that Robertson's voters were no more likely than other Republican primary voters to be casting their first ballot. Taken with the evidence above, this suggests that Robertson may have had more success in encouraging those who had rarely voted or who had not previously voted in primaries or caucuses, but that he did not succeed in encouraging those who had never voted to take their first political steps.

ROBERTSON AND BLACKS

Although most studies of support for the Christian Right have limited their analyses to whites, assuming that they constituted the target constituency (Shupe and Stacey 1983; Buell and Sigelman 1985; Wilcox 1987c), blacks are more likely than whites to hold conservative religious beliefs and to exhibit higher levels of public and private religiosity. Among respondents to the ANES Super Tuesday survey, blacks were significantly more likely than whites to report a born-again experience (72 percent to 50 percent), to believe in the inerrancy of the Scriptures (70 percent to 38 percent), and to attend church regularly (19 percent to 12 percent). Blacks were also more likely to take consistently conservative positions on social issues (24 percent to 7 percent).

This high degree of orthodox black religiosity suggests that there is a potential constituency for the New Christian Right among black Americans. Robertson was aware of this constituency. During his days on the television show the "700 Club," Robertson's cohost was black. His campaign actively reached out to blacks, holding rallies in black churches in some southern states.

Previous research suggests that blacks in Washington, D.C., showed a fair degree of support for Robertson prior to Super Tuesday (Wilcox 1990a). In that study, support for Robertson was correlated with religiosity, exposure to televangelists, born-again status, charismatic experiences, and conservative religious identities, although in multivariate analysis only religiosity and exposure to televangelists proved significant predictors. However, the vast majority of black supporters of Robertson in Washington, D.C., knew little about his political positions.

Among black respondents to the ANES Super Tuesday survey, knowledge of Robertson was again not widespread. Slightly more than one-half of black respondents were able to rate Robertson on a feeling thermometer, and one-third claimed to know at least a "fair amount"

TABLE 7.6
Preference among Republican Candidates (Discriminant Analysis)

	Function 1 [a]	Function 2 [a]	Function 3 [a]
Doctrine	.66		
Social issues	.64		
Moral traditionalism	.51		
Pentecostal denomination	.38	.29	
Ideology	.37		.30
Equality	−.33		−.20
Spending on liberal programs	.28		
Education	−.23		
Foreign issues	−.27	.59	−.35
Spending on Reagan defense	−.32	.66	
Partisanship	−.28	.51	
Age		.25	
Evangelical denomination		−.21	
Attendance	.30	−.30	−.39
Economic issues		.23	.36
Sex			.34
Spending entitlement			.22
Income			−.25

Canonical Discriminant Functions Evaluated at Group Means

	Function 1	Function 2	Function 3
Robertson	1.41	.15	.15
Bush	−.01	−.33	.05
Dole	−.46	.30	.05
Kemp	.25	.10	−.86
Percentage correctly classified	49	Modal category	45
Robertson	65	Sample probability	11
Bush	44	Sample probability	45
Dole	52	Sample probability	37
Kemp	47	Sample probability	7

[a]Entries are total structure coefficients, which represent correlations between function and variable. Only correlations of at least .20 are shown. All scales and items are coded, so high scores represent more conservative responses.

about Robertson. Of those who claimed this level of knowledge, one-half did not know that he was a conservative.

Blacks who were able to rate Robertson were more supportive than whites. Three in ten supported Robertson relative to all candidates, and one in three were warm relative to Republican candidates. More than one in four rated him as their first choice among Republican contenders.

TABLE 7.7
Black Support for Robertson (Correlation)

	Support/All	Support/Republican	First Republican
Pentecostal denomination	.05	.13	.07
	(.19**)	(.20**)	(.19**)
Evangelical denomination	.14*	.02	−.00
	(.08**)	(.06)*	(−.01)
Fundamentalist denomination	.07	.05	.03
	(−.01)	(−.01)	(−.02)
Southern Baptist	.15*	.04	.00
	(.09**)	(.05*)	(−.00)
Born-again	.03	.10	−.08
	(.30**)	(.28**)	(.22**)
Bible	−.00	.01	.06
	(.28**)	(.24**)	(.20)**
Church attendance	−.03	−.15	−.19*
	(.22**)	(.17**)	(.15**)
Social issues	.17*	.24**	.20*
	(.28**)	(.25**)	(.24**)
Moral traditionalism	.04	.07	.02
	(.25**)	(.23**)	(.21**)
Know Robertson	−.05	−.05	−.42**
	(.01)	(−.03)	(−.18**)

Note: Entries are Pearson product-moment correlations. Parenthesized entries are comparable correlations for whites.
$*p \leq .05$
$**p \leq .01$

Because of the small number of blacks who were able to evaluate Robertson, multivariate analysis is suspect—as missing data on other variables comes into play, the number of cases becomes distressingly small. Table 7.7 presents the correlations between a number of variables and the three measures of support for Robertson. The coefficients in the table are Pearson's r correlations, with the corresponding figure for whites in parentheses below.

Few of the religious variables that predict support for Robertson among whites are significant among blacks. Although there are many fewer blacks (94) than whites (1,108) in this table, the differences are not solely due to smaller sample sizes: the size of the coefficients for blacks is generally small, and in some cases the direction is reversed.

Only social-issue conservatism emerges as a consistent predictor. *In*fre-quent church attendance is associated with greater support for Robertson among blacks—a surprising reversal of the direction of the relationship among whites. It is possible that those who attend infre-quently are among the most likely to watch religious television and therefore to be exposed to Robertson's program. Lack of knowledge of Robertson is the strongest correlate of Robertson preference.

SUMMARY

This analysis has suggested that Robertson's support in the South was confined to those who shared his religious, moral, and social-issue positions. Although Robertson tried to distance himself from his tele-vangelist past, he does not appear to have succeeded. No other political issues predict Robertson support. However, his campaign may have reached its greatest possible support, for increasing knowledge of Robertson was associated with decreased support.

Religious differences may have limited Robertson's support. Al-though Robertson received strong support from those who attended pentecostal churches, his support among evangelicals was not signifi-cantly higher than that among other whites. His support among Catholics was slightly lower than among others, and his support among fundamentalists was far lower still. Although fundamentalists and most evangelicals shared with the pentecostals the belief in the authori-ty of the Scriptures, in the born-again experience, and a conservative outlook on social issues and moral values, religious doctrine appears to have prevented them from supporting Robertson.

ROBERTSON SUPPORT IN OTHER SURVEYS

It is possible that the sources of Robertson's support among those who actually voted might differ from the sources of his support among the general public or among likely voters. Detailed analysis of data from the CBS and ABC Super Tuesday exit polls suggests that this is not the case. These studies revealed that the sources of Robertson support among the primary and caucus electorate were confined to religious variables, moral traditionalism, and social issues.

With the large samples of the ABC and CBS Super Tuesday exit polls (over fourteen thousand cases for each data file), small relation-ships achieve statistical significance. Some modest but statistically sig-nificant relationships from analyses of these studies suggest that

Robertson did better than most other Republicans among black voters (though Kemp did even better), young voters, women, and those with lower levels of education. He did less well among working women. In other surveys, he did somewhat better among Democrats voting in Republican primaries and caucuses. Evidence from the ABC Super Tuesday tracking polls suggested that Robertson's support among blacks and among young voters increased over time. However, it is important to remember that these relationships were relatively weak and were statistically significant only in large, pooled sets of exit polls.

These surveys suggest that Robertson's voters were not disproportionately first-time voters, however. In none of the surveys were Robertson's voters significantly more likely than voters for other Republican candidates to be casting their first ballot. These results do not necessarily contradict the findings above that Robertson's supporters turned out at a rate greater than predicted by their demographic variables. Robertson voters may have been either erratic voters in the past or recently mobilized voters, but there were not new voters.

CONCLUSIONS

Although Robertson attempted to expand his base by denying his televangelist past many times before the southern rooster crowed, his support never expanded beyond his narrow base. His support was highest among those who attended pentecostal churches and other evangelicals who believed in biblical inerrancy and reported a born-again experience. The political sources of his support were limited to social issues and to basic moral traditionalism. Robertson's base was exceedingly narrow.

Even in this base, Robertson's support was not overwhelming. Among those respondents to the ANES Super Tuesday survey who attended pentecostal churches *and* were born-again *and* believed in the inerrancy of the Scriptures, Robertson was preferred to Bush 45 percent to 40 percent. Among those very few white southerners who met this religious test and were conservative on social issues and moral values, Robertson was preferred by 50 percent to 35 percent.

Religious doctrine seemed to play a role in limiting Robertson's support. Catholics were somewhat less supportive of Robertson than Protestants. Those who attended fundamentalist Baptist churches— the core base of the Moral Majority—were less supportive of Robertson than other whites. Among those who attended evangelical, nonfundamentalist, and nonpentecostal churches, support was about the same level as other whites. However, those who identified themselves as evangelicals, and those evangelicals who held orthodox theological views and attended church regularly, were more supportive.

CHAPTER 8

Elites in the Charismatic Right: Contributors to and Delegates for Robertson

By one standard, Robertson's presidential campaign was a colossal failure. Although he spent as much as Bush and Dole, he won only thirty-five pledged delegates. His only victories came in low-turnout caucus states, and, although the media made much of his supposed strength in the South, he lost badly even in states where he outspent Bush by at least three to one. With the sole exception of the 1976 campaign of John Connally, no recent presidential nomination campaign has been so comparatively well funded, yet secured so few delegates.

By another standard, however, Robertson's campaign was surprisingly successful. The opposition was formidable, including the sitting vice-president and former Senate majority leader, as well as a popular conservative congressman. Bush, Dole, and Kemp (and, to a lesser extent, Du Pont) could count on a circle of influential supporters who could help raise money and mobilize their political machines to help their favored candidates. Robertson could count on no such advantages. Despite these long odds, he managed to raise as much money as Bush and Dole and to win caucuses in Washington and such scattered states as Hawaii and Alaska, and probably Michigan's first balloting. Although he lost all of the Super Tuesday southern primaries, he did almost as well as Dole.

Moreover, Robertson's thirty-five official delegates understate his presence at the national and statewide Republican conventions. Although many southern states had rules that pledged delegates to Bush, they selected these delegates separately through caucuses. In many southern states, Robertson won delegates to the national convention, even though the delegates were pledged to vote for Bush. More importantly, his campaign was successful in winning control of several state Republican party committees and in building a strong presence in many others. In Virginia (Robertson's home state), Bush handily won the primary election on 8 March, but many Robertson supporters were able to win slots to the national convention. McGlennon (1989) reports that, among the Virginia GOP delegates, 41 percent preferred Bush and 38 percent supported Robertson. In Michigan, although many Robertson supporters eventually boycotted the state convention, others attended it and fought for a continuing presence of New Christian Right supporters in Michigan Republican politics.

This chapter discusses activists in the Robertson campaign. Chapter 6 demonstrated that activists in the Christian Anti-Communism Crusade and the Moral Majority were different from passive supporters of those groups, and the same is true for Robertson. More importantly, Robertson's activists are quite different from other Republican activists, and they constitute a major split within Republican party ranks.

The discussion is divided into two sections. The first contrasts political elites who contributed to Robertson to those who gave to other Republican candidates. The second compares those delegates to the 1988 GOP National Convention who supported Robertson (regardless of their pledged vote) to those who supported other candidates.

ROBERTSON'S EARLY BACKERS: CAMPAIGN CONTRIBUTORS

The data for this section come from a mail survey of contributors to Republican and Democratic prenomination presidential candidates, conducted between December 1988 and May 1990. The survey resulted in 1,265 valid surveys, which represents a return rate of 36 percent.[1] The survey contained an oversample of Robertson contribu-

1. The data were collected in collaboration with Clifford Brown of Union College and Lynda Powell of the University of Rochester. The survey was funded in part by a grant from the Society for the Scientific Study of Religion and by two research grants from Union College.

Our sample was drawn from paper reports filed with the Federal Elections Commission, which list all contributors who gave more than two hundred dollars to the campaign. Because those who gave more than once have a greater probability of being sampled, I have weighted the data. For the multivariate analysis, I have also weighted the data to reflect the proportion of contributors to each candidate.

tors, which received a slightly different questionnaire with additional items on religious orientations.

Green and Guth (1988) studied early contributors to Robertson's Political Action Committee (PAC) and compared them to contributors to other presidential PACs and to contributors to party committees. My survey differs from that of Green and Guth in two important ways. First, the sample is drawn from individuals who gave to Robertson's presidential committee at any time during the campaign, and not merely from those who gave early to his PAC. The sample therefore includes those who gave relatively late in the campaign and those who gave early to Robertson's PAC. This distinction is important: Green and Guth sampled primarily those strong Robertson supporters who were sufficiently politically astute to be aware of Robertson's presidential efforts before his formal campaign. These data doubtlessly include some of those early contributors (who could legally give again to Robertson's presidential campaign), but also include those who gave to the campaign in March, when Robertson was often visible on national television. It is likely that Green and Guth's sample constitutes a more sophisticated political elite than the sample in this chapter.

A second difference in our samples is also important. Green and Guth sampled those who had contributed at least $500 to Robertson's PAC, to other presidential PACs, or to Republican committees, whereas I sampled those whose contributions throughout the primary season to Robertson's campaign totaled at least $200. Many Robertson contributors pledged $19.88 per month to join the 1988 Club, and these small contributors are doubtlessly less wealthy than those who are able to give $500. The inclusion of these smaller contributors is especially important in the case of Robertson, who received 90 percent of his money in contributions of less than $500. This figure is far larger than for other Republican presidential candidates: Kemp received 68 percent of his funds in these smaller contributions, Du Pont received 45 percent, Dole received 36 percent, and Bush received 22 percent.

Robertson's Activists and the GOP: A Religious Insurgency

How do contributors to Robertson's campaign differ from those who gave to the campaigns of other Republicans? Table 8.1 provides the bivariate differences. Predictably, campaign contributors to Robertson (as to other candidates) are a well-educated, wealthy elite. Nonetheless, there are interesting demographic differences between Robertson contributors and those who gave to other Republicans. Robertson contributors are more likely to be women, to have no more than a college education, to have incomes less than $250,000 a year, and to come from

TABLE 8.1
Republican Presidential Campaign Contributors:
Demographics and Religious Attributes (Bivariate Results)

	Robertson (%)	Kemp (%)	Bush (%)	Dole (%)	Du Pont (%)
Demographics					
Male	62	66	75	87	82
More than college education	35	54	50	58	50
Income ≥ $250,000	3	27	43	55	29
Less than 40 years old	19	20	11	8	25
Live in South/border states	58	29	41	22	10
Religion					
Episcopal/Presbyterian	10	22	35	27	39
Baptist	6	9	2	4	0
Pentecostal/Holiness	19	0	0	0	0
Nondenominational	26	4	0	2	4
Catholic	5	19	20	22	19
Jewish	0	5	9	17	5
Atheist/agnostic/none	2	15	8	7	9
Bible literally true	71	14	9	1	13
Attend church more than weekly	48	10	11	11	3
Identify as fundamentalist	42	11	4	2	1
Evangelical	55	10	4	9	7
Charismatic	63	0	0	1	1
Born-again Christian	79	14	5	9	7
Mainline Christian	10	13	29	19	12
Liberal Christian	0	6	7	14	14
Agnostic/atheist	0	10	5	10	6
Religion very important in candidate choice	86	33	14	20	13
attitudes toward					
Abortion	97				
Death penalty	89				
Budget deficit	65				
Détente with Soviet Union	68				
Watch religious T.V.					
Never	29				
3 or more hrs. weekly	39				
Watched "700 Club"	93				
Contributed to "700 Club"	85				
Christians can disagree on meaning of Bible	66				
State should assure teacher competence in religious schools	55				
Strongly agree—U.S. laws should be consistent with Bible	66				

Note: Percentage of contributors to each candidate in each cell. Final items asked only in oversample of Robertson contributors.

southern and border states. Unlike contributors to some other candidates, Robertson's contributors were not disproportionately home-state givers, but were scattered throughout the South and border states.

Not surprisingly, there are important differences in religious variables as well. Robertson contributors were much more likely than other contributors to relate their religious beliefs to candidate selection, to believe that the Bible is literally true, to attend church more than weekly, and to identify as a fundamentalist, an evangelical, a charismatic, and/or a born-again Christian. Nearly one-third identified as a fundamentalist, an evangelical, *and* a charismatic, with another one-third identifying as either a charismatic only or as a charismatic and an evangelical. Nearly all Robertson contributors who identified as fundamentalists also identified as charismatics and evangelicals.

Many Robertson contributors received a special survey that contained a few additional religious items, which are also shown in table 8.1. Large majorities reported that their religious beliefs influenced their political views on matters such as abortion, the death penalty, the budget deficit, and détente with the Soviet Union.

In some ways, Robertson supporters defy common stereotypes. Fully 66 percent believed that Christians can disagree about what the Bible means. Although most supporters believe the Bible is literally true, they allow for conflicting interpretations of biblical passages. Moreover, a plurality of Robertson contributors believed that states should certify Christian schoolteachers, despite the public pronouncements on this issue by many Christian Right groups.

Most interesting is the connection with Robertson's "700 Club" television program. More than 70 percent reported watching religious television weekly, and an overwhelming majority have watched the "700 Club" at some time, with more than one-third reporting that they watched frequently. Fully 85 percent of Robertson contributors have contributed to the program, with more than one-half classifying themselves as frequent givers. These data indicate that Robertson solicited contributions from his "700 Club" direct-mail lists for his presidential campaign.

Robertson contributors were also distinctive in their political beliefs. They were more conservative than other contributors on nearly every issue, including some issues (e.g., the gold standard and taxes) that were sounded by other candidates. Robertson contributors are especially distinctive on national health insurance, spending on education, the gold standard, Contra aid, defense spending, détente with the Soviet Union, pledging allegiance to the flag, school prayer, pornography, women's roles, and abortion—issues that include economic policy, foreign policy, and (of course) social matters.

TABLE 8.2
Republican Presidential Campaign Contributors:
Political Attitudes (Bivariate Results)

	Robertson (%)	Kemp (%)	Bush (%)	Dole (%)	Du Pont (%)
Political Attitudes					
Extremely conservative	25	12	3	1	7
Extremely conservative on					
Economic policy	25	22	10	6	11
Defense policy	25	20	8	3	9
Social issues	68	26	8	6	11
Strongly Agree					
Budget deficit is top priority	64	63	51	61	63
Do not raise taxes	61	60	34	24	37
Free trade is important	21	14	33	11	21
Return to gold standard	35	23	3	7	5
No national health insurance	46	16	22	9	6
Childcare not government responsibility	58	46	22	25	26
Do not reduce defense spending	28	27	15	9	4
Continue Contra aid	57	37	31	31	27
Business has right to drug tests	61	52	46	26	57
Mandatory death for murder	58	54	44	37	44
Require students and teachers to pledge allegiance	82	69	46	39	51
Mandatory school prayer	43	13	7	2	12
Regulate adults reading pornography	55	12	8	3	15
Prohibit abortion	85	25	10	21	5
Conservative Position on					
Affirmative action for blacks	58	71	45	46	55
Government job guarantees	81	87	68	83	65
Ordered society ≥ freedom	35	23	22	27	29
Defense spending	51	39	31	38	28
Détente	72	54	25	44	28
Women's role in society	49	20	12	9	15
Government untrustworthy	28	17	11	23	23
Country run for the few	47	37	20	31	33

Note: Percentage of contributors to each candidate taking conservative positions on each issue.

The surprising support among Robertson contributors for the gold standard provides some indirect support for Wald's (1989b) contention that Christian Right supporters are distinguished by a cognitive style that prefers judgments by authority and absolute standards. For those who regard the Bible as an absolute moral standard, there may be a certain attraction to absolute standards in other domains as well.

What emerges from these data is that, although Robertson contributors are especially distinctive in their social-issue attitudes, they are more conservative than most other contributors on other issues as well. This distinctiveness is evident in the responses to a series of three items which asked contributors to place themselves on seven-point liberal-conservative scales. Robertson contributors were more likely than those who gave to other candidates to consider themselves "extremely conservative" on economic, defense, and social issues, and the social-issue differences are largest.

These data suggest that Robertson supporters may constitute an insurgent force within Republican politics which may not be readily integrated into existing party coalitions. Table 8.3 provides additional evidence for this point. The figures in this table are adjusted feeling thermometers toward political and social groups and toward political figures. These data suggest that group affect is an important part of the difference between Robertson's Republicans and the party mainstream. Robertson contributors stand out as the only supporters of the Moral Majority and of the National Rifle Association, as well as the most ideologically polarized—rating conservatives a full 79 points higher than liberals. Robertson's supporters were the coolest of Republican contributors toward civil-rights leaders, feminists, and the American Civil Liberties Union. These data suggest a symbolic politics explanation of support for Robertson, although I prefer the more parsimonious interpretation that Christian Right supporters dislike their political opponents.

Although Christian Right contributors are somewhat quicker than the passive supporters of the Christian Right to perceive the ideological shift in the Supreme Court, Robertson supporters remain less positive toward the court than other Republican contributors. Moreover, Robertson supporters are less concerned than other Republican contributors with the traditional economic cleavage, for they are the least positive toward big business, and among the least negative toward unions.

The data on partisan affect show that Robertson contributors are politically polarized as well. They are enthusiastic Republicans who rate Republicans higher than contributors to other Republican candidates, while rating Democrats more coolly. Robertson did not attract contributions from Democrats: Du Pont, Dole, and Bush all had

TABLE 8.3
Republican Presidential Campaign Contributors:
Political and Social Affect (Bivariate Results)

	Robertson[a]	Kemp[a]	Bush[a]	Dole[a]	Du Pont[a]
Adjusted Affect Toward					
Moral Majority	34	−5	−8	−13	−11
NRA	11	3	−0	−8	−7
Conservatives	44	36	26	26	20
Big business	11	17	20	17	13
Supreme Court	12	28	30	32	30
Labor unions	−12	−18	−12	−15	−6
A.C.L.U.	−35	−16	−17	−4	−13
Liberals	−29	−22	−16	−13	−8
Feminists	−33	−12	−10	−7	−3
Civil-rights leaders	−11	−9	−5	−4	−2
Republicans	37	37	31	28	23
Democrats	−18	−14	−10	−10	−5
Bush	42	44	45	40	38
Dole	30	30	26	32	21
Kemp	33	42	23	16	14
Du Pont	14	20	13	16	36
Robertson	49	4	−13	−10	−15
Percentage rated Robertson at 0°	0	12	19	13	18
Percentage rated Robertson lower than					
Dukakis	1	14	35	30	47
Jackson	1	16	27	34	33

Note: Percentage of contributors to each candidate who rated Robertson in manner described.
[a]Entries represent degrees on feeling thermometers above or below each respondent's personal mean for social groups.

higher percentages of Democratic contributors than Robertson, and Robertson, Kemp, and Bush all had equally high proportions of strong Republicans among their contributors, far more than Dole or Du Pont.

Robertson's contributors rated the other Republican candidates warmly, but this positive regard was not reciprocated. Republican contributors to Bush, Dole, or Du Pont were markedly cool toward Robertson, and Kemp's contributors were at best neutral. These data confirm the comments of one Virginia Robertson activist in 1988, who noted that mainstream Republicans "really don't want us in this party. We are not welcome."

The depths of the antagonism that the old-line Republicans feel toward the Robertson insurgency is seen in the data at the bottom of this table. Between 10 percent and 20 percent of contributors to the other Republican candidates rated Robertson at 0°, the most negative possible score. Fully one-third of Bush contributors and nearly one-half of Du Pont contributors rated Robertson less favorably than they rated Dukakis. Even among Kemp delegates, a sizable minority were openly hostile to Robertson and rated Dukakis more warmly. Even more surprisingly, nearly one-third of contributors to Bush, Dole, and Du Pont rated Jackson higher than Robertson.

Robertson's Recent Republicans

The data presented above show that Robertson contributors are distinct from other Republicans. They are more consistently conservative, and they are quite different in cultural, religious, and moral values and attitudes. The Republican party does not seem to welcome their presence, yet they are enthusiastic in their affect for the party and its candidates.

This enthusiasm is that of the recent convert. Although my survey contained no items to determine exactly how long Robertson's contributors had been active in Republican politics, table 8.4 suggests that they are not longtime Republican activists. Of those who reported voting in 1976, fully one-third had voted for Carter. They had switched en masse to support Reagan in 1980 and 1984, and they stayed with Bush in 1988. These data do not tell us whether the Carter vote was motivated by his status as a born-again Southern Baptist or whether it represented a longstanding Democratic partisanship. The data do indicate that Robertson Republicans have not been longstanding loyalists to the party.

A series of questions asked respondents how often in the past they had contributed to various types of political candidates, and a small minority of Robertson contributors indicated previous contribution activity. Although over one-half of the contributors to Bush, Dole, and Kemp had contributed in most previous presidential elections, only 25 percent of Robertson contributors had done so. Robertson Republicans were similarly less likely to have contributed to Senate, House, or local candidates on a regular basis in the past.

Taken together, the data on past votes and past contributions suggest that at least some of Robertson's contributors have been drawn to the Republican party in the past decade. This reinforces the conclusion in chapter 7 that at least some of Robertson's support in the mass public came from Democrats or recently converted Republicans.

Table 8.4 also shows responses to questions asking about other

TABLE 8.4
Republican Presidential Campaign Contributors:
Political Involvement and Behavior (Bivariate Results)

	Robertson (%)	Kemp (%)	Bush (%)	Dole (%)	Du Pont (%)
Political Activity					
Worked in informal groups	43	26	28	26	17
Worked in formal groups	32	35	35	33	31
Worked in party	27	41	35	15	26
Wrote policymaker	71	63	46	51	53
Spoke to policymaker	22	32	33	26	35
Spoke to staff of policymaker	35	31	31	35	44
Demonstrated	13	3	3	1	6
Helped form new group	44	36	48	39	32
Party position	13	21	18	8	12
Elected office	1	12	11	2	7
Appointed office	6	16	22	10	14
In Most Elections, Have					
Contributed to pres. candidate	25	54	66	62	34
Contributed to Senate candi-date	11	24	55	44	43
Contributed to local candidate	8	30	55	46	37
Worked for pres. candidate	5	11	21	3	8
Worked for local candidate	5	8	19	8	17
Two-Party Vote					
Voted for Ford in 1976	67	92	91	83	86
Voted for Reagan in 1980	93	99	93	93	95
Voted for Reagan in 1984	97	99	95	92	91
Voted for Bush in 1988	97	99	98	93	91

Note: Percentage of those who contributed to each candidate which falls into each category.

types of political participation. These data show that Robertson's contributors are less well connected to the political machinery. They are less likely than other sets of contributors to hold party, elected, or appointed office. They are less likely than contributors to any other candidate to have personal contacts with policymakers and are less likely than many others to work within the party. However, they are more likely to have worked in informal political groups, to have written letters to policymakers, and to have participated in demonstrations. Although the differences in this table are not especially large, they suggest that, when Bush contributors want to voice their opinion, they call their congressman or other policymaker personally. When

Robertson's contributors seek to express their viewpoint, they write letters, organize citizen groups, or demonstrate.

These differences in political activity are mirrored in data on contribution behavior in table 8.5. Robertson's contributors were less likely during the 1987–88 election cycle to contribute to Senate or House candidates or to PACs than those who gave to other candidates.

The table also presents information on how the first contribution by each contributor was solicited, as well as what motivated the donation. The data show that Robertson and Kemp relied on direct-mail appeals, whereas Bush, Dole, and Du Pont used networks of solicitors who asked personal friends to contribute. Interestingly, Robertson is unique in having a significant proportion of his contributors initially solicited personally by a stranger. This may involve solicitation by activists through church networks.

There are also important differences in the motivations for giving.

TABLE 8.5
Contribution Behavior in 1988 (Bivariate Results)

	Robertson (%)	Kemp (%)	Bush (%)	Dole (%)	Du Pont (%)
Method of Original Solicitation					
Asked by personal friend	18	28	61	57	40
Asked by stranger	12	1	4	1	0
Mail request, friend	19	15	13	12	22
Mail request, stranger	39	41	16	24	28
Motivations for Giving					
Factor very important					
Friendship with candidate	20	18	39	35	49
Influence policy	59	48	39	30	41
Expected of my position	4	5	10	10	1
Social contacts	2	2	8	6	13
Personal recognition	1	2	3	8	3
Community obligation	29	29	28	30	32
Affect election outcome	70	61	44	32	46
Business reasons	3	17	19	15	4
Gave to both parties	0	5	7	7	5
Solicited from others	19	28	38	12	22
Gave to PACs in 1987–88	44	60	40	79	39
Gave to party committees	51	55	72	41	43
Gave to Senate candidates	23	51	53	42	49
Gave to House candidates	24	33	47	33	47
out of state	5	22	20	27	17

Note: Percentage of each group which falls into each category.

Respondents were allowed multiple responses to these items, so the totals do not sum to 100. Note that Robertson (and, to a lesser extent, Kemp) contributors were more likely to be motivated by a desire to influence policy or to affect the election outcome. Robertson contributors were also much less likely to list a business reason for their contribution.

Multivariate Analysis

The analysis above suggests that Robertson contributors are distinct from other Republican contributors in many ways. To determine which are the most important differences, I performed discriminant analysis. Table 8.6 shows the results. Four statistically significant functions correctly predict 84 percent of the cases and predict fully 97 percent of Robertson contributors. The first function accounts for 75 percent of the variance, and it discriminates between those who gave to Robertson and those who gave to other Republican candidates. The importance of this function suggests that the split between Christian Right and old-line Republicans is by far the most salient. I present only those variables with at least a .20 correlation with the discriminant function.

Robertson's support among political contributors was strongly motivated by religion, and religious attributes and attitudes on religious and moral issues dominate the function. The variable with the highest correlation with the function is charismatic identity, followed by born-again identity. Evangelical and fundamentalist identities also load on this function, as do affect toward the Moral Majority, the connection between religion and politics, interpretation of the Bible, and church attendance. Narrowly missing the .20 cutoff were pentecostal denomination and nondenominational churches.

Social issues are also important. Abortion, pornography, and women's roles are all correlated with support for Robertson. Among other issues, only détente and the gold standard are strong predictors of support for Robertson. Negative affect toward feminists, the American Civil Liberties Union, and the Supreme Court and positive affect toward conservatives are also predictors.

The second function predicts support for Du Pont. Compared with other Republican contributors, Du Pont contributors were less orthodox in their view of the Bible, less likely to attend church regularly, more liberal on abortion, school prayer, and social issues in general, and more likely to call themselves moderates on economic issues. They were less supportive of national health insurance, but warmer toward unions.

The third function distinguishes Dole contributors from all oth-

TABLE 8.6
Candidate Choice among Republican Contributors
(Discriminant Analysis)

	Function 1[a]	Function 2[a]	Function 3[a]	Function 4[a]
Charismatic identity	.49			
Born-again identity	.44			
Abortion attitude	.38	−.25		
Affect, Moral Majority	.37			
Salience of religion to candidate choice	.37	−.23		
Interpretation of Bible	.36	−.27		
Evangelical identity	.35			
Pornography attitude	.32			
Income	−.28			
Affect, feminists	−.27			
Affect, A.C.L.U.	−.27			
Gold standard	.24			.22
Détente	.23		.21	
Women's role	.22			
Fundamentalist identity	.22			
Affect, conservatives	.21			
Affect, Supreme Court	−.20			
Conservative self-placement, social issues	.33	−.39		
Affect, Republicans		−.34		
Church attendance	.30	−.32	.20	
Health insurance		.28		−.22
Contra aid		−.27		
School prayer		−.24		
Personal contact with policymakers		.23		
Affect, labor unions		.22		
Conservative self-placement, economic issues		−.21		
Conservative self-placement, general		−.21		
High status denomination			.20	
Defense spending				.50
Not raise taxes				.29
Affect, liberals	−.23	.25		−.28
Child care				.24
Affirmative action for blacks				.24
Budget deficit top priority				−.23
Conservative self-placement, defense				.22

(continued)

TABLE 8.6 (*continued*)

	Function 1 [a]	Function 2 [a]	Function 3 [a]	Function 4 [a]
Government guarantees job			.20	

Canonical Discriminant Functions Evaluated at Group Means

	Function 1	Function 2	Function 3	Function 4
Bush	−1.89	−0.85	0.73	−0.01
Dole	−1.47	−0.41	−1.61	−0.96
DuPont	−2.35	2.54	−.66	−0.60
Kemp	−1.73	0.47	−0.88	1.50
Robertson	3.01	0.06	0.07	−0.01

Modal category				45
Percentage predicted correctly				84
Bush	Prior probability	22	Correctly predicted	79
Dole	Prior probability	10	Correctly predicted	88
Du Pont	Prior probability	9	Correctly predicted	73
Kemp	Prior probability	14	Correctly predicted	65
Robertson	Prior probability	45	Correctly predicted	97

[a]Correlations with discriminant function. Only correlations ≥ .20 shown.

ers, especially from those who gave to Bush. Dole supporters were more liberal on détente, less likely to attend church regularly, and less likely to affiliate with a high-status Protestant denomination.

The fourth function discriminates between those who gave to Kemp and those who gave to other candidates. Kemp supporters were more supportive of the gold standard, defense spending, and holding the line on taxes, and less supportive of national health insurance, affirmative action for blacks, child care, and government job guarantees. They were also less likely to believe that the budget deficit was a top priority.

The multivariate results suggest that, despite the strong attitudinal differences between Robertson contributors and other Republicans, the primary cleavage is religious. Like Robertson supporters, his contributors were motivated primarily by religious identity, doctrine, and practice, as well as by social-issue attitudes that sprang from their religious views.

The results confirm many of the findings of Green and Guth. They also found Robertson's contributors to be more conservative on social issues, foreign policy, and economic policy, and they found some antipathy for Robertson among contributors to other candidates. However, whereas they anticipate an eventual accommodation, I am less sanguine. The depths of resentment of Robertson by contributors to other candidates is remarkable, and it is not clear that Robertson Republicans will continue to feel positively about a party that does not welcome them into its fold. At this point, the likelihood that Robertson's forces will be integrated into Republican politics seems too close to call.

ROBERTSON'S DELEGATES

Campaign contributors are a distinct type of political elite. Although many are active in party politics in a variety of ways, others are content to sit by the sidelines and write checks. The elites that are the focus of the rest of this chapter are more active. As delegates to the Republican National Convention, these activists were involved in the day-to-day political struggles of the Robertson insurgency. Many won their posts as a result of a multistage caucus process, in which they had to marshal votes in local, county, regional, and then state meetings.

The data for this study come from a *New York Times* survey of delegates to the Republican National Convention. The survey included a random sample of 739 delegates, and it determined the initial candidate preference of each delegate, not merely the candidate for whom they were pledged to vote. Although three-fourths of the delegates initially favored Bush, 6 percent favored Robertson, 5 percent favored Kemp, and the remainder favored Dole.

Although there has been no published work to date on the full contingent of the national delegates for Robertson, researchers have described his delegates in Virginia and Michigan. McGlennon (1989) reported differences between the Robertson and Bush delegations from Virginia. He found some demographic differences in the delegations, with the Robertson delegates younger, more female, less affluent, and more religious. He reported that Robertson delegates were more conservative on many issues (especially moral ones), but less committed to economic conservatism. Finally, his delegates were relatively new to party activity, with fully 75 percent active for less than five years.

Smidt and Penning (1990) focused on differences between Robertson and Bush delegates to the contentious Michigan State Republican Convention. Like McGlennon, Smidt and Penning report that Robertson delegates were younger, more female, less affluent, and more religious than Bush delegates. Also like McGlennon, the authors report that Robertson delegates had different religious identities than those pledged to Bush—they were more likely to call themselves charismatic or evangelical Christians. The Michigan delegates of

Robertson were much more conservative than Bush supporters on moral and foreign-policy issues, though the differences on economic issues was slight. Finally, Robertson delegates were more likely to be recent Republicans and new to electoral politics.

Table 8.7 provides further confirmation of these earlier results. Robertson's delegates are younger, less well educated, and less affluent than those of the other candidates. There was no gender difference, primarily because Bush and Kemp made conscious efforts to assure a sizable bloc of female delegates to the national convention.

The differences on issue positions is even more striking. Robertson delegates are consistently more conservative than those who initially supported other candidates. Note the large difference in the percentage of delegates who chose the most conservative position on a seven-point scale. Although nearly three-fourths of Robertson delegates considered themselves very conservative, less than one-fourth of the delegates who supported other Republican candidates fell into this category. Predictably, Robertson delegates were the most conservative on social and moral issues. They were most likely to think that the government should uphold traditional moral values, ban abortion,

TABLE 8.7
Initial Candidate Choice among Delegates
to 1988 Republican National Convention

	Robertson (%)	Kemp (%)	Bush (%)	Dole (%)
Demographics				
White	95	92	96	97
Male	61	62	62	71
More than college education	27	62	42	42
Income ≥ $50,000	46	56	75	86
Protestant	82	39	69	85
Less than 40 years old	51	12	13	17
ATTITUDES				
Strongest conservative	70	24	16	19
Increase Spending				
Military	38	20	10	3
Education	10	38	49	43
Day care	11	17	45	44
Combating drugs	78	83	83	75
Homeless	32	36	35	34
Infrastructure	46	20	37	31

(*continued*)

TABLE 8.7 (*continued*)

	Robertson (%)	Kemp (%)	Bush (%)	Dole (%)
Federal Government Should				
Restrict imports	44	4	36	28
Uphold traditional values	91	78	66	58
Guarantee a job	29	33	40	33
Guarantee medical care	22	29	30	21
Support anti-Communists	95	86	84	83
Support human rights	88	83	81	76
Not raise taxes	66	73	65	59
If taxes raised, not tax rich	91	83	86	87
Constitutional convention to balance budget	34	31	40	49
Oppose big government	95	96	90	94
Abortion not allowed	44	46	8	9
Abortion legal as now	2	13	37	33
Deny Planned Parenthood funds	93	71	45	47
No AIDS education	76	55	33	36
Death penalty	90	84	84	77
Get tough with Soviets	64	46	18	20
INF a mistake	70	50	10	15
Use military in drug war	87	74	73	75
Groups U.S. Is Paying Too Much Attention to				
Blacks	29	25	10	12
Blue-collar workers	14	8	3	3
Middle class	25	4	8	2
Business corporations	41	20	19	22
Women	36	32	7	9
Small businessmen	13	8	4	6
Partisan Attitudes and Behavior				
First Republican convention attended	96	65	56	67
Active in Republican politics less than 10 years	66	27	12	8
Works for candidates and issues, not party	58	19	16	11
Reagan not conservative enough	68	61	25	31

Note: Percentage of delegates who initially favored each candidate falling into each category.

deny funds to Planned Parenthood and AIDS education, and invoke the death penalty.

Robertson supporters were also much more conservative than other delegates on foreign policy. They were much less likely than others to approve of the INF treaty, much more likely to oppose détente with the Soviet Union, much more likely to favor increased military spending, and somewhat more likely to favor increased aid to anti-Communist movements. The only surprise in foreign policy comes from the slightly stronger support for human rights among Robertson supporters.

There are remarkable differences in economic policy as well. The table shows the percentage of delegates who favored increases in spending on a range of issues. Robertson delegates were much more likely to oppose increased spending on education and day care. Robertson delegates were somewhat more conservative on government guarantees of jobs and medical care as well, despite their somewhat lower level of affluence. Robertson delegates were more opposed to raising taxes and less likely to favor taxing the rich should taxes need to be raised. Thus, on economic issues as well, Robertson delegates were the most conservative.

The survey also contained a set of items asking whether the government paid too much attention to a series of groups. Robertson supporters were more likely than those who supported other Republican candidates to say that the government listened excessively to blacks, which might be interpreted as evidence of racism. Yet further analysis suggests a different interpretation. Robertson delegates were more likely to mention *all* groups in the list, implying that they believe that the government listens too much to special interests in general. Indeed, the gap between Robertson and other Republicans is greater in their beliefs that the government listens too closely to the middle class and big business than in their beliefs that the government pays too much attention to blacks.

Finally, table 8.7 confirms the findings of Smidt and Penning and of McGlennon, as well as the evidence in the contributor survey above, that Robertson supporters are recently mobilized into Republican politics. Fully 96 percent of Robertson delegates were attending their first national convention: the comparative figure for other candidates was around two-thirds. Two-thirds of Robertson delegates had been working in Republican politics for less than ten years, a figure more than twice that of the Kemp delegation. Although part of this difference may be reflected in the different age structure of the delegations, controls for age do not substantially alter this pattern. Even more striking is the difference in political motivation. Nearly 60 percent of Robertson supporters were motivated by candidates or issues, compared with fewer than 20 percent for Kemp.

I reported that many of Robertson's contributors seem to have been brought into Republican party politics by Reagan in 1980. If this

TABLE 8.8
Initial Candidate Choice among Republican Convention Delegates
(Discriminant Analysis)

	Function 1[a]	Function 2[a]	Function 3[a]
INF Treaty	.52		
Spending, education	−.41	.26	
Ideology	.39		
Spending, day care	−.37		
Women too much influence	−.34		
Income	.33		
Abortion	−.33		
Détente	−.33		
Planned Parenthood	−.32		
Years as Republican	.32		
AIDS education	−.28		
Blacks too much influence	−.25	−.24	
Government assures morals		−.33	
Death penalty		−.23	
Big government		.19	
Military spending		−.19	
Age	.24		−.35
Drugs			−.26
Job guarantee			.25
Support anti-Communists			.23
Restrict imports			.20
Tax rich			.20
Spend on medical care			.20

Canonical Discriminant Functions Evaluated at Group Means

	Function 1	Function 2	Function 3
Bush	.37	−.17	.00
Dole	−.32	1.28	.32
Kemp	−1.61	.24	−1.40
Robertson	−3.20	−.80	.77

Modal Category			77
Percentage predicted correctly			71
Bush	64	Prior probability	77
Dole	48	Prior probability	12
Kemp	62	Prior probability	5
Robertson	87	Prior probability	6

[a]Correlations with discriminant function. Only correlations ≥ .20 shown.

is true of Robertson delegates, they appear to have been disappointed in Reagan. Fully 68 percent felt that Reagan was not sufficiently conservative.

Table 8.8 shows the results of a multivariate discriminant analysis, which allows us to see which variables are most useful in distinguishing Robertson delegates from other delegates. All three functions distinguish between delegates for one or more other candidate and those for Robertson, suggesting that once again the dominant cleavage in the Republican party is between Robertson and other political figures. The functions do an especially good job of predicting Robertson delegates.

The first function centers on ideology, distinguishing especially Robertson delegates (and, to a lesser extent, Kemp delegates) from those of Bush and Dole. This function is by far the most important, accounting for more than one-half of the variance. Robertson delegates are unique in their opposition to the INF, to spending on education and day care, to abortion, to détente, to funding for Planned Parenthood and AIDS education, and to government attention to women and blacks. Robertson delegates are also distinguished by their lower levels of income and their recent involvement in Republican politics. Because this survey did not include useful religious items, the attitudinal sources of Robertson Republicans versus other Republicans cleavage show up strongly in these data.

The second and third functions were not statistically significant, but are presented for their heuristic value. The second function distinguishes between Dole delegates and Robertson delegates. Robertson delegates are more interested in moral traditionalism, more supportive of the death penalty and increased military spending, whereas Dole delegates are more opposed to big government.

Finally, the third function shows the variables that help identify Robertson supporters compared with Kemp supporters. Robertson's delegates were younger, more opposed to government guarantees of jobs and medical care, more supportive of aid to anti-Communist movements, more supportive of restrictions on imports, and less willing to tax the rich if taxes must be raised.

CONCLUSIONS

The distinguishing characteristics of Robertson supporters in the mass public were primarily religious. The same is true of elite support for Robertson. By far the most important factors that separate Robertson supporters from supporters of other Republican presidential candidates are their religious identity, religious doctrine, and religiosity, as well as the social-issue positions that derive from them.

Like the elites of the Moral Majority and unlike those of the Crusade, political elites who supported Robertson were consistently conservative. Their conservatism stands out even in contrast to other contributors to, and delegates for, Republican presidential candidates, including conservatives such as Kemp. Their conservatism is especially strong on social and moral issues, but is also strong on foreign policy, in which the historical connection between anticommunism and the Christian Right remains in force. Their conservatism is also evident on economic issues. Although the traditional labor-management cleavage is of less interest to Robertson backers than to backers of other Republicans, they are more strongly opposed to spending on education, day care, government jobs, and medical care than other Republican activists.

The concern with education and day care echoes another common theme in Christian Right movements—a strong concern for inculcating moral values in their offspring. Robertson endorsed the Christian school movement throughout his campaign and argued that government day care would lead to a decline in the ability of Christian parents to teach their children.

These data also show a vast cultural and political gap between Robertson Republicans and the rest of the Republican party. Although Robertson contributors are enthusiastic for their party and other party figures, the old-line Republicans are less than enthusiastic about the Robertson insurgency. Whether this gap will be bridged in the next few years, as Green and Guth predict, remains to be seen. Wilson (1973) suggested that one way that insurgent movements become integrated into political organizations is that their primary ideological or purposive motives become subordinated to material or solidary motives. Robertson Republicans seem unlikely to quickly become enamored by the possible material gains of politics, and it is difficult to picture that they would value the solidary benefits of rubbing shoulders with other Republicans who do not share their religious or cultural values. If the Republican mainline cannot buy them off with material or solidary benefits, they will need to accommodate them on policy. Not all Republicans, even conservative ones, are willing to do so. The marriage between Robertson backers and the Republican party is likely to be at best a rocky one, with a high probability of divorce.

CHAPTER 9

Lingering Support for the Christian Right: Robertson and Christian Right Groups in 1988

By November 1988, the New Christian Right was in retreat. The Moral Majority had disbanded, and Robertson had sent word to his followers that he would not run in 1992 if Bush won the presidential election. Yet the disbandment of the Moral Majority and Robertson's retreat did not mean that the New Christian Right was moribund. Local activity continued, and public support for Robertson and for political action by the New Christian Right remained. The fading of the Christian Right was not due to weakening public support.

Support for the Moral Majority was never widespread, but the level of support did not decline in 1988.[1] The demise of the Moral Majority was caused by falling revenue, not falling support. Direct-mail revenues of conservative groups fell in the late 1980s, as the potential donor market became saturated with competing solicitors. By 1988, potential donors were increasingly besieged with direct-mail requests. In addition, after eight years of Reagan's presidency, Moral Majority supporters may have found it less credible that their $25 was needed to save the Republic. Declining direct-mail revenues were not unique to organizations of the Christian Right: secular Right organizations and Republican party committees experienced a similar decline. Moral Majority revenues fell to only $3 million in 1988, slightly more than one-fourth of the peak of $11.1 million in 1984 (Niebuhr 1989). By the time

---

1. Data from the 1987 ANES Pilot Study indicate an increase in support, to 19 percent. Although I am suspicious of this figure for a variety of reasons, this result suggests that at least support for the Moral Majority did not decline.

Falwell dismantled the Moral Majority, direct mailings were no longer breaking even.

Similarly, Robertson's withdrawal from presidential politics was due to the structure of the American political system, not to declining support. In a European-styled parliamentary system, Robertson would head a small, religious party in the legislature. Although he would have little influence on policy, he would remain visible and active in politics. However, in the U.S. system Robertson must wait at least four years and most probably eight to challenge the presidency.

After the dismantlement of the Moral Majority and Robertson's withdrawal from presidential politics, there remained lingering public support for the Christian Right. It is important to determine this support because it can help us determine the potential for a renewed effort by Christian Right elites in the 1990s. Moreover, if we can distinguish among those who supported Robertson, those who supported other Christian Right organizations, and those who supported both, it will be possible to determine the likelihood for a broader Christian Right coalition.

This chapter assesses the sources of lingering support for the Christian Right in 1988. I examine the sources of support for Robertson and for Christian Right groups in fall 1988, after the demise of the Moral Majority and Robertson's candidacy. First, I test the various theories of support discussed in chapter 2, then distinguish between the sources of support for Robertson and those for Christian Right groups. Second, I explore the political consequences of Christian Right support in electoral behavior in 1988. Finally, I explore the possibility of a black constituency for the Christian Right.

THE DATA

The data come from the 1988 American National Election Study (ANES). In addition, I make somewhat greater use of the 1989 pilot survey. As before, support for the Christian Right will be operationalized by adjusting the feeling-thermometer items for differences in individual responses.[2] Once again, the analysis first focuses on

2. I have chosen to adjust the feeling thermometer for Robertson by subtracting the mean of the feeling thermometers toward political and social groups, not political figures. In chapter 7, I adjusted the Robertson feeling thermometer relative to affect toward other candidates. (The Super Tuesday survey did not contain feeling thermometers toward social groups.) During a general election campaign, partisan affect becomes more polarized, affecting responses to feeling thermometers toward obviously partisan figures. Therefore, feeling thermometers toward social and political groups are better measures of response tendencies.

whites, then examines support among blacks. The 1988 ANES contained feeling-thermometer items toward Robertson and toward "evangelical groups active in politics." Because the Moral Majority had disbanded, it was no longer included as a referent for this item. The exclusion of the Moral Majority altered the meaning of the item, for now the focus was on *evangelical groups,* not the more concrete (and controversial) Moral Majority. Moreover, without the Moral Majority as a referent, this item does not clearly refer to right-wing groups. It is possible that liberal evangelicals could interpret this item as support for like-minded evangelical groups. However, closer examination of the response patterns demonstrates that most whites responded to this question as indicating support for Christian Right groups. The adjusted feeling thermometer was correlated with conservative positions on political issues among whites, and with support for other conservative groups. However, without the obvious referent of the Moral Majority, the item became a "harder" question. Those who had heard of the Moral Majority but could not interpret the more vague reference to "evangelical groups active in politics" doubtlessly responded with more neutral scores, regardless of their feelings toward Falwell's organization.

EXPLAINING SUPPORT FOR THE CHRISTIAN RIGHT

In the 1988 ANES, 100 white respondents were classified as supporters of Christian Right groups, who constituted approximately 7 percent of white respondents. Support for Robertson was somewhat higher, with 133 supporters, who constituted 10 percent of white respondents. There was some overlap between these two sets of Christian Right supporters, with over 13 percent of white respondents classified as supporters of the Christian Right (i.e., supporters of either Robertson or Christian Right groups).

In this section, I explore each of the explanations discussed in chapter 2—first in bivariate analysis, then in multivariate probit analysis. In chapters 4 and 5, I presented two sets of bivariate figures: the composition of supporters of the Christian Right and the relationship between the independent and the dependent variable. In this chapter, I compare the sources of support for two different Christian Right referents. To avoid confusing and cluttered tables, the bivariate analysis presents only the correlations between the independent and the dependent variables.

Personality Explanations

Once again there are no items that directly measure personality traits. Separate factor analysis of social groups again failed to find evidence of dogmatism or cognitive simplism. The factor solution for supporters of both Christian Right referents closely resembled that of other whites, although once again the Christian Right was seen as part of Middle America.

Other indirect evidence against a personality explanation comes from feeling-thermometer items toward racial and religious minorities. Some personality theories suggest that supporters of the Right will project their own inadequacies (and, in some formulations, self-loathing) onto out-groups. The most frequently mentioned out-groups are racial and religious minorities (Lipset and Raab 1978).

In table 9.1 (under symbolic politics), it is evident that supporters of the Right do not project hatred toward blacks, Hispanics, Catholics, or Jews. Indeed, supporters of both Robertson and Christian Right groups are significantly *warmer* toward Jews than are other whites, perhaps reflecting the biblical view of Jews as God's chosen people, as well as the importance of the restoration of Israel in evangelical interpretations of the final days.

Both sets of supporters are markedly cooler toward gays and lesbians, however. Homophobic rhetoric was a prominent feature of the direct-mail appeals of the Moral Majority, and activists in the Ohio Moral Majority voiced it frequently to me. Yet this negative affect may not have a personality source. The emphasis of evangelicals, fundamentalists, and pentecostals on the authority of the Scriptures may lead Christian Right supporters to their antihomosexual affect. In the Old Testament, homosexual behavior is one of a rather long list of capital offenses, and Saint Paul castigates homosexuals (as well as fornicators and adulterers) in his epistles. Those who accept the authority of the Scriptures are likely to be cooler toward those labeled by the Bible as sinners. Christian Right supporters are more likely to be responding to religious doctrine in their feelings toward gays and lesbians than projecting their own insecurities outward. It would be possible to test this interpretation if the survey had contained feeling thermometers toward other groups that evangelicals would have considered sexual sinners (e.g., unmarried couples living together). Unfortunately, no such items were included in the survey.

Alienation

There is again weak evidence for an alienation explanation of support for the Christian Right. Supporters of Robertson and of Christian

TABLE 9.1
Lingering Support for the Christian Right: Bivariate Relationships
(Correlations)

	Robertson	Christian Right Groups
Alienation		
Social group attachment		
Average group affect	.02	.10**
Number of group	.04	.06*
identifications		
Political involvement		
Turnout	−.03	.03
Other electoral activities	.03	.06*
Interest	.01	.04
External efficacy	−.03	.01
Cynicism	.10**	.07**
Internal efficacy	−.05*	−.01
Sees difference between parties	.00	.06*
Social Status		
Status anxiety		
Identifies as middle class if		
Bottom third in education	.00	.00
Bottom third in income	.11*	.00
Bottom third in occupation	.01	−.02
Feels close to own class		
Middle	−.01	−.04
Working	.00	−.01
Generational mobility	−.02	.01
Income ahead of inflation	.12**	.03
Expect to be better off next year	−.02	.01
Symbolic Politics		
Middle America	−.02	−.02
Establishment	−.01	−.02
Minorities	−.09**	−.11**
Liberal groups	−.17**	−.22**
Blacks	−.02	.07**
Hispanics	.03	.05*
Catholics	−.04	−.01
Jews	.05*	.09**
Homosexuals	−.12**	−.21**
Feminists	−.23**	−.19**
Antiabortionists	.18**	.19**
Christian fundamentalists	.22**	.24**
Religion		
Doctrine		
Born-again	.25**	.25**
Bible inerrant	.16**	.18**

(*continued*)

TABLE 9.1 (*continued*)

	Robertson	Christian Right Groups
Both	.26**	.26**
Bible literal	.24**	.30**
Denomination		
Fundamentalist	−.02	.05*
Pentecostal	.20**	.12**
Southern Baptist	.02	.07**
Other evangelical	.04	.06*
Catholic	−.09**	−.09**
Religiosity		
Church attendance	.16**	.17**
Religious salience	.16**	.21**
Prayer	.17**	.21**
Televangelists	.24**	.21**
Religious identity		
Fundamentalist	.01	.13**
Evangelical	.17**	.21**
Charismatic	.12*	.19**
Fundamentalist and charismatic	.13*	.17**
Fundamentalist and evangelical	.11*	.20**
Evangelical and charismatic	.21**	.22**
All three	.20**	.19**
Pastor preaches politics	.24**	.24**
Political Values and Attitudes		
Moral traditionalism	.20**	.21**
Equality	.07**	.10**
Anti-Communism	.14**	.11**
Patriotism	.05*	.05*
Partisanship	.04	.08**
Ideology	.22**	.15**
Social programs	−.00	.09**
Taxes	−.09**	.01
Spending on poor	.00	.01
Spending on elderly	−.02	−.00
Spending on liberal programs	.14**	.11**
Spending on Reagan defense	−.05*	−.03
Social issues	.23**	.22**
Death penalty	.02	.00
Racial attitudes	.04	.02
Strong defense	.06*	.06**
Negotiate with Soviet Union	.17**	.14**
Isolationism	.00	.08**

Note: Pearson's *r* correlations between dichotomous support measure and independent variables.
* $p \le .05$
** $p \le .01$

Right groups showed attachments to social and political groups that rivaled or exceeded attachments of the rest of the white population and were equally involved in politics. Support was not linked to external efficacy (the belief that government listens), but support for Robertson was slightly but significantly higher among those with low levels of internal efficacy—that is, among those who feared that they were not as officious and knowledgeable about politics as other Americans. Finally, support for both Christian Right groups and for Robertson was linked to greater cynicism about the political process, although these relationships were rather modest.

Social Status Explanations

There were significant differences between Robertson supporters and nonsupporters on only one status indicator. Robertson supporters were significantly less well educated than nonsupporters, but this was not true for Christian Right groups. Because of the vagueness of "evangelical political groups," better-educated respondents were doubtlessly better able to interpret and respond to the item. The data support this interpretation: better-educated respondents assigned to Christian Right groups markedly higher and markedly lower scores. Fewer chose the neutral categories that are often used when a respondent has little knowledge of a political or social group.

I have once again tested the status inconsistency theory in three ways (see chapter 4 for details). In none of these methods did supporters of Robertson or supporters of Christian Right groups display higher levels of status inconsistency. Indeed, in some tests supporters of Christian Right groups were significantly more consonant in their status indicators than nonsupporters.

Evidence is again weak for status anxiety as well. Only one of the several indicators shows a positive correlation with support for the Christian Right: supporters of Robertson who were in the bottom one-third of the population in income were significantly more likely than nonsupporters to call themselves middle class. Robertson supporters were disproportionately widows, who have lower incomes than other citizens because of their age and gender. Many of these widows had undoubtedly been married to men with middle-class jobs and incomes and considered themselves middle class because of their previous life circumstances. When widows were excluded from the analysis, this relationship was reduced to nonsignificance.

Symbolic Politics Explanations

In chapter 3, I described the scales formed from the factor analysis of the feeling thermometers that asked respondents to rate social groups. There is some evidence for a symbolic crusade in the pattern of group affect in table 9.1. Supporters of Robertson and supporters of Christian Right groups are not markedly warmer toward the symbols of Middle America, nor are they warmer or cooler toward the political establishment. They are markedly cooler toward minorities (chiefly gays and lesbians) and liberal groups, especially feminists. They are also significantly warmer toward antiabortion activists and Christian fundamentalists.

It is possible to read these findings as support for a symbolic politics explanation. Because racial attitudes are among those most frequently assigned symbolic status, the markedly lower affect of supporters of the Christian Right toward minorities seems to support such an explanation. However, note that the lower scores for the minority scale come primarily from affect toward gays and lesbians. Supporters of the Christian Right are not cooler toward racial minorities, or more conservative on racial attitudes (see table 9.1).

Supporters of the Right are cooler toward groups that might symbolize lifestyle conflict, however, including feminists and gays and lesbians, and warmer toward groups that are generally supportive of their lifestyles; for example, Christian fundamentalists and antiabortion activists. Although this pattern probably reflects simple political reality (supporters are cool toward the political opposition and warm toward sympathetic groups), it also provides some tentative evidence for a symbolic politics explanation.

Religious Explanations

The data in table 9.1 again suggest that religion is among the strongest predictors of support. Supporters of both Christian Right referents are more likely than other whites to belong to evangelical denominations, to hold evangelical doctrinal beliefs, and to show high levels of religiosity. Predictably, those who attended pentecostal churches were warmer toward Robertson, whereas fundamentalists and Southern Baptists were not. However, both of these latter groups were significantly more likely to support Christian Right groups.

The 1989 pilot survey added two important sets of items. Respondents were asked if they considered themselves evangelicals, fundamentalists, or charismatics. Religious identity was a strong predictor of support for the Christian Right, although the patterns were somewhat surprising. Nearly all doctrinally conservative religious identities (and combinations thereof) were more strongly correlated with support for Christian Right groups than with support for Robertson. Predictably, self-identified fundamentalists were more supportive of Christian Right groups than other whites and, predictably, were not more supportive of Robertson. However, self-identified charismatic Protestants were also more supportive of Christian Right groups than they were of Robertson.[3] These data provide some support for an explanation of support for the Christian Right which centers on politicized religious identity.

Finally, those who attended churches in which politics was frequently preached from the pulpit were significantly more supportive of both Robertson and Christian Right groups. These relationships were even stronger among those who attended conservative Protestant churches, where the content of the political message was likely to be conservative. Respondents were asked whether their churches were evangelical, fundamentalist, charismatic, conservative, and/or liberal. Among those who attended churches that they labeled as evangelical, charismatic, or fundamentalist, pastoral involvement in politics was associated with greater support. But among those who attended Protestant churches that they labeled liberal, the relationship was negative.

Political Explanations

Supporters of the Christian Right in 1988 were generally more conservative than other whites, but neither set of supporters was as consistently conservative as supporters of the Moral Majority. Supporters of Christian Right groups were somewhat more conservative than Robertson supporters. The differences between supporters of the Christian Right and other whites were greatest on basic values, social issues, spending on liberal programs, and defense-related issues. Somewhat surprisingly, there were no significant differences on the death penalty.

Robertson supporters were fairly moderate on economic issues— and significantly more liberal than other whites on taxes and on spending for Reagan's defense programs. Robertson supporters were also not significantly different from the rest of the population in their par-

3. Among Catholics, the interaction effect approached statistical significance. The correlation between a charismatic identity and support for Robertson was .06, and the correlation with support for New Christian Right groups was −.12. Neither correlation was statistically significant (there were fewer than one hundred cases for each correlation), but the difference between them was significant at .10.

tisanship (although the correlation was nearly significant, $p \le .08$). However, Robertson supporters were significantly and substantially more likely than other whites to identify themselves as conservative.

MULTIVARIATE ANALYSIS

To sort out the independent effects of these variables, I have estimated two separate sets of probit equations. The results are shown in table 9.2. I have first estimated equations with a full list of independent variables, then estimated parsimonious models with a shorter list of statistically significant predictors.

Once again, support for the Christian Right seems to come from religious and political beliefs and values, not from social strain. There is also evidence that symbolic politics are involved in the lingering support for the Christian Right. The equations do a better job explaining support for Robertson, probably because of the vague nature of the item tapping support for Christian Right groups.

Support for Christian Right groups is predicted by evangelical doctrine, exposure to televangelists, social-issue attitudes, moral traditionalism, attitudes toward isolationism and Reagan defense programs, and partisanship. Supporters are also warmer toward Middle America and cooler toward liberal groups. Finally, supporters of Christian Right groups are less trusting of government than other whites.

Support for Robertson is also associated with evangelical doctrine, exposure to televangelists, social-issue attitudes, coolness toward liberal groups, and attitudes toward isolationism. However, Robertson's support is more closely linked to specific denominations, with those who attended fundamentalist churches or churches in the Southern Baptist Convention less supportive, and those who attended pentecostal churches more supportive. Finally, support for Robertson is associated with low levels of external efficacy (the belief that government does not listen to its citizens), anticommunism, conservative ideology, and low levels of income.

It is interesting that support for both Christian Right symbols is associated with some form of alienation from government. The 1988 ANES was conducted after eight years of a Reagan presidency, which sought to nurture a Christian Right constituency. Although supporters of Christian Right groups were warmer toward Reagan and more positive about the accomplishments of his presidency than other whites, Robertson supporters were not. Moreover, after controls for partisanship, supporters of the Christian Right were not more favorable toward Reagan than other whites. This may hint at a dissatisfaction with the

TABLE 9.2
Support for Christian Right Groups and Robertson (Probit Analysis)

	Christian Right Groups				Robertson			
	Full		Parsimonious		Full		Parsimonious	
	MLE	T	MLE	T	MLE	T	MLE	T
Alienation								
Cynicism	.00	.02			.01	.15		
Internal efficacy	-.01	-.15			.00	.00	-.15	-1.98*
External efficacy	.01	.07			-.21	-1.87		
Group attachment	.05	.87			.01	.06		
Trust government	.17	1.38	.16	2.38	.07	.70		
Social Status								
Status inconsistency/anxiety	-.04	-.35			-.01	-.10		
Education	.01	.12			-.01	-.18		
Income	-.01	-.31			-.05	-2.56*	-.04	-3.12**
Occupation, head of household	-.01	-.37						
Symbolic Politics, Affect								
Middle America	.01	1.26	.01	2.41*	-.00	-.44		
Establishment	.01	1.10			-.00	-.30		
Minorities	-.00	-.18			.00	.48		
Liberals	-.00	-.09			-.02	-2.50*	-.01	-2.80*
Religion								
Evangelical denomination	-.36	-.90			-.48	-1.41	-1.38	-1.98*
Fundamentalist denomination	-1.35	-1.45			-1.70	-1.68	.84	2.72*
Pentecostal denomination	-.62	-1.28			1.00	2.57*	-.72	-2.28*
Southern Baptist	.53	1.20			-.45	-.89		
Catholic	-.15	-1.20			-.10	-.87		

(*continued*)

TABLE 9.2 (continued)

| | Christian Right Groups | | | | Robertson | | | |
| | Full | | Parsimonious | | Full | | Parsimonious | |
	MLE	T	MLE	T	MLE	T	MLE	T
Evangelical doctrine	.60	2.42*	.53	3.95**	.44	1.97*	.45	2.88*
Religiosity	.11	.78			.12	.89		
Televangelists	.39	1.68	.40	3.08**	.53	2.63*	.43	2.91*
Political Attitudes								
Partisanship	.10	1.57	.09	1.99*	.00	.18		
Ideology	.11	1.15			.22	2.24*	.20	3.10**
Moral traditionalism	.14	1.12	.18	2.46*	.09	.82		
Equality	−.08	−.70			.11	.98		
Anti-Communism	.07	.55			.27	2.07*	.17	2.02*
Patriotism	.11	.80			.08	.69		
Social issues	.84	3.86**	.41	3.77**	.44	2.40*	.30	2.31*
Death penalty	.00	.03			.06	.54		
Racial attitudes	.25	1.08			.06	.30		
Social programs	.16	1.17			.07	.54		

Taxes	.10	.95			-.06	-.70		
Spending on poor	.04	.26			-.05	-.43		
Spending on liberal programs	.07	.61			.17	1.55		
Spending on elderly	.08	.66			-.12	-1.11		
Spending on Reagan defense	.31	2.59*	.15	1.96*	.06	.45		
Defense	.10	.58			.12	.78		
Negotiate with Soviet Union	.08	.63			-.00	-.06		
Isolationism	.17	1.07	.25	2.82*	.36	2.65*	.20	2.25
Geography								
South	-.03	-.14			.06	.29		
Rural-born	.05	.75			-.02	-.39		
Moved recently	-.00	-.13			.00	.19		
Other Demographics								
Age	.01	1.18			.00	.64		
Sex	-.08	-.37			-.11	-.49		
Intercept	-4.66	-.28	-3.95	-5.10**	-.74	-3.96**	-1.42	-7.64**
N	683		1265		640		866	

Note: Entries are maximum likelihood estimates from probit analysis and corresponding T values.
*$p \leq .05$
**$p \leq .01$

accomplishments of the Reagan years. Although Reagan's speeches were full of promises on the Christian Right agenda (Moen 1990a), little in the way of concrete policy was forthcoming. The early successes of Reagan were focused on economic and defense policy, and his efforts on behalf of the social agenda of the Christian Right were never vigorous. Some Christian Right supporters may have blamed the Washington establishment for failing to implement the social programs that Reagan had promised them, whereas others may have begun to question his commitment to their agenda.

Supporters of the Christian Right were also less likely than were other whites to perceive the rightward tilt of the Supreme Court after Reagan's appointments. For those who did not support the Christian Right, affect toward the Supreme Court had a strong negative correlation with warmth toward liberal groups. However, for supporters of both Robertson and Christian Right groups, the correlation was positive. For Christian Right supporters, then, the Supreme Court remains a liberal institution.

DISTINGUISHING AMONG SUPPORTERS
OF THE CHRISTIAN RIGHT

Not all of those who supported Christian Right groups also supported Robertson. Fewer than one-half of those who supported Christian Right groups also supported Robertson (46 percent), whereas only one-third of Robertson supporters also supported Christian Right groups. If the Christian Right is ever to achieve the mass-movement status to which its leaders seem to aspire, some sort of unity seems essential. Yet fewer than one-fourth of those who supported either of these Christian Right referents in 1988 supported *both* Robertson and Christian Right groups.

To determine the potential for a unified Christian Right, it is useful to compare those who support one or the other Christian Right referent with those who support both. Table 9.3 presents the results of a multivariate discriminant analysis. I include all independent variables from table 9.2 in the analysis, but only present those variables with correlations of at least .20 with one of the discriminating functions. Three statistically significant functions resulted from this analysis. The first function contains variables that are associated with the degree of Christian Right support. In other words, the first function distinguishes among those who support neither Christian Right object, those who support either referent, and those who support both.

Those who are frequently exposed to televangelists or religious

TABLE 9.3
Support for Christian Right Groups and Robertson
(Discriminant Analysis)

	Function 1 [a]	Function 2 [a]	Function 3 [a]
Televangelists	.67	.34	
Evangelical doctrine	.56	−.22	.28
Social issues	.53		
Moral traditionalism	.48		
Religiosity	.44		
Pentecostal denomination	.37	−.26	−.36
Negotiate with Soviet Union	.35		
Spending on liberal programs	.30		
Affect, liberal groups	−.27		
Anti-Communism	.26		
Social programs		.41	
Isolationism		.40	
Partisanship		.34	
Education		.31	
Income	−.20	.31	
External, efficacy		.25	
Spending on elderly		.22	
Affect, Middle America			.33
Southern Baptist			.31
Fundamentalist denomination			.28
Evangelical denomination			.26
South			.24

Canonical Discriminant Functions Evaluated at Group Means

	Function 1	Function 2	Function 3
Neither	−.22	.04	−.01
Evangelical Right	.91	−.29	1.15
Robertson	1.04	−.88	−.37
Both	2.60	.90	−.23
Percentage of groups classified correctly	71	Modal Category	86
Evangelical Right	67	Sample probability	4
Robertson	51	Sample probability	7
Both	67	Sample probability	3

[a]Correlations with discriminant function. Only correlations ≥ .20 shown.

radio are the most supportive of both Christian Right referents, as are those who hold evangelical doctrine, exhibit high levels of religiosity, and attend pentecostal churches. In addition, support is linked to political attitudes and values, including social issues, moral traditionalism, opposition to spending on liberal programs, and negative affect toward liberal groups. Support is also higher among those with strongly anti-Communist values and those who oppose negotiations with the Soviets. Therefore, those who support both Christian Right groups are consistently conservative on social, economic-policy, and foreign-policy issues, as well as highly religious doctrinal evangelicals.

The second function distinguishes between those who support both groups from those who support only one, especially those who support Robertson. Variables with high positive correlations with this function are predictors of support for both referents, and those with high negative correlations are predictors of support for Robertson. His supporters are distinguished by their affiliation with pentecostal churches and their evangelical doctrine, whereas those who support both Robertson and Christian Right groups are more likely to watch televangelists and to be conservative on social programs, isolationism (i.e., favor intervention), and spending for the elderly, and to be better educated, financially better off, Republican, and have lower levels of external efficacy.

The third function discriminates between those who support Christian Right groups only from those who support Robertson. High positive correlations on this factor are associated with support for only Christian Right groups. High negative correlations are associated with support for Robertson. Such support is associated with membership in a pentecostal church. Support for only Christian Right groups is associated with membership in fundamentalist, Southern Baptist, or other nonpentecostal evangelical churches, with evangelical doctrine, with high levels of religiosity, southern residence, and affect for Middle America.

The first function explains the greatest share of the variance, suggesting that support for the Christian Right can be conceived as additive: the most important difference is among those who support neither referent, one, or both. At the same time, there are important differences between supporters of these two Christian Right referents. Support for Robertson is strong in pentecostal churches, and weak in fundamentalist, Southern Baptist, and other evangelical churches. Those who support only Robertson are less consistently conservative than those who also support Christian Right groups, and those who support the latter are more likely to hold evangelical beliefs, to show high levels of religiosity, and to attend nonpentecostal denominations than those who also support Robertson.

These results contain some important implications for the possibility of a unified Christian Right. First, those who attend pentecostal churches are more likely to support a wide range of Christian Right figures than are those who attend other evangelical denominations. This suggests that the theological cleavages within the evangelical community remain a serious barrier to a united movement.

In addition, the results modify somewhat the suggestion that a pentecostal/charismatic Right has more potential for a broad-based movement than does a fundamentalist Right. Although these results support the notion that pentecostals would welcome evangelicals and fundamentalists into their political coalition, they also suggest that evangelicals and fundamentalists are unlikely to warm to such an invitation. Instead, pentecostals are more likely to support a fundamentalist or evangelical political figure than vice versa. For grass-roots mobilization, then, a pentecostal Right may have greater potential to build inclusive coalitions. However, a fundamentalist or evangelical candidate may attract a wider range of voters.

One additional implication can be derived from these results. Robertson attracted some highly religious supporters who were conservative on social issues but moderate on other issues. These moderate Robertson supporters were not supporters of Christian Right groups. It seems likely that many of these Robertson supporters might have been unaware of his conservative positions on economic- and foreign-policy issues. Further analysis provides tentative confirmation for this suspicion. Among those who supported only Robertson was a group who was moderate on economic- and foreign-policy issues, and who had markedly lower levels of political information than other supporters of the Christian Right. The number of cases here is small, so all conclusions must be tentative. These supporters had higher levels of weekly exposure to religious television and radio broadcasts. The moderate Robertson supporters echoed the moderation of supporters of the Christian Anti-Communism Crusade more than the consistent conservatism of supporters of the Moral Majority or Christian Right groups of the 1980s.

POLITICAL CONSEQUENCES OF SUPPORT
FOR THE CHRISTIAN RIGHT

The 1988 data provide little evidence of continued electoral mobilization by Christian Right organizations or leaders. The turnout of supporters of the Christian Right was not significantly higher than that of other whites, and controls for demographic variables did not change that pattern. Although Christian Right supporters did vote for Bush at a higher rate than other whites, this difference is entirely explained by differences in partisanship and ideology. Indeed, after controls for

TABLE 9.4
Political Consequences of Support

	Robertson		Evangelical Right	
	Support	*Nonsupport*	*Support*	*Nonsupport*
Reported voting, 1988	74%	77%	78%	73%
Adjusted for demographics	74%	77%	77%	74%
Voted for Bush	67%*	58%	78%**	58%
Adjusted for partisanship, ide-ology, and demographics	60%	61%	61%	61%
Voted for Republican in House	62%*	44%	73%**	43%
Adjusted for partisanship, ide-ology, and demographics	64%*	53%	68*	54%*
Affect for Bush	65°	64°	72°*	63°
Adjusted for partisanship, ide-ology, partisan affect, and demographics	62°*	68°	67°	68°
Partisanship	3.71**	3.20	4.15**	3.11
Adjusted for demographics and parents' party	3.73**	3.17	4.10**	3.17

Note: Percentages and mean values for supporters and nonsupporters. Partisanship values are means on seven-point scale, ranging from 0 (strong Democrat) to 6 (strong Republican).
*$p \leq .05$
**$p \leq .01$

partisanship, partisan affect, ideology, and demographics, supporters of the Christian Right (particularly those of Robertson) were somewhat cooler than other whites toward Bush. The details are in table 9.4. However, Christian Right supporters were significantly more likely than other whites to report a vote for House Republican candidates, and this difference persisted after controls for partisanship, ideology, and demographic variables.

Some Christian Right supporters might have recently identified with Republicans. Both supporters of Christian Right groups and supporters of Robertson are significantly more Republican in their partisanship than other whites. This greater Republican affiliation is not due to demographic characteristics such as income or region, nor is it due to parental partisanship. Both sets of supporters of Christian Right groups are significantly more Republican than would be predicted from their demographic backgrounds and the partisanship of their parents. Moreover, supporters of Christian Right groups are more likely than other whites to have defected from their mother's Demo-

cratic partisanship. Whereas approximately one-third of nonsupporters with Democratic mothers consider themselves Republicans, more
than one-half of supporters of Christian Right groups with Democratic
mothers are now Republicans. However, these data do not allow us to
determine whether the Christian Right helped bring these partisans
into the Republican fold.

BLACKS AND THE NEW CHRISTIAN RIGHT IN 1988

Once again there is evidence for a potential black constituency for the
Christian Right. Blacks were slightly more supportive than whites of
the Christian Right in 1988: 12 percent supported Christian Right
groups, and 14 percent were classified as supporters of Robertson.
Fully 21 percent supported a Christian Right figure.

Because of the relatively small number of black respondents to the
1988 ANES, multivariate analysis is suspect. However, bivariate correlations suggest that support for the Christian Right is associated with
many of the same variables for blacks as for whites: evangelical doctrine, pentecostal denomination, televangelists, religiosity, and conservative positions on social issues and foreign policy. The correlations are
presented in table 9.5. The small number of black respondents to the
1988 ANES again indicates that fairly sizable correlations do not
achieve statistical significance. Therefore, in comparing these coefficients with those in table 9.1, it is important to compare the magnitude
of those coefficients that are not statistically significant.

Although supporters of Robertson are generally more conservative than nonsupporting blacks, supporters of "evangelical political
groups" are in some cases more liberal than nonsupporting blacks.
Black evangelical churches have often preached liberal political messages. For blacks, then, this item may not tap support for Christian
Right groups among all respondents: some may be responding with
their affect for an evangelical Left.

CONCLUSIONS

In November 1988, after the Moral Majority had disbanded and
Robertson had announced his withdrawal from the electoral arena,
support for the Christian Right in the United States remained un-
diminished. The sources of this support were religious and political,
although there may have been a symbolic component to affect for the
Christian Right. Yet this lingering support for the Christian Right was

TABLE 9.5
Black Support for the Christian Right, 1988
(Correlations)

	Robertson	Evangelical Right
Religious Variables		
Evangelical denomination	−.06	−.02
Pentecostal denomination	.13*	.09
Fundamentalist denomination	−.08	.00
Southern Baptist	−.03	.03
Evangelical doctrine	.22**	.15*
Televangelists	.17**	.07
Religiosity	.16*	.06
Political Variables		
Moral traditionalism	.05	−.06
Anti-Communism	.10[a]	−.03
Patriotism	.03	.01
Equality	.13*	−.09
Ideology	−.05	.09
Partisanship	.18**	.00
Social issues	.20**	.18**
Death penalty	.00	−.00
Racial attitudes	.04	−.12
Social programs	−.03	−.15[a]
Taxes	−.05	.05
Spending on poor	−.08	−.08
Spending on liberal programs	−.10	−.01
Spending on elderly	−.01	−.05
Spending on Reagan defense	.01	.15*
Defense	.11[a]	.05
Negotiate with Soviet Union	.25**	−.06
Isolationism	.19**	−.06

Note: Pearson correlations.
[a]$p \leq .10$
*$p \leq .05$
**$p \leq .01$

fragmented, with only one-fourth of those who supported either Christian Right figure backing both Robertson and Christian Right groups.

There were two barriers to these differing sets of supporters merging into a larger coalition. The first relates to sectarian disputes: pentecostals were willing to support both Christian Right groups and Robertson, but evangelicals and, especially, fundamentalists were unwilling to support the charismatic Robertson. In addition, a segment of

Robertson supporters were moderates who responded to his religious message and stands on social issues, but may have been unfamiliar with his positions on economic- and foreign-policy matters. These moderate supporters were poor prospects for a renewed Christian Right.

There remained a potential constituency for the Christian Right among black Americans. Although the general liberalism of black Americans on economic policy and many foreign-policy issues would mean that a black Christian Right would need a limited political agenda, the greater religiosity and social-issue conservatism of blacks makes such a movement not impossible. Moreover, the lack of racism among white supporters of the Christian Right suggests the potential for a multiracial movement.

CHAPTER 10

The Potential Christian Right

Religious disputes prevented a unified Christian Right from emerging in the 1980s. Potential support existed for the Christian Right in 1988, even after the Moral Majority and Robertson had at least temporarily left the political scene.[1] It is possible that the next decades will mark a period of quiescence for the Christian Right, much like the periods that followed the activity of the 1920s and 1950s. It is also possible that a new set of political and religious entrepreneurs will soon attempt to build new Christian Right organizations, in order to capitalize on lingering support for the Christian Right.

When Falwell disbanded the Moral Majority, he claimed that it had accomplished its goals. In a narrow sense, he was correct. The goal of the secular New Right activists who planned and helped organize the Christian Right was to develop a Republican voting bloc among white evangelical Christians. In both 1984 and 1988, an overwhelming majority of white evangelicals cast Republican ballots.

Yet when the Moral Majority dissolved, the issue agenda of the Christian Right was almost entirely unrealized. School prayer was restricted, and, although the Reagan Supreme Court was willing to countenance more public displays of religion, it did not support an open, public advocacy of Christianity, which the Christian Right had sought. Abortion remained largely legal, and, although in the *Webster* v. *Reproductive Health Services* decision the Supreme Court hinted at an even-

---

1. Although it seems likely that Falwell has permanently retired from politics, Robertson may well be contemplating another presidential bid, though he has stated that he will not challenge an incumbent Bush.

tual reversal of *Roe* v. *Wade,* right-to-life advocates faced a state-by-state battle to limit abortion. Although only a few localities passed laws liberalizing their approach to homosexuality, few stiffened their enforcement of existing bans. Feminists continued to win battles against gender discrimination, and the public remained supportive of greater gender equality. Moreover, younger Americans were more liberal on social issues than their grandparents, suggesting that the natural process of generational replacement will likely lead to even more social change. In short, the core of the social-issue agenda remained unfulfilled.

The lingering public support for a Christian Right, coupled with the unfinished social-issue agenda, suggests that the Christian Right could rise like Lazarus from the grave in the 1990s. Such a revival seems unlikely today, but the possibility cannot be readily dismissed. If there is public support for values and policy positions that constitute the Christian Right agenda, or if there is an untapped set of potential supporters, then political and religious entrepreneurs might attempt to put together a new set of organizations to again mobilize conservative Christians into political action.

This chapter explores the issues surrounding the likely future of the Christian Right. It focuses on three questions. First, how widespread is support for the Christian Right platform? If there is substantial support for it, then it seems likely that a new Christian Right may form sooner, rather than later. Second, are there groups of citizens who are potential Christian Right supporters, but who did not support the Christian Right of the 1980s? The existence of a well of untapped potential support would also suggest the formation a new set of organizations in the future. Finally, what have been the recent trends in white evangelical electoral politics? Such trends have important implications for the likely behavior of entrepreneurs who might seek to form new Christian Right organizations.

POPULAR SUPPORT FOR THE CHRISTIAN RIGHT PLATFORM

A good deal of scholarly research has reported that in the 1980s there was more support for the Christian Right agenda than for its organizations and leaders. Such a finding is important because it implies an untapped potential support that could attract future religious and political entrepreneurs, who might form new organizations. Lingering support for the policy positions of the Christian Right could indicate that the next wave of activity will be sooner and not later.

In a widely cited article, Simpson (1983) reported the general public's widespread support of the Moral Majority platform. Using sophisticated statistical analysis of the 1977 General Social Survey (GSS) data, Simpson concluded that a plurality of Americans endorsed the Moral Majority position on four issues: homosexual relations, school prayer, women's roles, and abortion. Moreover, Simpson argued that a substantial majority of Americans held a set of beliefs close enough to that of the Moral Majority platform to be called "fellow traveling conservatives," a group who give general support to the Christian Right platform.

Yinger and Cutler (1982) reported similar results, again using GSS data. They define the Christian Right agenda as including intolerance toward antireligious and homosexual writings, opposition to legalized marijuana, abortion, extramarital and homosexual relations, and pornography. Yinger and Cutler report that approximately one-third of respondents in 1973 supported the Moral Majority platform, although that support had declined slightly by 1980.

Kellstedt (1989) focused on support for Falwell's platform among white evangelicals. Kellstedt's analysis used data from the Evangelical Voter study to assess support for the following positions: school prayer, tuition tax credits for parents whose children attended religious schools, defense spending, aid to Israel, and opposition to the Equal Rights Amendment, birth-control information in schools, a nuclear freeze, the National Organization for Women, and abortion. In addition, Kellstedt includes the belief that AIDS is God's punishment for homosexuals as part of the Moral Majority platform. Kellstedt does not report the proportion of white evangelicals who adopt a position of consistent support for the Christian Right agenda, although he does note that, on most of these issues, the average position for white evangelicals was in the direction of the Moral Majority platform.

The studies above suggest that the range of items which can be considered part of the Christian Right platform is broad. Stockton (1984) included other items, and Falwell has taken positions on nearly every issue that faces the polity. Christian Right elites in the 1980s took positions on a subminimum wage for teen-agers, a balanced budget, the gold standard, capital-gains taxes, and other specific economic issues, and on aid to South Africa, Pakistan, the Contras, the Afghanistan resistance, the Cambodian resistance, U.S. participation in the United Nations, a wide variety of weapons systems, nuclear energy, gasoline-import taxes, and many other issues. Very few Americans supported this entire agenda, although the same could be said for any equally lengthy set of positions on controversial issues.

One difficulty, then, in assessing support for the Christian Right platform is to define the core of the Christian Right agenda. A second difficulty is determining exactly which political positions can be thought of as supporting the platform. For example, the Christian Right has generally opposed abortion in all circumstances, yet one Ohio activist told me (after requesting that I turn off my tape recorder) that although "the others in this movement won't agree," she favored abortion in cases of rape and incest. Was this Moral Majority member a supporter of the platform? Although she was more liberal on abortion than the official Christian Right position, she supported most of the actions by Christian Right elites to limit abortion on demand, which she strongly opposed.

A related question concerns the intensity of an attitude. Does it matter if someone merely agrees with a position, or must he or she strongly agree to be considered a supporter of the Christian Right agenda? Sigelman and Presser (1988) noted that Simpson chose to label as supportive of the Moral Majority platform those who merely agreed with the statement that men should be the achievers while women stayed at home. A different choice—classifying as supporters only those who strongly agreed—would have drastically reduced the level of support for the Moral Majority platform.

A different picture would have emerged had Simpson used a more restrictive abortion item (e.g., one that asked if abortion should be allowed in cases of rape and incest), instead of one that asked about abortion on demand. Although only one-third of respondents agreed with abortion on demand, there were more prochoice respondents in the 1977 GSS than strictly prolife partisans. Had Simpson required that those who he defined as supporting the Christian Right platform opposed abortion in all cases, the set of supporters would have been much smaller.

A final problem relates to the treatment of those with no opinion on a political issue. Sigelman and Presser note that Simpson does not include respondents who had no opinion on any of the four issues in his index. Although this is a fairly common procedure, it creates the appearance of more support for the Christian Right platform than actually exists. For example, those who are uncertain of their views on abortion are not included in Simpson's analysis, yet they are surely *not* supporters of the Christian Right platform on abortion.

Support for the Christian Right Agenda in 1988

Smelser (1963) argued that social movements by evangelical Christians were best conceived as value-oriented movements. Therefore, the core of the Moral Majority platform might be best conceived as involving three sets of values: moral traditionalism, patriotism, and anticommunism, as well as attitudes on policies that involve these values—social and foreign issues. In the analysis below, those without opinions on some of the values and issues in the survey are included in the analysis, but those who are consistently unable to express opinions on these issues are excluded. I adopt a fairly liberal criteria for support of the Christian Right position, classifying as supportive those who take conservative positions on each issue. This operational decision overstates the actual support for the Christian Right agenda, but such a wide net captures nearly all potential supporters.

I am interested not only in the extent of support for the Christian Right platform but also in the extent of support among certain target constituencies. Table 10.1 separately examines support for Christian Right positions among three potential target constituencies: white evangelical nonsupporters, white Catholic nonsupporters, and black nonsupporters. Whites and blacks are separated in table 10.1, and, because of the small number of black respondents to the survey, black nonsupporters are not further differentiated. Table 10.1 also presents the attitudes of black and white supporters of the Christian Right (either Christian Right groups or Robertson), as well as a column that represents the entire population.

The values of moral traditionalism, patriotism, and anticommunism are central to the Christian Right. Each of the movements in the twentieth century has extolled these values, although the relative emphasis among them has varied. Table 10.1 suggests that many of the potential constituencies of the Christian Right share these values with its supporters. Two other findings are noteworthy. First, the actual supporters of the Christian Right are not unanimously supportive of these values, or of the issue positions of the Christian Right discussed below. Previous research that set a standard for support which required agreement with *all* of the positions of the Christian Right has set an unrealistic standard because not even the current supporters agree with the entire platform.[2]

Second, nonsupporting evangelicals are as consistently conservative as actual supporters of the Christian Right, and often more so. This conservatism is due to the inclusion of nonevangelicals among Christian Right supporters. White evangelicals who support the Christian Right are more conservative than nonevangelical supporters, as well as slightly more conservative than evangelical nonsupporters.

Any attempt to define the Christian Right policy agenda must begin with social issues because the organizations of the 1980s empha-

2. This finding is doubtlessly not unique to the Christian Right. Indeed, most supporters of a political group that stakes positions on a wide range of issues will probably disagree with a few of the positions taken by the group.

TABLE 10.1
Support for the Christian Right Platform (1988 ANES Data)

	Whites			
	Supporters (%)	Other Evangelicals (%)	Other Catholics (%)	Public (%)
Moral Traditionalism				
3–4 Conservative	58	64	36	32
Anticommunism				
2–3 Conservative	76	80	60	62
Patriotism				
3–4 Conservative	86	97	90	56
Social Issue Attitudes				
3–5 Conservative	72	72	46	44
Foreign Policy/Defense				
3–5 Conservative	34	34	25	23
Economic Policy				
2–4 Conservative	47	47	38	38

	Blacks	
	Supporters (%)	Nonsupporters (%)
Moral Traditionalism		
3–4 Conservative	36	32
Anticommunism		
2–3 Conservative	53	62
Patriotism		
3–4 Conservative	45	62
Social Issue Attitudes		
3–5 Conservative	48	41
Foreign Policy/Defense		
3–5 Conservative	14	16
Economic Policy		
2–4 Conservative	23	26

Note: Percentage of each group selecting conservative alternatives on the given number of scale items. Support-supporters of Christian Right groups or Robertson. Other evangelicals is nonsupporting evangelicals. Other Catholics is nonsupporting Catholics. Public is all respondents. For this table, those without opinions on some items were included in the analysis, but coded as having a nonconservative position on those items for which they had no opinion.

sized these issues. Articles condemning abortion, homosexuality, the Supreme Court ruling on school prayer, and feminism, as well as endorsing the death penalty, were common in the pages of the *Moral Majority Report* and in publications by Christian Voice, and these issues were by far the most frequently mentioned in Moral Majority direct-mail appeals. Also highly visible in Christian Right direct mail and publications were pronouncements on foreign policy. At the core of the Christian Right foreign-policy agenda were increased spending on defense and a deep distrust of the Soviets. Less attention was given to economic issues, although Falwell often took positions on them.

Table 10.1 suggests that there may be a strong potential constituency among white evangelicals, as well as a smaller one among white nonevangelical Catholics. As was the case in the analysis of values, white nonsupporting evangelicals are as conservative as actual supporters of the Christian Right. The potential constituency among white Catholics is more limited, for, although Catholic nonsupporters are somewhat conservative on abortion and gay and lesbian rights, they are relatively liberal on gender equality and economic issues.

Among blacks, there is a larger proportion of conservatives among nonsupporters than among supporters, although there are many more liberals among the nonsupporting ranks as well (not shown). As a group, black supporters are marginally more conservative than nonsupporters when the full range of positions on these scales is taken into account, but they were not more likely than nonsupporters to take consistently conservative positions. Nonetheless, there appears to be a limited untapped constituency among blacks.

These results suggest that there is a large untapped potential constituency for the Christian Right among white evangelicals, as well as a smaller one among white Catholics. However, to more fully assess the potential constituency for a unified Christian Right, it is important to look at combinations of attitudes across issue areas. Although potential supporters need not agree with the entire program of the Christian Right, they may not support a movement that strongly stakes positions that they oppose on important issues. If conservative positions on social issues are linked to conservative positions on other issues, the Christian Right has potential to mobilize new support. However, where conservative positions on social issues are held by those who are liberal on foreign-policy and economic issues, a future Christian Right would need to radically repackage itself to gain wide appeal. Therefore, to more fully explore the potential for a future Christian Right movement, it is important to examine the issue groups within the potential Christian Right constituency.

ISSUE GROUPS AND THE POTENTIAL CHRISTIAN RIGHT: WHITE EVANGELICALS

Clearly the constituency with the greatest potential for Christian Right support is white evangelicals. In chapter 3, we examined the issue

TABLE 10.2
Support for the Christian Right among White Evangelical Issue Groups
(1988 ANES Data)

	Christian Right Groups (%)	Robertson (%)	Percentage of White Evangelicals (%)
Conservatives	57	37	21
Liberals	4	13	40
Economic conservatives	0	11	8
Economic moderates	14	16	31
			100
Total	18	19	

Note: Percentage of each cluster supporting Christian Right groups or Robertson, as well as the proportion of all white evangelicals belonging to each group.

groups within the white evangelical community. Table 10.2 shows the current levels of support for the Christian Right among each cluster of evangelicals from the 1988 ANES data. Not surprisingly, those white evangelicals in the conservative cluster are generally supportive of the Christian Right, but there are sufficient nonsupporters in this cluster to note the potential for the Christian Right to expand its support here. However, support is low among liberals and economic conservatives. Economic conservatives are moderate on social issues and foreign policy, which the Christian Right stresses more frequently than economic issues. Finally, economic moderates are only slightly more supportive of the Christian Right than the rest of the white population, despite their conservatism on social and foreign-policy issues.

The most promising potential constituency for the Christian Right in these data are unmobilized conservatives, but economic moderates seem to constitute an additional opportunity. Although the Moral Majority took a consistently conservative line on economic issues, Robertson often sounded a populist theme in promising opportunity for the disadvantaged. An issue package of conservatism on social and foreign-policy issues, combined with either moderation or populism on economic issues, seems the most promising line for a future Christian Right movement that seeks to maximize its support among white evangelicals.

We can get an additional look at the issue clusters of white evangelicals by performing a similar cluster analysis among white evangelicals in the Evangelical Voter data. Although the survey did not contain economic issues, it had a range of foreign- and social-issue items. The best solution has five clusters. The largest cluster is distinguished by its relatively liberal positions on social issues, and it is fairly cool toward the

TABLE 10.3
Support for the Christian Right among White Evangelical Issue Groups
(Evangelical Voter Study)

	Moral Majority (%)	Falwell (%)	Percentage of White Evangelicals (%)
Social-issue liberals	28	24	30
Conservatives	55	60	24
Liberals	33	24	17
Social-issue conservatives	33	42	16
Doves	29	34	13

Note: Percentage of each cluster supporting Moral Majority or Falwell, as well as the proportion of all white evangelicals belonging to each group.

Moral Majority and Falwell. This cluster, which I call the Social Issue Liberals, disproportionately consists of those who hold evangelical doctrinal beliefs but do not attend evangelical churches. Evangelicals in this cluster are the least likely of all to perceive a strong connection between their religious and political beliefs. They tend to be young and to live outside the South.

The second cluster is composed of consistent Conservatives. The Conservatives are older, more southern, and are the most likely to attend fundamentalist and charismatic churches, to show high levels of religiosity, and to perceive a strong connection between their religion and politics. More than one-half support the Moral Majority and Falwell.

A third cluster contains consistent Liberals. Support for Falwell and the Moral Majority is relatively low in this cluster. The fourth cluster contains evangelicals who are distinguished by their conservative positions on social issues, especially abortion. This doctrinally conservative cluster of Social-Issue Conservatives contains fewer fundamentalists than other clusters and is not particularly supportive of the Christian Right. The smallest cluster is the Doves, who take consistently liberal positions on foreign policy. This group is also cool toward the Christian Right. The details are presented in table 10.3.

As is the case with the ANES data, the best target for future mobilization would be the consistent Conservatives, and, although the Moral Majority already commanded the support of over one-half of this cluster, there is still room for further recruitment. Additional support could come from the Social-Issue Conservatives, although this cluster was not particularly conservative on foreign-policy issues. Even if the

Christian Right were to fully mobilize the most likely clusters of evangelicals, it would still fall short of constituting a majority of even white evangelicals. To become a truly important social movement, the Christian Right would need to mobilize among sympathetic Catholic, mainline Protestant, and possibly black constituencies.

The Christian Right's prospects are even dimmer for gaining support among these other possible constituencies. A cluster analysis of white nonevangelical Catholics from the 1988 ANES data found only one small cluster that was likely to be supportive of the Christian Right. These respondents were doctrinally conservative, taking positions that were close to those of evangelical doctrine, and were conservative on social issues, but liberal on economic and foreign-policy issues. This cluster represented only 8 percent of white Catholics, and, even among this set, only 25 percent supported Robertson, with 13 percent supportive of the Moral Majority. The relatively low levels of support among this group suggests that religious cleavages might constitute an important barrier to gaining support among Catholics.

There was some support for other issues of the Christian Right platform among Catholics, but this support would not be easy to mobilize. For example, a somewhat larger cluster (17 percent of white nonevangelical Catholics) were strongly anti-Communist and hawkish on foreign policy, but this cluster was liberal on social issues and quite cold toward the Christian Right.

Similarly, a cluster analysis of white mainline Protestants revealed one fairly small cluster (11 percent) that seemed a likely target for Christian Right mobilization. These Social-Issue Conservatives also took hawkish foreign-policy positions and were moderately conservative on economic issues. However, the Christian Right already had the support of 40 percent of this cluster, and no other clusters seem particularly promising for recruitment.

Finally, a cluster analysis of black Americans revealed no promising clusters for mobilization for a Christian Right that takes positions on economic and foreign-policy issues. Although a fairly sizable cluster is conservative on social issues, and it is disproportionately composed of religious conservatives, its economic- and foreign-policy positions are quite liberal.

These data suggest that there is some untapped potential for a larger Christian Right movement, but it would be difficult to mobilize these potential supporters behind a movement with a wide issue agenda. A movement that focuses only on social issues has the widest possibility of success, but, even if that movement were to gain the support of every citizen who took conservative positions on those issues, the Christian Right would not truly constitute a "Moral Majority."

THE POLITICS OF WHITE EVANGELICALS AND
THE FUTURE OF THE CHRISTIAN RIGHT

The fundamentalist and pentecostal Right of the 1980s was formed in part to bring into politics a previously apolitical evangelical constituency, which was likely to support Republicans at the presidential level. Secular conservative leaders sought to increase the turnout and change the vote direction of white evangelicals, and they used their available resources to help form Christian Right groups to achieve these ends.

If this task remains unaccomplished, such resources may again be forthcoming. However, if evangelicals are now firmly in the Republican camp, then there will be less impetus for secular elites to seek to aid the formation of future Christian Right groups.

Table 10.4 presents the electoral behavior and partisanship of

TABLE 10.4
White Evangelical Electoral Politics, 1972–88

	1972 (%)	1976 (%)	1980 (%)	1984 (%)	1988 (%)
Reported Turnout					
Denominational evangelicals	61	66	65	65	61
Other whites	78**	75*	75**	78**	74**
Reported Turnout					
Doctrinal evangelicals			76	70	71
Other whites			72	80**	72
Voted Republican for President					
Denominational evangelicals	81	44	55	70	67
Other whites	68	55	60	62*	58*
Voted Republican for President					
Doctrinal evangelicals			65	74	67
Other whites			55	60**	57**
Republican Partisanship					
Denominational evangelicals	33	38	25	45	46
Other whites	38	44	38**	44	47
Republican Partisanship					
Doctrinal evangelicals			42	51	52
Other whites			36	44*	45*

Note: Percentage of each group in each category. Data unavailable for doctrinal evangelicals prior to 1980.
*$p \leq .05$
**$p \leq .01$

white evangelicals in the period 1972–88. Because the doctrinal questions that I have used to identify evangelicals throughout the book were not used in ANES surveys prior to 1980, I present data derived from both denominational and doctrinal definitions.

The data using the denominational definition of evangelicalism shows an increase in turnout in 1976, with the candidacy of Carter, and a further increase in 1980, when Carter was opposed by Reagan, a conservative favorite. In 1984, with Carter off the ticket, turnout among white evangelicals declined slightly, and it declined further in 1988. The data using a doctrinal definition show a similar pattern of decline after 1980, although the better-educated doctrinal evangelicals vote at a higher rate than those who attend evangelical churches.

Evangelical voting has become solidly Republican in the past two elections, and evangelical partisanship is following suit. These data suggest that secular conservative leaders no longer need seek to convert the evangelical vote to Republicanism. Although evangelical turnout still lags behind that of other citizens, this is mainly due to the lower levels of education of evangelicals. After controls for demographic variables such as education, age, and region, evangelical turnout in 1988 was no lower than that of other whites.

Evangelicals supported Republican presidential candidates in large numbers in 1972 and since 1984. In 1976 and 1980, evangelicals were attracted to the candidacy of Carter. Perhaps more importantly, the partisanship of evangelicals has become increasingly Republican over the period covered in this table. By 1988, denominational evangelicals were just as likely as other whites to identify as Republicans, and doctrinal evangelicals were more so.

Other studies (Kellstedt and Green 1990; Smidt and Kellstedt 1990) have reported that changes in partisanship are greatest among younger, southern evangelicals. Their evidence is persuasive. To the extent that partisan change is a process of generational replacement, the growing Republicanism among younger evangelicals suggests a strong Republican bloc in future elections.

One implication of the changing partisanship of white evangelicals is that secular elites have less incentive to help form political groups to bring evangelicals into Republican politics. However, another implication suggests a growing political voice for evangelicals. Whether new extraparty organizations are formed to mobilize white evangelicals, their growing importance to Republican electoral politics suggests that they will have a voice within the party. Christian Right politics of the 1990s and beyond may be an intramural struggle between contending groups of Republican activists. This struggle may not be a friendly one.

CONCLUSIONS

There is some support for the values and policies advocated by the Christian Right. This support is highest on basic values such as patriotism, anticommunism, and moral traditionalism. There is fair support for some of the social-issue agenda as well, although this support is largely confined to white evangelicals. However, even among actual supporters of the Christian Right, there is less support for the economic conservatism that has marked the policy pronouncements of Christian Right leaders.

These data suggest that there is more support for the platform of the Christian Right than for its organizations and leaders. This seemingly implies that there might be a sizable untapped constituency for the Christian Right. However, closer examination suggests that it will not be easy for a future Christian Right to take advantage of support for some of its programs. Social-issue conservatism does not always go hand in hand with conservatism on foreign and economic policy. The cluster analysis suggests that there is only limited potential for a Christian Right to expand beyond its core of conservative evangelicals, particularly if it continues to take positions on foreign-policy issues and, especially, economic-policy ones. Conservative positions on economic issues will alienate some potential supporters, and conservative positions on foreign policy will alienate still others. However, a Christian Right that focuses exclusively on social and moral issues has a fairly large potential constituency among white evangelicals, Catholics, and blacks.

The barriers to tapping this potential support are religious as well as political. As long as religious particularism remains a strong source of negative affect toward potential political and religious allies, an inclusive Christian Right cannot emerge. Fundamentalist antipathy toward Catholics, pentecostals, charismatics, and even other evangelicals remains strong, and recent evidence suggests that the hostility now runs two ways (Jelen 1990a).

CHAPTER 11

Conclusions

In 1991, New Christian Right activity is almost invisible in American politics. Yet such activity continues, as it has throughout the twentieth century. Local organizations continue to form over issues such as school texts, "indecent" art, and other issues of the day. A number of scholars have suggested that local activity may be the future of the Christian Right (Leege 1990; Moen 1990a; Morken 1990). It is often suggested that a shift to local activism is a carefully planned strategy on the part of Christian Right elites, although to me it echoes Muhammad Ali's famous "rope-a-dope" boxing strategy—inspiration borne of necessity. National Christian Right organizations were unable to raise much direct-mail money in the latter half of the 1980s, leaving local activity the only viable alternative.

Many of the national organizations continue to exist, however, including the Christian Anti-Communism Crusade and Christian Voice. Robertson now heads an organization called the Christian Coalition, and, in a full-page ad in the *Washington Post* and other newspapers in June 1990, he warned members of Congress that the organization might pass out one hundred thousand reproductions of Robert Mapplethorpe and Serrano art to registered voters in districts where the member voted for National Endowment for the Arts funding. He warned: "There may be more homosexuals and pedophiles in your district than there are Roman Catholics and Baptists. You may find that the working folks in your district want you to use their money to teach their sons how to sodomize one another. You may find that the Roman

Catholics in your district want their money spent on pictures of the Pope soaked in urine. BUT MAYBE NOT."

Robertson's explicit appeals to Catholics and Baptists—two groups that might be expected to sympathize with his positions but that did not rally to his presidential campaign—may mark the beginning of a new attempt to bridge particularistic religious barriers. Yet Falwell also unsuccessfully attempted to forge a union of conservative Catholics, Jews, and Protestants in his Moral Majority.

WHO ARE THE SUPPORTERS OF THE CHRISTIAN RIGHT?

In the Introduction, I posed five questions that this book would address. The first focused on passive supporters of the Christian Right. The data in this book have described supporters of three distinct Christian Right movements—the Crusade in 1964, the Moral Majority in 1984, and Robertson in 1988. There are some interesting similarities and differences in supporters of these three groups and figures. One somewhat surprising difference is that although supporters of the Moral Majority and Robertson were generally consistently conservative, those who supported the Crusade were not. There was a secular, highly conservative element among Crusade supporters, but the religiously motivated Crusade supporters were quite moderate on most issues.

In chapters 4, 5, and 9, I tested various explanations for support for the Christian Right. The general conclusion I draw from these analyses is that support for the Christian Right is not due to psychological abnormality, social-status anxiety, or other sources of strain. Instead, citizens who are motivated to support Christian Right groups are those who find the religious and political values and positions expressed by the groups congruent with their own. Support for the Christian Right is *rational* in at least two senses of the word. First, it is rational in that it does not result from pathological psychological forces. Second, and more importantly, it is rational in the sense used by political scientists to explore vote choice—citizens are supporting groups that espouse their values and beliefs.

Of course, the evidence here does not constitute definitive tests of psychological or status theories because often the tests for these theories have been indirect. Only in my exploration of the sources of support for the Crusade were direct measures of personality characteristics available, and these were perhaps not optimal. Nonetheless, the analysis revealed that Crusaders were not particularly strong-minded, distrusting of others, or nostalgic. Moreover, there is no evidence that

Christian Right supporters project self-hatred onto blacks, Jews, or Catholics, and no evidence that they see the world as a struggle between forces of good and evil. More sensitive tests may well reveal the "authority mindedness" that Wald et al. (1989b) have described, but, as they note, this would not be evidence of personality disorders, but rather of a certain cognitive style.

There is no evidence that support for the Christian Right is linked to alienation, at least as this term is conceived by mass-society theorists. Supporters were as attached to social groups and involved in politics as nonsupporters, and they were not the isolated individuals that some theorists have portrayed as "easy prey" for right-wing groups. Activists were even more involved in religious and political networks. There is some evidence of a certain policy dissatisfaction with government, which might be described as a different sort of alienation. Yet policy dissatisfaction is always highest among those on one or the other extreme end of the policy spectrum, and strong conservatives or liberals generally perceive that the government is farther from their preferred policies than is evident in the views of the rest of the public.

The tests for social-status inconsistency were quite direct and show no evidence to support this hypothesis. Measures of status anxiety were less direct, but there seems to be no connection between status mobility and support, and no evidence in the multivariate analysis to link status exaggeration or fear for future income to support for the Christian Right.

Unfortunately, the data have provided no measures to test the group status concept. Wald et al. (1989a) found that Christian Right supporters believed that churchgoers, ministers, hardworking people, and law-abiding people did not get enough respect. My in-depth interviews with Christian Right activists picked up on this theme, although most indicated that this was a peripheral concern. Indeed, many suggested that the declining respect for religiously motivated citizens foretold a time when religious values would be threatened.

The data in this book demonstrate, however, that the best predictors of support for the Christian Right are religious identities, doctrines, behaviors, affiliations, and political beliefs. Conservative religious identities, orthodox doctrine, high levels of public and private religiosity, and affiliation with conservative denominations are all positive predictors of support for the Christian Right. Religious identities matter most when they are politicized, usually through exposure to televangelists or other political and religious elites. Conservative positions on moral issues, foreign-policy issues, and, to a lesser extent, economic issues are also predictors, especially for the Christian Right of the 1980s.

Some of the political issues that resonate from the in-depth interviews I conducted involve a defense of lifestyle. Christian Right supporters feel threatened by the open expression of values and lifestyles that counter their own, and they increasingly see threats to their ability to socialize their children to their own values. The continuing theme throughout the twentieth century on education was especially evident in the Ohio Moral Majority. At state meetings of the executive council, education was usually the foremost topic. This confirms the contention of McAdam (1982, 1983) that public policies are an important factor in motivating social-movement activists.

One other explanation of Christian Right support is tentatively confirmed in these data. All three sets of Christian Right supporters were motivated by negative affect toward certain out-groups— Communists, feminists, gays and lesbians, the American Civil Liberties Union, and others. This confirms the major finding of Jelen (1991a), who found that out-group affect was a major source of support for Falwell, Robertson, and the Moral Majority. It is possible to interpret these findings as evidence of symbolic politics. Many others have suggested that the Christian Right is a symbolic crusade. Yet these same data may be interpreted merely as rational group affect toward political and social groups that oppose the Christian Right program. The antipathy is certainly reciprocal, for dislike of the Moral Majority is a significant predictor of warm affect for feminists in the 1988 ANES data as well, yet few have labeled the feminist movement a symbolic crusade.

The contrast between supporters of the Christian Right and supporters of two other "right-wing" groups in chapters 4 and 5 tells us even more about the sources of support for the Christian Right. In many ways, John Birch Society supporters resembled the "irrational" rightists portrayed by scholars in the 1950s. They were less trustful of others, alienated from government, and had higher levels of status inconsistency. These factors suggest that there may be no universal set of theories and explanations which accounts for support for all right-wing groups. Supporters of the prolife movement did not fit the label "right-wing" at all. Many were moderate on other issues, including other social ones. In this sense they more closely resembled the moderate, one-issue Crusaders from 1964 than the Moral Majority of 1984.

There is a final conclusion about support for the Christian Right. Religious particularism has been a major barrier to the formation of a unified religious coalition in support of conservative moral politics. The antipathy between pentecostals, fundamentalists, and some other evangelicals prevents them from supporting one another (see also Jelen 1991a). Only the pentecostals and charismatics rallied to support

Robertson, whereas fundamentalist Baptists who formed the backbone of the Moral Majority were less supportive. Similarly, when compared with mainline Protestants, pentecostals were slightly (though not significantly) negative toward the Moral Majority.

The depth of this cleavage will surprise those outside of these religious traditions, for pentecostals, evangelicals, and fundamentalists share much of a common doctrine. As Jelen (1991a) notes, they also share a common perception of who the enemy is (e.g., feminists, liberals, gays and lesbians). Finally, they share opposition to abortion and legal "pornography," support for school prayer and defense spending, and other political attitudes. Given these common elements, it may seem surprising that doctrinal disputes prevent a harmonious coalition.

Yet seen from within these religious traditions, the doctrinal dispute is a vital one. For those who believe that the Bible is the ultimate and only source of revealed truth, the pentecostal belief in experiential revelation seems wrong. Although many pentecostal churches teach that one must "test the Spirit" by comparing insights with the Scriptures, fundamentalists doubt the efficacy of such a test and believe that experiential revelation leads to spiritual error. Not all of the conflict is quite so cerebral; the austere fundamentalists also object to the free emotional expression of pentecostal services. Fundamentalists frequently refer to pentecostals as "holy rollers" or "chandelier-swingers" (Jelen 1991a).

WHO WERE THE ACTIVISTS IN THE CHRISTIAN RIGHT?

The second question I posed in the Introduction concerned activists in the Christian Right. One straightforward conclusion from the analysis in this book is the importance of distinguishing between activists and passive supporters of political organizations. Previous studies have often generalized freely from one to the other, and my data suggest that activists are quite different from passive supporters.

Many of these differences are not unique to the Christian Right, for activists in all types of political groups differ from passive supporters. Activists in the Christian Right were more affluent, better educated, and more politically involved than passive supporters. Activists had more political information than supporters. As a consequence, the attitudes of activists were more constrained, and they were more consistently conservative. Once again, the exception is the Crusade, whose activists were generally moderate on domestic issues and divided on questions of foreign policy.

Activists in the Moral Majority and in Robertson's campaign, however, were conservative on all issues. On political issues alone, it would be impossible to distinguish between these two sets of activists, but there were important differences. Once again, these differences centered on religious particularism, with the Moral Majority activists heavily recruited from Bible Baptist Fellowship churches and Robertson's activists disproportionately recruited from pentecostal or charismatic churches.

Activists in the Christian Right differ from other conservative activists primarily in their religious values and identities and in their emphasis on moral and social issues. They are also deeply conservative on foreign-policy questions that involve communism. However, on economic issues, although they may not be as centered on the labor-management dimension, they are strongly opposed to welfare programs and spending on other liberal programs, as well as increased spending on public education.

One of the other explanations for the Christian Right has particular relevance for activism. Resource mobilization theory stresses the importance of preexisting networks of groups which provide resources to aid in the formation of still other groups. In the case of the Moral Majority, the network of Bible Baptist Fellowship churches was an important recruiting opportunity for activists. Robertson's campaign likewise used existing pentecostal churches, and both the Moral Majority and Robertson used television networks to recruit contributors and members.

THE POLITICAL CONSEQUENCES OF THE CHRISTIAN RIGHT

A third important question concerns the political consequences of the Christian Right. Do the claims of political mobilization made by Crusade, Moral Majority, and Robertson spokespersons have any validity? The evidence is inconclusive.

The evidence for mobilization is particularly weak in the case of the Crusade. The turnout rate of Crusaders was higher than their demographic profile would predict. However, it is likely that this rate merely reflects a prior political activism among Crusaders. In addition, they were almost as likely to vote for Johnson as for Goldwater. Clearly, it was not the Crusade's strong endorsement of Goldwater that brought Crusaders to the polls.

Some supporters of the Moral Majority were newly mobilized between 1976 and 1984. Moral Majority supporters turned out at higher rates in 1980 and 1984 than would be predicted by their demographic and past participatory profiles. They voted in large numbers for Reagan in 1980 and 1984, crossed party lines in 1980 to support Reagan more often than nonsupporters, and were much more Republican than their parents' partisanship would predict. Moral Majority supporters were less likely than nonsupporters to report being lifelong supporters of their current party, as well as more likely to say they supported their party because of issues and ideology. All of this evidence suggests a recent conversion to Republican politics and an increased politicization.

How much of this conversion is due to the Moral Majority is open to debate. Evangelical turnout increased in 1976 with the candidacy of Carter, and it remained high in 1980 when Carter faced Reagan, an ideological favorite. However, in 1984, turnout of evangelicals, including Moral Majority supporters, declined. One alternative explanation is that the candidacy of Carter brought Moral Majority supporters and other evangelicals into the electorate.

Turnout was up in 1980 among all evangelicals, not only Moral Majority supporters. Among white evangelicals, turnout in 1980 was not correlated to support for the Moral Majority, suggesting that the increased participation of Moral Majority supporters may be due to other factors. Nonetheless, these data do provide tentative support for at least some of the claims of Moral Majority leaders. Moral Majority supporters did increase their participation in the 1980s, and many appear to have switched their partisanship.

The claims by Robertson spokespersons to have brought previously apolitical citizens into electoral politics have even more support here. Robertson supporters in the Super Tuesday states were more likely to vote than their demographic profile would predict, although exit polls suggested that they were not first-time voters. In addition, Robertson drew support among Democrats as well as Republicans. Moreover, Robertson activists were fairly new to Republican politics. A substantial proportion had supported Carter in 1976, and large numbers had been active in party politics for less than ten years.

These data suggest that many Christian Right supporters are newly mobilized into politics and disproportionately Republican. However, the data do not prove that the organizations of the Christian Right are responsible. Kellstedt and Green (1990) and Smidt and Kellstedt (1990) have provided substantial evidence of large-scale partisan shifts among all white evangelicals (whether or not they support the Christian Right), and especially among young evangelicals in the South. These studies suggest that cultural factors may create a large-scale shift in partisan sentiment among evangelicals, and this shift could also be responsible for the patterns we see in supporters for the Moral Majority and Robertson.

From the perspective of practical politics, this distinction is not particularly meaningful. Christian Right supporters have been mobilized and are now more active and more Republican than before. However, from the perspective of political science, the causal ordering here is ambiguous. Did the Moral Majority mobilize sympathetic fundamentalists, or did cultural and political factors mobilize the broader evangelical community, and did some of these newly mobilized fundamentalists support the Moral Majority? Only panel-survey data can answer this question.

THE CHRISTIAN RIGHT PLATFORM

How widespread was support for the Christian Right platform among supporters and nonsupporters of the Christian Right? The question is less relevant for the Crusade, for Schwarz did not take positions on many issues. However, even when the Crusade staked a position, supporters were not opposed to negotiations with Communists and were not universally opposed to Medicare. This moderation is true not only of the passive supporters of the Crusade but also of those who attended the School of Anti-Communism.

In contrast to the Crusade, the Moral Majority and Robertson staked out positions on a wide range of issues, including fairly esoteric economic and foreign-policy issues. Supporters of the fundamentalist and pentecostal Right in the 1980s were largely conservative on these issues, although sizable minorities took liberal positions on many economic issues. Activists were more consistently and strongly conservative on every issue.

Among the general public, there was support for some elements of the Christian Right platform. Among nonsupporting white evangelicals, there is fairly strong support for the social-issue positions of the Christian Right, and sizable minorities of Catholics and mainline Protestants also support these positions. Although few support the entire issue package of the Christian Right, this may be too high a standard, for even staunch supporters of a political group may disagree with at least some of its provisions.

THE POTENTIAL CHRISTIAN RIGHT

If there is untapped support for the Christian Right platform, does this mean that there are untapped constituencies for the Christian Right? The data suggest that support for a potential Christian Right would be higher if the organizations or figures did not stake consistently conservative positions on economic and foreign-policy issues. For example, among black Americans there is substantial support for moral conservatism, but very little support for economic conservatism and increased defense spending. Among white evangelicals, there is a cluster of social-issue conservatives which is moderate on other issues and which might support a Christian Right that focused only on social issues.

A New Christian Right movement that focused only on social issues would still need to overcome the essential barrier of religious particularism. Although Jelen (1991a) has suggested that there is a basic symmetry between fundamentalist antipathy for pentecostals and pentecostal dislike of fundamentalists, the data in chapter 5 show that pentecostals were only slightly negative toward the Moral Majority, whereas the data in chapters 7 and 9 show fundamentalists to be quite negative toward Robertson. These data suggest that a fundamentalist organization might have more potential to attract pentecostal support than vice versa. However, if the Ohio Moral Majority is any indication, fundamentalist elites may be incapable of building truly inclusive religious coalitions. Although charismatic elites might welcome fundamentalists, Catholics, and others into a New Christian Right, the data in chapters 7 and 9 indicate that fundamentalists are unlikely to cross that welcome mat. Religious particularism is a major barrier to a truly unified and effective Christian Right.

This book has revealed one relatively untapped source of support for the Christian Right which has gone virtually unnoticed by academics and journalists. Many black Americans hold doctrinally orthodox religious views, attend orthodox churches, frequently watch religious television shows, and have high levels of personal religiosity. Moreover, blacks are somewhat more conservative than whites on some moral issues, such as abortion. This research suggests that there is a real, if limited, potential constituency for the Christian Right among blacks.

THE CHRISTIAN RIGHT IN THE TWENTIETH CENTURY

One of the most surprising findings in this book is that supporters and activists of the Crusade are different from those in the Moral Majority and the Robertson campaign. The general political moderation of the religious supporters of, and activists in, the Crusade might be taken as evidence that it was not an organization of the Christian Right.

Wolfinger et al. (1969) argued persuasively, however, that the rhetoric of Crusade leaders was clearly part of the American Right. Moreover, the constant themes of antimodernism in education and anticommunism—which link anti-evolution groups, anti-Communist groups, and organizations of the 1980s such as the Moral Majority and Christian Voice—were quite evident in Schwarz's message.

Why, then, did the Crusade attract political moderates, whereas the Moral Majority and Robertson attracted consistent conservatives? The first answer is the single-issue focus of the Crusade's appeal. Many moderate evangelicals are fervently anti-Communist, and the combined message of Christianity and anticommunism attracted these moderate supporters. The second answer lies in the much lower levels of public information about the Crusade, which may have kept potentially conservative supporters from supporting the group and allowed moderates to support the organization in the absence of full information about its program.

It seems likely that if we had survey data on supporters of the anti-evolution crusades of the 1920s, they would be even less consistently conservative. The populist anticorporate economic message of Bryan had great appeal among evangelicals of this period, and it is possible that supporters of the Flying Fundamentalists would have been liberal on many economic issues.

Christian Right groups in the twentieth century, then, have expanded their agenda and taken increasingly conservative positions on all types of issues. The analysis in this book suggests that this tactic may limit their support. A Christian Right that focuses only on social issues might be able to appeal to otherwise-moderate Christians, much as did the Crusade of the 1960s, and might thereby constitute a more substantial political force. However, until conservative Protestants can resolve their religious rivalries, a unified Christian Right is unlikely, in this century or the next.

Bibliography

Abcarian, Gilbert, and Sherman Stanach. 1965. "Alienation and the Radical Right." *Journal of Politics* 27: 776–96.

Adorno, T., W. Frenkel-Brunskik, D. Levinson, and R. Sanford. 1950. *The Authoritarian Personality.* New York: Harper.

Aldrich, John H., and Forrest Nelson. 1984. *Linear Probability, Logit, and Probit Models.* Beverly Hills, Calif.: Sage.

Altemeyer, Bob. 1988. *Enemies of Freedom.* San Francisco: Jossey-Bass.

Ammerman, Nancy. 1982. "Comment: Operationalizing Evangelicalism: An Amendment." *Sociological Analysis* 43: 170–71.

———. 1987. *Bible Believers: Fundamentalists in the Modern World.* New Brunswick, N.J.: Rutgers University Press.

Andersen, Kristi. 1988. "Sources of Pro-Family Beliefs: A Cognitive Approach." *Political Psychology* 9: 229–43.

Beatty, Kathleen, and Oliver Walter. 1982. "Religious Beliefs and Practice: New Forces in American Politics." Presented at the annual meeting of the American Political Science Association, Denver.

———. 1983. "The Religious Right and Electoral Change." Presented at the annual meeting of the Midwest Political Science Association, Chicago.

———. 1988. "Fundamentalists, Evangelicals and Politics." *American Politics Quarterly* 16: 43–59.

———. n.d. "Clergy as Group Leaders: Linking Religion with Political Tolerance." Unpublished manuscript.

Bell, Daniel, ed. 1963. *The Radical Right.* Garden City, N.Y.: Doubleday.

Brown, L. B. 1962. "A Study of Religious Belief." *British Journal of Psychology* 53: 259–72.

Broyles, J. Allen. 1966. *The John Birch Society: Anatomy of a Protest.* Boston: Beacon.

Bruce, Steve. 1987. "Status and Cultural Defense: The Case of the New Christian Right." *Sociological Focus* 20: 242–46.

——. 1988. *The Rise and Fall of the New Christian Right.* Oxford: Oxford University Press.

Buell, Emmett, and Lee Sigelman. 1985. "An Army That Meets Every Sunday? Popular Support for the Moral Majority in 1980." *Social Science Quarterly* 66: 426–34.

Carpenter, Joel. 1984. "From Fundamentalism to the New Evangelical Coalition." In *Evangelicalism and Modern America*, edited by G. Marsden. Grand Rapids, Mich.: Eerdmans.

Chandler, Ralph. 1984. "The Wicked Shall Not Bear Rule: The Fundamentalist Heritage of the New Christian Right." In *New Christian Politics*, edited by D. Bromley and A. Shupe. Macon, Ga.: Mercer University Press.

Chesler, Mark, and Richard Schmuck. 1969. "Social Psychological Characteristics of Super-Patriots." In *The American Right Wing*, edited by R. Schoenberger. New York: Holt, Rinehart and Winston.

Christie, R., and M. Jahoda. 1969. *Studies in the Scope and Method of "The Authoritarian Personality."* Glencoe, Ill.: Free Press.

Clabaugh, Gary. 1974. *Thunder on the Right.* Chicago: Nelson Hall.

Cole, Stewart. 1931. *The History of Fundamentalism.* Westport, Conn.: Greenwood Press.

Conover, Pamela. 1983. "The Mobilization of the New Right: A Test of Various Explanations." *Western Political Quarterly* 36: 632–49.

——. 1984. "The Influence of Group Identifications on Political Perception and Evaluation." *Journal of Politics* 46: 760–85.

Conover, Pamela, and Stanley Feldman. 1984. "Group Identification, Values, and the Nature of Political Beliefs." *American Politics Quarterly* 12: 151–75.

——. 1986. "Religion, Morality and Politics: Moral Traditionalism in the 1980's." Presented at the annual meeting of the Midwest Political Science Association, Chicago.

Conover, Pamela, and Virginia Gray. 1981. "Political Activists and the Conflict over Abortion and the E.R.A.: Pro-Family vs. Pro-Women." Presented at the annual meeting of the Midwest Political Science Association, Cincinnati.

——. 1983. *Feminism and the New Right.* New York: Praeger.

Cook, Elizabeth. 1987. "Feminism and Group Consciousness in America 1972–1984." Ph.D. dissertation, Ohio State University.

Cook, Elizabeth, and Clyde Wilcox. 1990. "Religious Orientations and Political Attitudes among Blacks in Washington, D.C." *Polity* 22: 527–39.

Elms, Alan. 1969. "Psychological Factors in Right-Wing Extremism." In *The American Right Wing*, edited by R. Schoenberger. New York: Holt, Rinehart and Winston.

Falwell, Jerry. 1981. *The Fundamentalist Phenomenon.* Garden City, N.Y.: Doubleday.

Ferkiss, Victor. 1962. "Political and Intellectual Origins of American Radicalism, Right and Left." *Annals of the American Academy of Political and Social Science,* pp. 1–12.

Fitzgerald, Frances. 1990. "Reflections (the Bakkers)." *The New Yorker,* 23 April.

Fried, Amy. 1988. "Abortion as Symbolic Politics: An Investigation of a Belief System." *Social Science Quarterly* 69: 137–54.

Furniss, Norman. 1963. *The Fundamentalist Controversy, 1918–1931.* Hamden, Conn.: Archon Books.

Gargan, Edward. 1961. "Radical Catholics of the Right." *Social Order,* November, pp. 3–5.

Gatewood, William. *Controversy in the Twenties.* Nashville: Vanderbilt University Press.

Georgianna, Sharon. 1989. *The Moral Majority and Fundamentalism: Plausibility and Dissonance.* Lewiston, N.Y.: Edwin Mellon Press.

Gilbert, Christopher. 1989. "The Political Impact of Church-Discussion Partners." Presented at the annual meeting of the American Political Science Association, Atlanta.

Graber, Doris. 1984. *Processing the News.* New York: Longman.

Green, B., K. Turner, and D. Germino. 1963. "Responsible and Irresponsible Right-Wing Groups: A Problem of Analysis." *Journal of Social Issues* 19: 3–17.

Green, John, and James Guth. 1988. "The Christian Right in the Republican Party: The Case of Pat Robertson's Supporters." *Journal of Politics* 50: 150–65.

Grupp, Fred. 1968. "Social Correlate of Political Activists: The John Birch Society and the ADA." Ph.D. dissertation, University of Pennsylvania.

———. 1969. "The Political Perspectives of the John Birch Society Members." In *The American Right Wing,* edited by R. Schoenberger. New York: Holt, Rinehart and Winston.

Gusfield, Joseph. 1963. *Symbolic Crusade: Status Politics and the American Temperance Movement.* Urbana: University of Illinois Press.

Guth, James. 1983a. "The New Christian Right." In *The New Christian Right,* edited by R. Liebman and R. Wuthnow. New York: Aldine.

———. 1983b. "The Politics of the Christian Right." In *Interest Group Politics,* edited by A. Cigler and B. Loomis. Washington, D.C.: CQ Press.

———. 1984. "The Politics of Preachers: Southern Baptist Ministers and Christian Right Activism." In *New Christian Politics,* edited by D. Bromley and A. Shupe. Macon, Ga.: Mercer University Press.

———. 1989. "A New Turn for the Christian Right? Robertson's Support from the Southern Baptist Ministry." Presented at the annual meeting of the American Association for the Advancement of Science, San Francisco.

Guth, James, and John Green. 1987a. "God and the GOP: Varieties of Religiosity among Political Contributors." Presented at the annual meeting of the American Political Science Association, Chicago.

———. 1987b. "The Moralizing Minority: Christian Right Support among Political Activists." *Social Science Quarterly* 67: 598–610.

———. 1987c. "Robertson's Republicans: Christian Activists in Republican Politics." *Election Politics* 4:9–14.

Guth, James, Ted Jelen, Lyman Kellstedt, Corwin Smidt, and Kenneth Wald. 1988. "The Politics of Religion in America." *American Politics Quarterly* 16: 357–97.

Harrell, David E. 1981. "The South: Seedbed of Sectarianism." In *Varieties of Southern Evangelicalism*, edited by D. Harrell. Macon, Ga.: Mercer University Press.

———. 1988. *Pat Robertson: A Personal, Religious, and Political Portrait.* San Francisco: Harper and Row.

———, ed. 1981. *Varieties of Southern Evangelicalism.* Macon, Ga.: Mercer University Press.

Hertzke, Allen. 1988. *Representing God in Washington.* Knoxville: University of Tennessee Press.

———. 1989a. "American Political Parties and Strategic Assimilation: The Lessons of Jackson and Robertson." Presented at the annual meeting of the Western Political Science Association, Salt Lake City.

———. 1989b. "Pat Robertson's Crusade and the GOP: A Strategic Analysis." Presented at the annual meeting of the Midwest Political Science Association, Chicago.

Himmelstein, Jerome. 1986. "The Social Basis of Anti-Feminism." *Journal for the Scientific Study of Religion* 25: 1–15.

Hofstadter, Richard. 1955. *The Age of Reform.* New York: Vintage Books.

———. 1967. *The Paranoid Style in American Politics.* New York: Random House.

Huitema, Bradley. 1980. *The Analysis of Covariance and Alternatives.* New York. Wiley and Sons.

Hunter, James. 1981. "Operationalizing Evangelicalism: A Review, Critique and Proposal." *Sociological Analysis* 42: 363–72.

———. 1983. *American Evangelicalism: Conservative Religion and the Quandary of Modernity.* New Brunswick, N.J.: Rutgers University Press.

———. 1987. "The Evangelical Worldview since 1890." In *Piety and Politics*, edited by R. Neuhaus and M. Cromartie. Washington, D.C.: Ethics and Public Policy Center.

Jelen, Ted. 1987. "The Effects of Religious Separatism on White Protestants in the 1984 Presidential Election." *Sociological Analysis* 48: 30–45.

———. 1990a. "The Causes and Effects of Religious Group Identifications." Presented at the annual meeting of the Midwest Political Science Association, Chicago.

———. 1990b. "Religious Belief and Attitude Constraint." *Journal for the Scientific Study of Religion* 29: 118–25.

———. 1991a. *The Political Mobilization of Religious Belief.* New York: Praeger.

———. 1991b. "Politicized Group Identification: The Case of Fundamentalism." Forthcoming, *Western Political Quarterly.*

Johnson, Loch, and Charles Bullock III. 1986. "The New Religious Right and the 1980 Congressional Elections." In *Do Elections Matter?*, edited by Benjamin Ginsburg and Alan Stone. New York: M. E. Sharpe.

Johnson, Stephen. 1988. "The Christian Right in Middletown." In *The Political Role of Religion in the U.S.*, edited by Stephen Johnson and Joseph Tamney. New York: Westview.

Johnson, Stephen, and Joseph Tamney. 1984. "Support for the Moral Majority: A Test of a Model." *Journal for the Scientific Study of Religion* 23: 183–96.

———. 1985. "The Christian Right and the 1984 Presidential Election." *Review of Religious Research* 27: 124–33.

Johnson, Stephen, Joseph Tamney, and Ronald Burton. 1989. "Pat Robertson: Who Supported His Candidacy for President?" *Journal for the Scientific Study of Religion* 28: 387–99.

———. 1990. "Factors Influencing a Vote for a Christian Right Candidate." *Review of Religious Research* 31: 291–305.

Jorstad, Erling. 1970. *The Politics of Doomsday.* Nashville: Abingdon Press.

———. 1981. *Evangelicals in the White House.* New York: Edwin Mellon Press.

———. 1987. *The New Christian Right, 1981–1988.* New York: Edwin Mellon Press.

Kellstedt, Lyman. 1984. "Religion and Politics: The Measurement of Evangelicalism." Presented at the annual meeting of the American Political Science Association, Washington, D.C.

———. 1986. "Evangelicals and Political Realignment." Presented at the annual meeting of the American Political Science Association, Washington, D.C.

———. 1988. "The Falwell Issue Agenda: Sources of Support among White Protestant Evangelicals." In *An Annual in the Sociology of Religion,* edited by M. Lynn and D. Moberg. New York: JAI Press.

———. 1989. "The Meaning and Measurement of Evangelism: Problems and Prospects." In *Religion and Political Behavior in the United States,* edited by Ted Jelen. New York: Praeger.

Kellstedt, Lyman, and John Green. 1990. "Religion, Partisanship and Political Behavior: Regional Variation." Presented at biannual Citadel Symposium on Southern Politics, Charleston, S.C.

Kellstedt, Lyman, and Corwin Smidt. 1985. "Defining and Measuring Fundamentalism: An Analysis of Different Conceptual and Operational Strategies." Presented at the annual meeting of the American Political Science Association, New Orleans.

Kinder, Donald, and David Sears. 1981. "Prejudice and Politics: Symbolic Racism versus Racial Threats to the Good Life." *Journal of Personality and Social Psychology* 40: 414–31.

Klatch, Rebecca. 1987. *Women and the New Right.* Philadelphia: Temple University Press.

Knight, Kathleen. 1984. "The Dimensionality of Partisan and Ideological Affect: The Influence of Positivity." *American Political Quarterly,* July, pp. 305–34.

Knoke, David. 1976. *Change and Continuity in American Politics: The Social Basis of Political Parties.* Baltimore: Johns Hopkins University Press.

Koeppen, Sheilah. 1969. "The Radical Right and the Politics of Consensus." In *The American Right Wing,* edited by R. Schoenberger. New York: Holt, Rinehart and Winston.

Kornhauser, William. 1959. *The Politics of Mass Society.* New York: Free Press.

Langenbach, Lisa. 1987. "Mixed Blessings: Evangelical Elites and the Potential Robertson Presidential Candidacy." Presented at the annual meeting of the Northeastern Political Science Association, Philadelphia.

Latus, Margaret. 1983. "Ideological PACs and Political Action." In *The New Christian Right*, edited by R. Liebman and R. Wuthnow. New York: Aldine.

———. 1984. "Mobilizing Christians for Political Action: Campaigning with God on Your Side." In *New Christian Politics*, edited by D. Bromley and A. Shupe. Macon, Ga.: Mercer University Press.

Leege, David. 1990. "Coalitions, Cues, Strategic Politics, and the Staying Power of the Religious Right." Presented at the annual meeting of the American Sociological Association, Washington, D.C.

Leege, David, Joel Lieske, and Kenneth Wald. 1989. "Toward Cultural Theories of American Political Behavior: Religion, Ethnicity, and Class Outlook." Presented at the annual meeting of the Midwest Political Science Association, Chicago.

Lenski, Gerald. 1954. "Status Crystallization: A Non-Vertical Dimension of Social Status." *American Sociological Review* 19: 405–13.

Lichter, S. Robert, Daniel Admunndson, and Richard Noyes. *The Video Campaign*. Washington, D.C.: AEI.

Liebman, Robert. 1983. "Mobilizing the Moral Majority." In *The New Christian Right*, edited by R. Liebman and R. Wuthnow. New York: Aldine.

Lienesch, Michael. 1982. "Right-Wing Religion: Christian Conservatism as a Political Movement." *Political Science Quarterly* 97: 403–25.

Lipset, Seymour Martin. 1963a. "The Sources of the Radical Right." In *The Radical Right*, edited by Daniel Bell. Garden City, N.Y.: Doubleday.

———. 1963b. "Three Decades of the Radical Right: Coughlinites, McCarthyites, and Birchers." In *The Radical Right*, edited by Daniel Bell. Garden City, N.Y.: Doubleday.

———. 1982. "Failures of Extremism." *Society* 20: 48–58.

Lipset, Seymour Martin, and Earl Raab. 1978. *The Politics of Unreason.* Chicago: University of Chicago Press.

———. 1981. "The Election and the Evangelicals." *Commentary* 71: 25–31.

Lorentzen, Louise. 1980. "Evangelical Life Style Concerns Expressed as Political Action." *Sociological Analysis* 41: 144–54.

Luker, Kristen. 1988. *Abortion and the Politics of Motherhood*. Berkeley: University of California Press.

McAdam, Doug. 1982. *Political Process and the Development of Black Insurgency, 1930–1970*. Chicago: University of Chicago Press.

———. 1983. "Tactical Innovation and the Pace of Insurgency." *American Sociological Review* 48: 735–53.

McCarthy, John, and Mayer Zald. 1977. "Resource Mobilization and Social Movements: A Partial Theory." *American Journal of Sociology* 82: 1212–41.

McDonnell, Kilian. 1976. *Charismatic Renewal and the Churches*. New York: Seabury Press.

McEvoy, James. 1971. *Radicals or Conservatives? The Contemporary American Right*. Chicago: Rand McNally.

McGlennon, John. 1989. "Religious Activists in the Republican Party: Robertson and Bush Supporters in Virginia." Presented at the Midwest Political Science Association, Chicago.

McGuire, Meredith. 1982. *Pentecostal Catholics*. Philadelphia: Temple University Press.

McNall, Scott. 1969. "Social Disorganization and Availability: Accounting for Radical Rightism." In *The American Right Wing*, edited by R. Schoenberger. New York: Holt, Rinehart and Winston.

Marsden, George. 1980. *Fundamentalism and American Culture*. New York: Oxford University Press.

————, ed. 1984. *Evangelicalism and Modern America*. Grand Rapids, Mich.: Eerdmans.

Marshall, Susan E. 1986. "In Defense of Separate Spheres: Class and Status Politics in the Anti-Suffrage Movement." *Social Forces* 65: 327–51.

Menendez, Albert. 1977. *Religion at the Polls*. Philadelphia: Westminster Press.

Miller, Arthur, Patricia Gurin, and Gerald Gurin. 1978. "Electoral Implications of Group Identification and Group Consciousness: A Reintroduction of a Concept." Presented at the annual meeting of the American Political Science Association, New York.

Miller, Arthur, Patricia Gurin, Gerald Gurin, and Oksana Malunchuk. 1980. "Group Consciousness and Political Participation." *American Journal of Political Science* 25: 494–511.

Miller, Arthur, Grace Simmons, and Anne Hildreth. 1986. "Group Influences, Solidarity, and Electoral Outcomes." Presented at the annual meeting of the American Political Science Association, Washington, D.C.

Miller, W. E. 1985. "The New Christian Right and Fundamentalist Discontent: The Politics of Life Style Concern Hypothesis Revisited." *Sociological Focus* 18: 325–36.

Moe, Terry. 1980. *The Organization of Interests*. Chicago: University of Chicago Press.

Moen, Matthew. 1989. *The Christian Right and Congress*. Tuscaloosa: University of Alabama Press.

————. 1990a. "The Political Transformation of the Christian Right." Presented at the annual meeting of the American Political Science Association, San Francisco.

————. 1990b. "Ronald Reagan and the Social Issues: Rhetorical Support for the Christian Right." *Social Science Journal* 27: 199–207.

Morken, Hubert. 1990. "Religious Lobbying at the State Level: Case Studies in a Continuing Role for the New Religious Right." Presented at the annual meeting of the American Political Science Association, San Francisco.

Neuhaus, Richard. 1987. "What the Fundamentalists Want." In *Piety and Politics*, edited by R. Neuhaus and M. Cromartie. Washington, D.C.: Ethics and Public Policy Center.

Niebuhr, R. Gustav. 1989. "Why 'Moral Majority,' a Force for a Decade, Ran out of Steam." *Wall Street Journal*, 25 September, P A1.

Noll, Mark, ed. 1989. *Religion and American Politics*. New York: Oxford University Press.

Oldfield, Duane. 1989. "Pat Crashes the Party: Reform, Republicans, and Robertson." Presented at the annual meeting of the American Political Science Association, Atlanta.

————. 1990. "The Christian Right and State Republican Parties." Presented at the annual meeting of the American Political Science Association, San Francisco.

Olson, Mancur. 1965. *The Logic of Collective Action.* Cambridge, Mass.: Harvard University Press.

Ostling, Richard. 1984. "Evangelical Publishing and Broadcasting." In *Evangelicalism and Modern America,* edited by G. Marsden. Grand Rapids, Mich.: Eerdmans.

Page, Ann, and Donald Clelland. 1978. "The Kanawha County Textbook Controversy: A Study in the Politics of Lifestyle." *Social Forces* 57: 265–81.

Perkins, Jerry. 1989. "The Moral Majority as a Political Reference Group in the 1980 and 1984 Elections." In *Religion and Political Behavior in the United States,* edited by Ted Jelen. New York: Praeger.

Pierand, Richard, and James Wright. 1984. "No Hoosier Hospitality for Humanism: The Moral Majority in Indiana." In *New Christian Politics,* edited by D. Bromley and A. Shupe. Macon, Ga.: Mercer University Press.

Poloma, Margaret. 1982. *The Charismatic Movement.* Boston: G. K. Hall.

Polsby, Nelson. 1963. "Towards an Explanation of McCarthyism." *Political Studies* 8: 250–71.

Quebedeaux, Richard. 1983. *The New Charismatics II.* New York: Harper and Row.

Reichley, A. James. 1985. *Religion in American Public Life.* Washington, D.C.: Brookings Institution.

———. 1987. "The Evangelical and Fundamentalist Revolt." In *Piety and Politics,* edited by R. Neuhaus and M. Cromartie. Washington, D.C.: Ethics and Public Policy Center.

Rhodes, Lewis. 1960. "Authoritarianism and Fundamentalism of Rural and Urban High School Students." *Journal of Educational Psychology* 39: 97–105.

Ribuffo, Leo. 1983. *The Old Christian Right.* Philadelphia: Temple University Press.

Rifkin, Jeremy, with Ted Howard. 1979. *The Emerging Order.* New York: Ballantine.

Robbins, John. 1988. *Pat Robertson: A Warning to America.* Jefferson, Md.: Trinity Foundation.

Roelofs, H. Mark. 1988. "Liberation Theology: The Recovery of Biblical Radicalism." *American Political Science Review* 81: 549–66.

Rogin, Michael. 1967. *The Intellectuals and McCarthy: The Radical Spectre.* Cambridge, Mass.: MIT Press.

Rohter, Ira. 1965. "Some Personal Needs Met by Becoming a Radical Rightist." Presented at the annual meeting of the American Psychological Association, Chicago.

———. 1969. "Social Psychological Determinants of Radical Rightism." In *The American Right Wing,* edited by R. Schoenberger. New York: Holt, Rinehart and Winston.

Rothenberg, Stuart, and Frank Newport. 1984. *The Evangelical Voter.* Washington, D.C.: Free Congress Research and Education Foundation.

Rush, Gary. 1967. "Status Consistency and Right-Wing Extremism." *American Sociological Review* 32: 86–92.

Russell, C. Allyn. 1976. *Voices of American Fundamentalism.* Philadelphia: Westminster Press.

Salisbury, Robert. 1969. "An Exchange Theory of Interest Groups." *Midwest Journal of Political Science* 13: 1–32.

Sandeen, Ernest. 1970. *The Roots of Fundamentalism.* Chicago: University of Chicago Press.

Scott, Wilbur J. 1982. "Status Politics and the Equal Rights Amendment: A Struggle over How Women Should Spend Their Days." Presented at the annual meeting of the Southwestern Sociological Association, San Antonio.

Sears, David, Carl Hensler, and Leslie Speer. 1979. "Whites' Opposition to Bussing: Self-Interest or Symbolic Politics?" *American Political Science Review* 73: 369–84.

Sears, David, Richard Lau, Tom Tyler, and Harris Allen. 1980. "Self-interest vs. Symbolic Politics in Policy Attitudes and Presidential Voting." *American Political Science Review* 74: 670–84.

Shupe, Anson, and William Stacey. 1983. "The Moral Majority Constituency." In *The New Christian Right,* edited by R. Liebman and R. Wuthnow. New York: Aldine.

———. 1984. "Public and Clergy Sentiments toward the Moral Majority: Evidence from the Dallas–Fort Worth Metroplex." In *New Christian Politics,* edited by D. Bromley and A. Shupe. Macon, Ga.: Mercer University Press.

Sigelman, Lee, and Stanley Presser. 1988. "Measuring Public Support for the New Christian Right: The Perils of Point Estimation." *Public Opinion Quarterly* 52: 325–37.

Sigelman, Lee, Clyde Wilcox, and Emmett Buell. 1987. "An Unchanged Minority: Popular Support for the Moral Majority in 1980 and 1984." *Social Science Quarterly* 68: 876–84.

Simpson, John. 1983. "Moral Issues and Status Politics." In *The New Christian Right,* edited by R. Liebman and R. Wuthnow. New York: Aldine.

———. 1984. "Support for the Moral Majority and Its Sociomoral Platform." In *New Christian Politics,* edited by D. Bromley and A. Shupe. Macon, Ga.: Mercer University Press.

Smelser, Neil. *Theory of Collective Behavior.* 1963. New York: Free Press.

Smidt, Corwin. 1987. "Evangelicals and the 1984 Election: Continuity or Change?" *American Politics Quarterly* 15: 419–44.

———. 1988a. "Evangelicals vs. Fundamentalists: An Analysis of the Political Characteristics and Importance of Two Major Religious Movements within American Politics." *Western Political Quarterly* 41: 601–20.

———. 1988b. "The Mobilization of Evangelical Voters in 1980: An Initial Test of Several Hypotheses." *Southeastern Political Review* 16: 3–33.

———. 1989. " 'Praise the Lord' Politics: A Comparative Analysis of the Social Characteristics and Political Views of American Evangelical and Charismatic Christians." *Sociological Analysis* 50: 53–72.

Smidt, Corwin, and Lyman Kellstedt. 1987. "Evangelicalism and Survey Research: Interpretive Problems and Substantive Findings." In *The Bible, Politics, and Democracy,* edited by R. J. Neuhaus. Grand Rapids, Mich.: Eerdmans.

Smidt, Corwin, and Paul Kellstedt. 1990. "Evangelicals and the Post-Reagan Era: An Analysis of Evangelicals in the 1988 Presidential Election." Presented at the biannual Citadel Symposium on Southern Politics, Charleston, S.C.

Smidt, Corwin, and James Penning. 1990. "A House Divided: A Comparison of Robertson and Bush Delegates to the 1988 Michigan Republican State Convention." *Polity* 23: 127–38.

———. 1991. "Religious Self-Identification and Support for Robertson: An Analysis of Delegates to the 1988 Michigan Republican State Convention." Forthcoming, *Review of Religious Research*.

Speer, James. 1984. "The New Christian Right and Its Parent Company: A Study in Political Contrasts." In *New Christian Politics*, edited by D. Bromley and A. Shupe. Macon, Ga.: Mercer University Press.

Spittler, Russell. 1976. *Perspectives on the New Pentecostalism*. Grand Rapids, Mich.: Baker Book House.

Stockton, Ronald. 1985. "The Falwell Core: A Public Opinion Analysis." Presented at the annual meeting of the Society for the Scientific Study of Religion, Chicago.

Stone, Barbara. 1968. "The John Birch Society of California." Ph.D. dissertation, University of Southern California.

Szasz, Ferenc. 1982. *The Divided Mind of Protestant America, 1880–1930*. Tuscaloosa: University of Alabama Press.

Tamney, Joseph, and Stephen Johnson. 1983. "The Moral Majority in Middletown." *Journal for the Scientific Study of Religion* 22: 145–57.

Trow, Martin. 1957. "Right-Wing Radicalism and Political Intolerance." Ph.D. dissertation, Columbia University.

Truman, David. 1951. *The Governmental Process*. New York: Knopf.

Turner, Helen, and James Guth. 1989. "The Politics of Armageddon: Dispensationalism among Southern Baptist Ministers." In *Religion and Political Behavior in America*, edited by Ted Jelen. New York: Praeger.

Wald, Kenneth. 1986. "The Persistence of Religious Influences in American Electoral Behavior: A Study of Voting Patterns in 1980." Presented at the annual meeting of the Midwest Political Science Association, Chicago.

———. 1987. *Religion and Politics in the United States*. New York: St. Martin's Press.

Wald, Kenneth, Dennis Owen, and Samuel Hill. 1988. "Churches as Political Communities." *American Political Science Review* 82: 531–49.

———. 1989a. "Evangelical Politics and Status Issues." *Journal for the Scientific Study of Religion* 28: 1–16.

———. 1989b. "Habits of the Mind? The Problem of Authority in the New Christian Right." In *Religion and American Political Behavior*, edited by Ted Jelen. New York: Praeger.

———. 1990. "Political Cohesion in Churches." *Journal of Politics* 52: 197–212.

Walker, Jack. 1983. "The Origin and Maintenance of Interest Groups in America." *American Political Science Review* 77: 384–96.

Weber, Timothy. 1987. *Living in the Shadow of the Second Coming*. Chicago: University of Chicago Press.

Welch, Michael, and David Leege. 1991. "Catholic Evangelicalism and Political Orientations: A Case of Transcended Group Boundaries and Distinctive Political Values." *American Journal of Political Science*, pp. 197–212.

Wilcox, Clyde. 1986a. "Evangelicals and Fundamentalists in the New Christian Right: Religious Differences in the Ohio Moral Majority." *Journal for the Scientific Study of Religion* 25: 355–63.

———. 1986b. "Fundamentalists and Politics: An Analysis of the Impact of Differing Operational Definitions." *Journal of Politics* 48: 1041–51.

———. 1987a. "America's Radical Right Revisited: A Comparison of the Activists in the Christian Right in Two Decades." *Sociological Analysis* 48: 45–58.

———. 1987b. "Popular Backing for the Old Christian Right: Explaining Support for the Christian Anti-Communism Crusade." *Journal of Social History* 21: 117–32.

———. 1987c. "Popular Support for the Moral Majority in 1980: A Second Look." *Social Science Quarterly* 68: 157–67.

———. 1987d. "Religious Orientations and Political Attitudes: Variations within the New Christian Right." *American Politics Quarterly* 15: 274–96.

———. 1987e. "Religious Attitudes and Anti-Feminism: An Analysis of the Ohio Moral Majority." *Women and Politics* 7: 59–78.

———. 1988a. "The Christian Right in the Twentieth Century: Continuity and Change." *Review of Politics* 50: 659–81.

———. 1988b. "Political Action Committees of the New Christian Right: A Longitudinal Analysis." *Journal for the Scientific Study of Religion* 27: 60–71.

———. 1988c. "Seeing the Connection: Religion and Politics in the Ohio Moral Majority." *Review of Religious Research* 30: 47–58.

———. 1988d. "Sources of Support for the Old Right: A Comparison of the John Birch Society and the Christian Anti-Communism Crusade." *Social Science History* 12: 429–49.

———. 1989a. "Feminism and Anti-Feminism among White Evangelical Women." *Western Political Quarterly* 42: 147–60.

———. 1989b. "The Fundamentalist Voter: Politicized Religious Identity and Political Attitudes and Behavior." *Review of Religious Research* 31: 54–67.

———. 1989c. "The New Christian Right and the Mobilization of the Evangelicals." In *Religion and American Political Behavior*, edited by T. Jelen. New York: Praeger.

———. 1989d. "Popular Support for the New Christian Right: A Test of Alternative Explanations." *Social Science Journal* 26: 55–65.

———. 1989e. "Support for the Christian Right, Old and New: A Comparison of the Christian Anti-Communism Crusade and the Moral Majority." *Sociological Focus* 22: 87–97.

———. 1990a. "Blacks and the New Christian Right: Support for the Moral Majority and Pat Robertson among Washington, D.C. Blacks." *Review of Religious Research* 32: 43–56.

———. 1990b. "Evangelicals and the Moral Majority." *Journal for the Scientific Study of Religion* 28: 400–414.

———. 1990c. "Racial Differences in Abortion Attitudes: Some Additional Evidence." *Public Opinion Quarterly* 54: 248–55.

———. 1991. "Financing the 1988 Prenomination Campaigns." In *Nominating the President*, edited by E. Buell and L. Sigelman. Knoxville: University of Tennessee Press.

Wilcox, Clyde, and Elizabeth Cook. 1989. "Evangelical Women and Feminism: A Second Look." *Women and Politics* 9: 27–50.

Wilcox, Clyde, and Leopoldo Gomez. 1990. "The Christian Right and the Pro-Life Movement: An Analysis of Political Support." *Review of Religious Research* 31: 380–89.

Wilcox, Clyde, and Ted Jelen. 1990. "Evangelicals and Political Tolerance." *American Politics Quarterly* 18: 25–46.

Wilcox, Clyde, Lee Sigelman, and Elizabeth Cook. 1989. "Some Like It Hot: Individual Differences in Responses to Group Feeling Thermometers." *Public Opinion Quarterly* 53: 247–57.

Will, Jeffry, and Rhys Williams. 1986. "Political Ideology and Political Action in the New Christian Right." *Sociological Analysis* 47: 160–68.

Wilson, James Q. 1973. *Political Organizations*. New York: Basic Books.

Wilson, Kenneth, and Louis Zurcher. 1977. "Status Inconsistency and Participation in Social Movements: A Rejoinder to Bland and Wallis." *Sociological Quarterly* 18: 430–35.

Wolfinger, Raymond, Barbara Wolfinger, Kenneth Prewitt, and Sheilah Rosenhack. 1969. "America's Radical Right: Politics and Ideology." In *The American Right Wing*, edited by R. Schoenberger. New York: Holt, Rinehart and Winston.

Wood, Michael, and Michael Hughes. 1984. "The Moral Basis of Moral Reform: Status Discontent vs. Culture and Socialization as Explanations of Anti-Pornography Social Movement Adherence." *American Sociological Review* 49: 86–99.

Wuthnow, Robert. 1983. "The Political Rebirth of American Evangelicals." In *The New Christian Right*, edited by R. Liebman and R. Wuthnow. New York: Aldine.

Yinger, Milton, and Stephen Cutler. 1982. "The Moral Majority Viewed Sociologically." In *New Christian Politics*, edited by D. Bromley and A. Shupe. Macon, Ga.: Mercer University Press.

Zwier, Robert. 1982. *Born-Again Politics: The New Christian Right in America*. Downers Grove, Ill.: InterVarsity Press.

Index

Designed by Joanna Hill
Composed by The Composing Room of Michigan, Inc.,
in Baskerville text and Kabel display
Printed on 50-lb. Glatfelter Offset
and bound in Joanna Anestox cloth
by The Maple Press Company